China at the Crossroads: Nationalists and Communists, 1927–1949

Westview Replica Editions

This book is a Westview Replica Edition. The concept of
Replica Editions is a response to the crisis in academic and
informational publishing. Library budgets for books have been
severely curtailed; economic pressures on the university presses
and the few private publishing companies primarily interested in
scholarly manuscripts have severely limited the capacity of the
industry to properly serve the academic and research communities.
Many manuscripts dealing with important subjects, often representing the highest level of scholarship, are today not economically viable publishing projects. Or, if they are accepted for
publication, they are often subject to lead times ranging from
one to three years. Scholars are understandably frustrated when
they realize that their first-class research cannot be published
within a reasonable time frame, if at all.

Westview Replica Editions are our practical solution to the
problem. The concept is simple. We accept a manuscript in camera-
ready form and move it immediately into the production process.
The responsibility for textual and copy editing lies with the
author or sponsoring organization. If necessary we will advise
the author on proper preparation of footnotes and bibliography.
We prefer that the manuscript be typed according to our speci-
fications, though it may be acceptable as typed for a dissertation or prepared in some other clearly organized and readable
way. The end result is a book produced by lithography and bound
in hard covers. Initial edition sizes range from 600 to 800
copies, and a number of recent Replicas are already in second
printings. We include among Westview Replica Editions only works
of outstanding scholarly quality or of great informational value,
and we will continue to exercise our usual editorial standards
and quality control.

China at the Crossroads:
Nationalists and Communists, 1927–1949
edited by F. Gilbert Chan

Concentrating on a transitional epoch, 1927–1949, when
China was at the crossroads of revolution, the contributors
analyze the Kuomintang's inherent weaknesses as a revolutionary force and the Communists' success in the quest for new
formulas to guide the modernization movement. Rejecting the
suggestion that external factors determined the outcome of
the Kuomintang-Communist conflict, they stress instead the
more fundamental issues of the Chinese revolution, pointing
to problems such as factionalism in Nanking, the weakness of
the New Life Movement as an experiment in thought control
and mass mobilization, the failure of land reform in Chekiang,
and the ineffectiveness of the anti-Japanese boycott of 1931–
1932. The regional power in Sinkiang and the rural problems
in Chungking are also emphasized.

Dr. Chan, associate professor of history at Miami Uni-
versity, Oxford, Ohio, has previously taught at the Chinese
University of Hong Kong, Purdue University, and Wright State
University.

China at the Crossroads:
Nationalists and Communists,
1927–1949

edited by F. Gilbert Chan

Westview Press / Boulder, Colorado

A Westview Replica Edition

Published in 1980 in the United States of America by
    Westview Press, Inc.
    5500 Central Avenue
    Boulder, Colorado 80301
    Frederick A. Praeger, Publisher

Library of Congress Cataloging in Publication Data
Main entry under title:
China at the crossroads.
  (A Westview replica edition)
  Bibliography: p.
  Includes index.
  1. China--Politics and government--1912-1949--Addresses,
essays, lectures. 2. Communism--China--Addresses, essays,
lectures. I. Chan, F. Gilbert.
DS777.47.C495   951.04   80-13766
ISBN 0-89158-913-9

To Ssu-yü Teng
with respect and admiration

Contents

x

Acknowledgments

As a token of my appreciation for his impeccable
scholarship and unfailing friendship, this volume
is dedicated, with admiration and gratitude, to Professor Ssu-yü Teng of Indiana University.

Professor Teng came to the United States in the
1930s. In the following decades, Chinese studies
flourished in many American universities. He is among
the pioneering scholars who have contributed significantly to the understanding of China in this country. His writings have benefited numerous students,
among whom are the contributors to this volume.
We owe him our gratitude.

It is my personal privilege to have known Professor Teng since 1969, when we were colleagues at the
Chinese University of Hong Kong. He has since then
been a generous friend and, above all, an inspir-
ing teacher. I am particularly thankful for the many
long hours he has spent reading my manuscripts, always
helpful with constructive and illuminating comments.

It has been a pleasure to work with a group
of scholars who share with me an interest in a fas-
cinating period of Chinese history. I appreciate
their patience and indulgence, especially when
the publication of this volume seemed uncertain. I am
grateful for the invaluable assistance of Professor
Te-kong Tong, my former teacher at Columbia University, who is now associated with the City College
of New York. I am also indebted to Mervyn W. Adams
Seldon, whose support of this project has gone beyond
the responsibility of a consulting editor, as well
as to Henley McIntosh, my doctoral student at Miami
University, who has proofread a large portion of the
manuscript of this volume. Acknowledgments are due
to the East Asian Institute of Columbia University for
permission to publish Samuel Chu's article on the New

Life Movement in its revised form, and to Hong Kong
University Press for permitting me to include
parts of my earlier article on Sheng Shih-ts'ai
in the fifth chapter of this volume.

A misfortune was inflicted on my family in April
1976 when I was working on this project. During
one of my visits to New York, our house in Oxford,
Ohio, was seriously damaged by fire. In my absence,
my colleagues at Miami helped my wife, Rosalind,
and our two children, Edmund and Sharon, salvage my
books from the study. Among the items removed
from the fire was the manuscript of this volume. My
special thanks go to Richard M. Jellison, Dwight L.
Smith, Jay W. Baird, John N. Dickinson, David M.
Fahey, Maynard W. Swanson, and Edward B. Parsons. No
expression of appreciation is adequate for Mary Jane
and James H. Rodabaugh and Franca and Herbert L.
Oerter for sharing their homes with us when we lost
ours. Finally, I admire Rosalind, Edmund, and Sharon
for going through a very difficult period with
courage and understanding. Without the love and
affection of my family and friends, I would not have
been able to complete the work for this volume.

Introduction:
China at the Crossroads,
1927–1949

F. Gilbert Chan

This book concentrates on one crucial period of
the Chinese revolutionary movement, which spans the
years from the founding of the T'ung-meng-hui (Revolutionary Alliance) in 1905 to the post-Mao Tse-tung
era. It deals with a transitional stage, 1927-1949,
when China was at the crossroads of revolution.
Thanks partly to the tutelage of Soviet Russia, the
Kuomintang had risen to power in the 1920s with the
tide of nationalism. As George Sokolsky observed in
1929, "no governmental group in China started under
better auspices" than the Nationalists in Nanking.[1]
Nevertheless, shortly after its military victories of
1926-1928, the Kuomintang, headed by Chiang Kai-shek,
was transformed from a party of revolutionaries to
one of "traditionalist bureaucrats." In spite of the
revolutionary fervor generated by the nationalist
movement of the 1920s, the Nanking government was
characterized by "ineffective administration, corruption, political repression, and factionalism." Its
leaders were seemingly insensitive to the many social
and economic problems of the people. The rule of
the Nationalists was, in short, a classic example of
revolutionary failure.[2]
In contrast, the Kuomintang extermination campaigns notwithstanding, the Communist movement in
China was far from dead. In 1934-1935, the party
turned the disaster of the Long March into a moral
victory. In their search for revolutionary models,
the Communist leaders rejected Western democracy and
embraced the Russian system of "soviets" as an alternative form of government. In an era of social
revolution, they initiated land reform that promised
to change the rural structure of Chinese society.
They also took advantage of the development of peasant
nationalism during the war against Japan and transformed the politically inactive sector of the popula-

1

tion into a strong revolutionary force. In sharp
contrast to the Kuomintang failure, their successes
won them the support of the masses, thereby helping
to determine the outcome of the civil war in 1949.
More important, their experimentation during these
years of struggle laid the groundwork for their later
endeavors in national reconstruction.

This volume is not a comprehensive study of the
Chinese revolution in 1927-1949. It is, instead, a
selective analysis of the Kuomintang's inherent
weaknesses as a revolutionary force, as well as the
Communist success in the quest for new formulae to
guide the embattled movement. The book does not
delineate the important achievements of the Nanking
government; that subject has been sufficiently
treated by other scholars.[3] Moreover, with the
exception of the two studies on Sinkiang and Szechwan,
the chapters on the Nationalists concentrate on the
1927-1937 decade. They outline the chief shortcomings
of the Kuomintang in a period when its leaders were
supposedly successful in their "nation-building"
effort. Significantly, these shortcomings were apparent before the outbreak of the Sino-Japanese War.
Indeed, my chapter on Sheng Shih-ts'ai and Robert
Kapp's on the Kuomintang in Chungking (both covering
the post-1937 years) are generally supportive of this
argument. Historians should therefore look beyond
foreign aggression for causes of Chiang Kai-shek's
expulsion from the mainland.

The failure of the Nationalists, however, did
not fully explain the victory of the Chinese Communists. To a considerable degree, the successes of
Mao Tse-tung and his comrades were attributable to
their ability to offer themselves as an attractive
alternative to a government that had lost the "mandate
of heaven" to rule China. The two chapters on the
Communist movement examine the development of the
soviets and the implementation of the land reform as
successful examples of revolutionary modernization.
In 1949, the Chinese people were confronted with
a choice between a reactionary government with obvious
weaknesses and a revolutionary movement that promised
the nation a better future. Their decision was
scarcely affected by the policies of either Soviet
Russia or the United States.

In addition to the earlier classics by Edgar Snow
and Agnes Smedley, many books have been published
since 1960 on the Chinese Communist movement. Among
the authors who are particularly interested in 1927-
1949 are Chalmers A. Johnson, William Hinton, Mark
Selden, Dick Wilson, Jane L. Price, and Ilpyong J.

Kim.[4] Nevertheless, with the exception of the recent
publications of Lloyd E. Eastman and Hung-mao Tien,
little scholarly attention has been paid to the revolutionary failure of the Nationalists.[5] With the
hope of stimulating research interest in the subject,
this volume devotes more than two-thirds of its
space to discussing the weaknesses of the Kuomintang
government.

THE NATIONALISTS, 1927-1937: A CASE STUDY OF REVOLU-
   TIONARY FAILURE

For years, scholars have debated the relative
importance to assign to foreign and domestic elements
in the Kuomintang debacle of 1949. Anthony Kubek
blamed the American government for its "policy of appeasement," whereas Hu Shih, a prominent educator
in China, maintained that the victory of the Chinese
Communists was a product of "Stalin's grand strategy
of world conquest."[6] Both views overemphasize the
external factors of the Kuomintang-Communist conflict
and ignore the more fundamental issues of the Chinese
revolution. Indeed, however damaging it may have
been for the Nationalists, the war with Japan was not
the principal cause of their humiliating defeat in
1949; it only aggravated their problems and intensified their weaknesses.

As head of the Nanking government, Chiang Kai-
shek had his share of responsibility for its failure.
Nonetheless, to label him as "the man who lost China"
is simplistic;[7] no one can lose something he does
not own. Chiang was a tragic figure. In an era of
modernization, he championed an ideology reminis-
cent of the Self-Strengthening Movement of the nineteenth century. His military training and Methodist
beliefs gave him a high degree of inflexibility
that, in many ways, reinforced his obsession with the
struggle against Communism. He led a united China
to victory against the Japanese yet soon afterward
plunged the nation into a civil war that resulted in
his political exile to Taiwan. In the end, he
sympolized the weaknesses of the Kuomintang government and was overwhelmed by the tides of the Chinese
revolution.

In retrospect, many symptoms of the Nationalist
failure had been evident in the pre-1927 years. The
Kuomintang leadership was represented by a network of
personal relations centering on Sun Yat-sen. Many
of his comrades were loyal followers whose association
with him dated back to the T'ung-meng-hui period.
Hu Han-min and Wang Ching-wei were two notable exam-

ples. In this respect, Chiang Kai-shek was an inadequate successor with no comparable command of the loyalty of his associates. Moreover, the bitterness of the succession struggle after Sun's death in March 1925 remained to haunt him in his difficult task of bringing wealth and power to China. Without the unified support of the party, he had to rely on his unstable alliances with the militarists. This excessive dependence upon military forces undermined the civil authority of his government.

The Kuomintang learned about the political importance of mass mobilization from the Russian *sovetniki* during the period of party reorganization in 1924-1925. According to Ho Ying-ch'in, however, many of its members were "unwilling to do the real and lower-level work."[8] They were more interested in the form of mass movement than in its substance. The few selflessly committed leaders were ridiculously overburdened. Liao Chung-k'ai headed the Bureau of Workers and, later, concurrently the Bureau of Peasants. At one time, he held thirteen important positions in both the party and the government.[9] This practice of concurrent appointments continued into the 1930s. For instance, Chiang Kai-shek held twenty-one offices, Sun Fo thirteen, and Wang Ching-wei twelve. They paid little attention to the qualifications of the new recruits. Although the membership increased from 150,000 in 1926 to 2 million in 1937, only 10 percent of them were active in party affairs.[10]

The Three Principles of the People, as elaborated in Sun Yat-sen's 1924 lectures, were a Chinese patriot's blueprint for national regeneration. To demonstrate his support for the Kuomintang alliance with Soviet Russia, Sun made some rhetorical concessions to Communism. Nevertheless, despite Tai Chit'ao's contention, the principles lacked philosophical sophistication. Beyond such slogans as "land to the tiller," they failed to include any cohesive program of social transformation.[11] But, in the absence of a viable political ideology, the Nationalists adopted these principles as their party bible. While the Northern Expedition of 1926-1928 attracted the backing of "old-style mandarins and militarists," the purges of Chinese Communists deprived the Kuomintang of the chance to experiment with new ideas and new leadership.[12] In the 1930s, the Nanking government accomplished "unity of thought" through extensive indoctrination and political repression.

During the epoch of Kuomintang rule, China was at the crossroads of revolutionary modernization. The political movement of 1911 had not produced any institutional stability. After Yüan Shih-k'ai's abortive attempt to restore the monarchy, Ts'ao K'un further "debased" the Chinese republic with his accession to presidency.[13] While in power in Nanking, the Nationalists likewise did not give republicanism a fair trial. Under the guise of "tutelage," they established a party dictatorship which, according to some scholars, was not dissimilar to European Fascism.[14] Instead of being a transitional stage of the Chinese revolution, the Kuomintang regime appeared as a reactionary interregnum.

The first four chapters in this volume analyze some important aspects of the Nationalist failure. In his essay on "Factional Politics in Kuomintang China, 1928-1937," Hung-mao Tien stresses the institutional weaknesses of the Nanking government. Factionalism was both a symbol and a cause of the failure of the Nationalists to accomplish political integration in China. The result was devastating. To strengthen his ties with loyal factional leaders, Chiang Kai-shek offered them substantial "tangible rewards." Their domination of the government prevented the affiliation of many other talented party members. Moreover, as Tien suggests, "the weaknesses of the Kuomintang as a political institution facilitated the growth of military apparatus." This, in turn, "undercut the party's ability to function" as an effective organization.

Samuel Chu's chapter on the New Life Movement studies the ideological weaknesses of the ruling Kuomintang. While Chiang Kai-shek and his party comrades perceived the movement as a mass campaign, they distrusted the people too much to give New Life any chance of success. Moreover, according to Chu, the movement exhibited an "almost exclusive concern with the urban sector of China." Its leaders were "elitist and paternalistic," and they emphasized appearance over substance. More important, as Chu argues, these damaging characteristics reflected "some of the central aspects of Kuomintang ideology."

Noel Miner's article on "Agrarian Reform in Nationalist China" examines the rent reduction campaign in Chekiang during the decade of 1927-1937. The province had an agrarian economy with an inequitable distribution of landownership. It was politically controlled by party leaders loyal to Chiang Kai-shek. The campaign followed Sun Yat-sen's ideological guideline of "land to the tiller." Nevertheless, the local officials needed the political and financial support of the landlords, and they chose to sacrifice

the opportunity to earn the backing of the masses.
They "were not strongly motivated reformers," and they
were more concerned with their own base of power than
with the results of the campaign. Miner maintains
that this "ineptness in rural reform provided the setting for successful Communist activities."

While reflecting on the failure of the Nationalists, Donald Jordan's chapter on the boycott of
1931-1932 does not restrict its discussions to the
Nanking government. It stresses China's "vulnerability" to Japanese imperialism, illustrating the political impotence of the Shanghai financial, commercial,
and industrial elite. The boycott was an outburst of
"commercial nationalism." As Jordan concedes, however, the Chinese capitalists were not motivated
solely by their "strong nationalist sentiment." They
wanted to wage an economic war against foreign domination of the China market. Their disappointing
performance, besides demonstrating the weaknesses of
their leadership, revealed some of the problems
of the Kuomintang government. The party's ambivalent
support of the boycott suggested that the Nationalists
did not recognize the potential strength of the anti-
Japanese movement. Their inability to mobilize the
capitalists at a time of national crisis was a clear
indication of the failure of the Kuomintang. The
lack of a "unified political and military power in
China" partially accounted for the ineffectiveness of
the boycott.

THE SINO-JAPANESE WAR AND THE KUOMINTANG DEBACLE OF
  1949

The four chapters described above, constituting
the first section of this volume, center on the inherent weaknesses of the Kuomintang, still unaffected
by the devastation of the Sino-Japanese War. The next
section, with two chapters by Robert Kapp and me,
concentrates on the period following the Japanese invasion of Manchuria.

In his work on Chiang Kai-shek's "nation-building
effort," Arthur Young contends that China's "promising outlook in mid-1937" was "tragically interrupted
by Japan."[15] This argument is inept and unconvincing.
In fact, the Nationalist failure during the war resulted, to a considerable extent, from the deficiencies of Kuomintang leadership. In addition to the
obvious damages inflicted upon the Chungking government, the Sino-Japanese War offered Chiang and his
associates a new opportunity for political integration
and national reconstruction. Their inability to ex-

ploit the opportunity sealed their fate on China's
mainland.   The war against Japan was not the principal
reason for their debacle in 1949.

When Chiang returned to Nanking from Sian
on Christmas Day in 1936, his prestige reached a new
height.   As the outbreak of the Sino-Japanese War
approached in the following year, Mao Tse-tung and his
Communist comrades pledged their support for the
national resistance against Japanese aggression.   For
the first time since 1928, the Kuomintang forces
extended their influence to provinces known for regional separatism.   Kwangtung, Kwangsi, and Szechwan
were notable examples.   China was politically more
integrated than it had been since the decline of the
Manchu dynasty.

Furthermore, when the Nationalists moved their
seat of government to Chungking in 1937, they were in
control of the agriculturally wealthy province of
Szechwan.   With successful agrarian reform, they could
have attracted the support of the rural masses,
thereby reducing the threat of Communist challenge in
the postwar years.   Yet, the Kuomintang leaders were
too insensitive to the needs of the Chinese people
to initiate any radical program of social change.   If
political unity on the eve of the anti-Japanese campaigns had generated new hope for national revivification, the optimism was premature and, in many ways,
misguided.

Sheng Shih-ts'ai, the warlord in Sinkiang, was
the lone challenger to the Kuomintang's attempt at
centralization during the war years.   My chapter on
"Regionalism and Central Power" chronicles his resistance to Chiang's ineffectual endeavors to extend
Nationalist authority to this northwestern province.
During his governorship, Sheng "entertained a contemptuously low estimate" of the Kuomintang's capability to intervene in Sinkiang's affairs.   He adopted
an "independent foreign policy," which enhanced
Russia's influence in the province at the expense of
China's national interests.   His rule in Sinkiang
demonstrated the political weakness of the Kuomintang
government.   More important, in spite of their
desire to gain effective control of the province,
Chiang and his associates were conspicuously unsoli-
citous about its racial problems.   In 1944, when they
succeeded in luring Sheng to abdicate his power in
Sinkiang for a cabinet position in Chungking, they did
not propose any program of social and economic reconstruction to relieve the suffering of the subject
races.   Hostilities continued between the ruling
Chinese and other nationalities, and Chungking's in-

fluence in the province remained tenuous after Sheng's departure.

As illustrated by Robert Kapp's chapter on "The Kuomintang and Rural China," the Nationalist performance in Szechwan during 1937-1945 was, at best, lackluster. While the "refugee regime" was "unprecedentedly dependent" upon the preindustrial resources of interior China, its leaders failed to meet "the daunting challenges of applying central government control to the rural sector of Chinese society." The slogan of "national reconstruction" became hollowly rhetorical, and neither the New Hsien System nor the tax-in-kind program succeeded in halting the decline of the Kuomintang government.

In spite of the gloomy outlook, however, the Nationalists emerged from the catastrophe of the Sino-Japanese War in an apparently strong position. Politically, Chiang benefited from the general euphoria resulting from China's victory over its archenemy. His government was diplomatically recognized by all major powers, including Soviet Russia, and such recognition was often accompanied by financial assistance. On paper, his military forces were at least three times more numerous than those of the Chinese Communists.[16] Yet, in a few years, he would be compelled to yield the mainland to the Communists and lead his followers to exile on the island of Taiwan.

In their examination of the causes of the Kuomintang debacle, many scholars maintain that the civil war of 1946-1949 was mainly a military struggle, in which Chiang committed "organizational flaws and strategic errors." His interference in the conduct of war "muddled the command structure," and his insistance on undertaking the Manchurian campaign overextended his military strength. It ended with the loss of 300,000 of his best troops. Consequently, in 1948, the balance shifted "decisively in favor of the Communists."[17]

The Kuomintang government, it is likewise argued, also suffered from the economic damages of postwar inflation. In 1948, the Chinese yüan depreciated to such an extent that it required 12 million to exchange one American dollar. In August, the Nationalists issued a new currency, the gold yüan, at the official value of four to one American dollar. But, barely nine months afterward, the ratio of exchange dropped to 70 million to one. As the Kuomintang was facing political disaster, an embroidered linen handkerchief cost 750,000 gold yüan, and a party of six people had to pay 50 million for a Peking duck dinner. "It

was impossible," noted a foreign journalist, "to find
out how the desperately poor and the unemployed
managed to keep living."[18]

Nevertheless, military blunders and economic
mismanagement offered only superficial explanations
for Chiang's expulsion from China's mainland.
They were manifestations, and not causes, of the Kuomintang's inherent weaknesses. The ridiculously
low morale of the Nationalist troops could not have
been attributable to strategic errors alone; it
was the product of political corruption, as well as
social and economic stagnation. Similarly, the
Nanking government failed to control inflation mostly
because its officials were unwilling to offend "vested
interests." They lacked "courage and determination"
to adopt stringent and, perhaps, unpopular anti-
inflationary measures which would yield long-term
benefits.[19]

THE COMMUNISTS, 1927-1949: IN SEARCH OF REVOLUTIONARY MODELS

The Nationalist failure notwithstanding, the
Chinese Communists did not move into a political vacuum and win the civil war in 1949 by default. Their
leaders, notably Mao Tse-tung, Liu Shao-ch'i, and Chou
En-lai, had devoted their entire adult lives to the
search for revolutionary models that would bring
wealth and power to China. They had successfully
merged the demands of a war against Japanese aggression with the needs of a social revolution. Their
victory in 1949 concluded a significant stage of experimentation. The third section of the present
volume, with chapters by Ilpyong Kim and Jane Price,
analyzes two important aspects of the Communist
experience.

With the purges of 1927, the Chinese Communist
alliance with the Nationalists collapsed. The impact
of the failure of the "bloc within" strategy was
disastrous. The party membership dropped from 58,000
in April to "a little more than 10,000" by November.[20]
Without implicating the Comintern, Ch'en Tu-hsiu was
blamed by his Communist associates for the catastrophe
of Stalin's "united front" policy. In the following
years, Ch'en's vacated position in the party leadership was filled by Ch'ü Ch'iu-pai, Li Li-san, and
the "twenty-eight Bolsheviks." The Chinese Communists, free from their alliance with the Kuomintang,
were convinced that only they could bring about
radical changes in China. Yet, by following the orthodox urban orientation of the Comintern, they

suffered one setback after another. The Russian
revolutionary model had failed. On the eve of the
Long March in 1934, the party was obviously in urgent
need of new leadership and new direction.

The origins of "the Maoist strategy" can be
dated from Mao Tse-tung's completion of his "Report
on an Investigation of the Peasant Movement in
Hunan."[21] In this important document of 1927, the
future Chinese Communist leader ignored the Marxian
emphasis on the urban proletariat and stressed the
revolutionary strength of the peasantry. Mao
predicted that the peasants would "rise like a mighty
storm, like a hurricane." They would unleash "a
force so swift and violent that no power, however
great, will be able to hold it back." This uprising
against "the feudal landlords" would initiate "a
revolution without parallel in history." Thus, Mao
urged his comrades to change "all the wrong measures
... concerning the peasant movement."[22] Nevertheless,
his heretical plea fell on unsympathetic ears.

In 1927, Mao was "a vigorous young Communist,
unhampered by a deep knowledge of Marxism-Leninism."
His report on the peasant movement in Hunan was
"written in the white heat of passion."[23] It would be
a mistake to assume that he planned, at this early
stage, to challenge the orthodoxy of Soviet Russia by
devising a new theory of revolution for China. The
Sinification of Communism -- known to some scholars as
"Maoism" -- was the product of a long process of
adapting an alien, urban-oriented strategy to the
realities of an agrarian society.[24] It formed an integral part of the search for revolutionary models.

Mao's flight to Chingkangshan after the failure
of the Autumn Harvest Uprising gave him the first
opportunity to test his conception of a peasant revolution in China's hinterland. In defeat, he did
not have many choices. Chingkangshan was not an urban center. He could not rely on the industrial workers
to lead the peasantry. His inability to mobilize the
rural masses would result in a personal catastrophe, probably terminating prematurely his revolutionary
career. To gain the support of the peasants, he thus
adopted the policy of "complete confiscation and
thorough redistribution" of land.[25] With Chu Teh's
able assistance, he also blended the Chinese "peasant-
insurgent military tradition" with "the Russian-
imported political techniques of mass mobilization" to
develop the "nucleus" of the Red Army.[26] His guerrilla
tactics proved extremely useful in the party's later
struggles against both the Kuomintang and the Japanese
aggressors.

Despite his success in the hinterland, Mao's road to power in the Chinese Communist Party was rough and uneven. His ideological conflict with the "returned students" did not end with the Tsunyi Conference in January 1935, when he assumed political control of the party.[27] Nonetheless, the Long March strengthened his commitment to bringing about fundamental changes in China. By 1936, "the Maoist strategy" had taken "full form," and it transformed the "entire concept" of the Chinese revolution.[28] Mao and his comrades were further helped in 1937 by the outbreak of the anti-Japanese War, which enabled the Communists to exploit the nationalist sentiments of the peasantry. The support of the rural masses provided the party with a solid base for its eventual challenge of the Kuomintang government.[29]

In 1942, Mao reaffirmed his commitment to the "mass line" with his call for a rectification (cheng-feng) movement in Yenan. The Chinese revolution was a "people's war," and its political objective was to replace the Kuomintang "tutelage" with a "new democracy."[30] Ideologically, Mao's campaign of rectification "marked the final eclipse" of the "returned students." The "Yenan way" evolved amidst attacks on subjectivism, sectarianism, and formalism. This experience in mass indoctrination, based on a "broad vision of man and society in revolution," helped to create an ideal Communist who "transcended barriers of specialization and status." An activist in the party should combine in himself "the values and accomplishments of the laborer, the leader, the soldier, and the student."[31]

The last two chapters in this volume offer examples of the revolutionary experimentation of the Chinese Communist Party. This quest for new models contrasted sharply with the failure of the Nationalists. In "The Origins of Communist and Soviet Movements in China," Ilpyong Kim analyzes the development of soviets as "an organizational technique for mass political action." The adoption of this institution represented a forward step in China's march toward a proletarian-socialist revolution. In the process, the Chinese Communists adjusted the Russian model to suit the realities of their society. They turned an urban-oriented movement into one based upon the agrarian population of China.

In a complementary article, Jane Price discusses the intricate relationship between land reform and mass mobilization. During the civil war, the radicalization of the peasantry was a political necessity.

Yet, as Price argues, the reform was "never an end in itself." The Chinese Communist leadership was "ideologically committed to creating a nation in which private property would ultimately be abolished altogether." In spite of the tone of utopian idealism, this was an objective that helped the Communists to win a struggle spanning two decades.

IN PLACE OF CONCLUSION

As a revolutionary party, the Kuomintang was seriously defective. Both Sun Yat-sen and Chiang Kai-shek overlooked the importance of organization and discipline, while demanding personal allegiance from their followers. The party lacked the unifying force of a well-defined ideology, and many members indulged in factional politics. They were often more concerned with their selfish interests than with the social and economic problems of the populace. In 1928, these weaknesses were sublimated by the success of the Northern Expedition, but they became intensified in the following years as the Kuomintang regressed "from revolution to restoration."[32] Meanwhile, Chiang's obsession with anti-Communism diverted his government from the task of national reconstruction, and he prolonged the period of "party tutelage" under the pretext of Japanese aggression. In the end, the Kuomintang lost the support of the people, and its leaders had to seek political sanctuary on the island of Taiwan.

In contrast, the Chinese Communist Party accumulated an impressive record on revolutionary experimentation, despite its disastrous defeats in 1927 and 1934. Thanks to Mao Tse-tung's Sinification of Communism, the party formulated a successful strategy based upon land reform and mass mobilization. The Communist movement became a dynamic political force on the eve of China's victory over Japan, as the Kuomintang was dragged into the quagmire of inflation by its own inherent weaknesses. The civil war was a political struggle between the two parties, and the Communist triumph was as much the result of Mao's success as it was the product of Nationalist failure.

The Kuomintang-Communist rivalries during the critical years of 1927-1949 dramatized China's arduous experience in modernization. The military victory of the Northern Expedition created an illusion of revolutionary success. Chiang and the new ruling elites in Nanking did not initiate any lasting changes to improve the livelihood of the masses. They failed to give republicanism an opportunity to take root in

China. In 1949, the Communists overthrew a corrupt
and reactionary government, yet this remarkable accomplishment did not by itself lead the beleaquered
nation toward the path of revivification. As guard-
ians of the "mandate of heaven," they must bear
the awesome responsibility of bringing about China's
socialist transformation. The nation's future depends
upon their success in this formidable endeavor.

NOTES

1. Sokolsky, "The Kuomintang," in *China Year
Book, 1928*, ed. by H. G. W. Woodhead (Tientsin: Tientsin Press Ltd., n.d.), p. 1373.
2. My theme of revolutionary failure is inspired
by Lloyd E. Eastman, *The Abortive Revolution: China
under Nationalist Rule, 1927-1937* (Cambridge,
Mass.: Harvard University Press, 1974), although
we offer different explanations for the Kuomintang
weaknesses. The quotations appear in p. 9.
3. See, for example, Arthur N. Young, *China's
Nation-Building Effort, 1927-1937* (Stanford: Hoover
Institution Press, 1971); Paul K. T. Sih (ed.),
*The Strenuous Decade: China's Nation-Building Efforts,
1927-1937* (Jamaica, N.Y.: St. John's University
Press, 1970); and Paul K. T. Sih (ed.), *Nationalist
China During the Sino-Japanese War, 1937-1945*
(Hicksville, N.Y.: Exposition Press, 1977).
4. Chalmers A. Johnson, *Peasant Nationalism and
Communist Power: The Emergence of Revolutionary China,
1937-1945* (Stanford: Stanford University Press,
1966); Dick Wilson, *The Long March: The Epic of Chi-
nese Communism's Survival, 1935* (New York: Viking
Press, 1971); William Hinton, *Fanshen: A Documentary
of Revolution in a Chinese Village* (New York:
Random House, 1968); Mark Selden, *The Yenan Way in
Revolutionary China* (Cambridge, Mass.: Harvard
University Press, 1971); Jane L. Price, *Cadres, Com-
manders, and Commissars: The Training of the Chi-
nese Communist Leadership, 1920-45* (Boulder: Westview
Press, 1976); and Ilpyong J. Kim, *The Politics of
Chinese Communism: Kiangsi under the Soviets*
(Berkeley: University of California Press, 1973).
See also Hsiao Tso-liang, *The Land Revolution in China,
1930-1934* (Seattle: University of Washington Press,
1969); Tetsuya Kataoka, *Resistance and Revolution in
China: The Communists and the Second United Front*
(Berkeley: University of California Press, 1974); and
Lyman P. Van Slyke, *Enemies and Friends: The United
Front in Chinese Communist History* (Stanford: Stanford
University Press, 1967).

14

5.   Eastman, *Abortive Revolution*; and Tien, *Government and Politics in Kuomintang China* (Stanford: Stanford University Press, 1972).

6.   Kubek, *How the Far East Was Lost: American Policy and the Creation of Communist China, 1941-1949* (Chicago: Henry Regnery Co., 1963); and Hu, "China in Stalin's Grand Strategy," in *Foreign Affairs*, Vol. XXIX, No. 1 (October 1950), p. 11.   Cf. Pichon P. Y. Loh (ed.), *The Kuomintang Debacle of 1949: Conquest or Collapse?* (Lexington, Mass.: D. C. Heath & Co., 1965); and Chiang Kai-shek, *Soviet Russia in China: A Summing-Up at Seventy* (New York: Farrar, Straus & Cudahy, 1957).

7.   Brian Crozier, *The Man Who Lost China: The First Full Biography of Chiang Kai-shek*, with the collaboration of Eric Chou (New York: Charles Scribner's Sons, 1976).

8.   Quoted from Eastman, *Abortive Revolution*, p. 7.

9.   Tsou Lu, *Chung-kuo kuo-min-tang shih-kao* /A Draft History of the Kuomintang/ (Taipei, 1965), Vol. I, p. 384.

10.   Eastman, *Abortive Revolution*, pp. 10, 285-86. Similarly, the Chinese Communist Party has often appointed its leaders to concurrent positions, although such practice is less common in Western democratic nations.

11.   Tai Chi-t'ao traced the principles to the teachings of the Chinese sages.   See *Tai Chi-t'ao hsien-sheng wen-ts'un tsai-hsu-pien* / Additional Supplement to Mr. Tai Chi-t'ao's Collected Works_/, ed. by Ch'en T'ien-hsi (Taipei, 1968), Vol. II, p. 657.   For the details of the principles, see Paul Myron Anthony Linebarger, *The Political Doctrine of Sun Yat-sen: An Exposition of the San Min Chu I* (Baltimore: Johns Hopkins Press, 1937).

12.   Eastman, *Abortive Revolution*, pp. 5-9.

13.   Andrew J. Nathan, *Peking Politics, 1918-1923: Factionalism and the Failure of Constitutionalism* (Berkeley: University of California Press, 1976), pp. 201-20.

14.   See, for example, Lloyd E. Eastman, "Fascism in Kuomintang China: The Blue Shirts," in *The China Quarterly*, No. 49 (January-March 1972), pp. 1-31.

15.   Young, *China's Nation-Building Effort*, p. v.

16.   A. Doak Barnett, *China on the Eve of Communist Takeover* (New York: Frederick A. Praeger, Publisher, 1963), p. 11.   Cf. F. F. Liu, *A Military History of Modern China: 1924-1949* (Princeton: Princeton University Press, 1956), p. 254.

17.   Loh (ed.), *Kuomintang Debacle*, p. viii; Liu,

Military History, pp. 259, 260; and Barnett, *China*, p. 11.

18.   Robert P. Martin, "China in the '40s," and Laurence S. Kuter, "China in the '40s," both in *U. S. News & World Report*, October 2, 1978, pp. 37-38.   While Martin was a journalist and Kuter a commander of American air forces, they were in China during the critical years of 1948-1949.

19.   Chang Kia-ngau, *The Inflationary Spiral: The Experience in China, 1939-1950* (Cambridge, Mass.: M. I. T. Press, 1958), p. 365.

20.   James Pinckney Harrison, *The Long March to Power: A History of the Chinese Communist Party, 1921-72* (New York: Praeger Publishers, 1972), p. 119.

21.   The report appears in *Selected Works of Mao Tse-tung* (Peking: Foreign Languages Press, 1965), Vol. I, pp. 23-59.   For an analysis of "the Maoist strategy," see John King Fairbank, *The United States and China*, third edition (Cambridge, Mass.: Harvard University Press, 1971), pp. 267-69; Benjamin I. Schwartz, *Chinese Communism and the Rise of Mao* (Cambridge, Mass.: Harvard University Press, 1964), pp. 189-204; and Conrad Brandt, Benjamin Schwartz, and John K. Fairbank (eds.), *A Documentary History of Chinese Communism* (Cambridge, Mass.: Harvard University Press, 1952), pp. 77-79.   Cf. Karl A. Wittfogel, "The Legend of 'Maoism,'" in *The China Quarterly*, No. 1 (January-March 1960), pp. 72-86; and No. 2 (April-June 1960), pp. 16-34.

22.   *Selected Works*, Vol. I, pp. 23, 25.

23.   Wittfogel, "Legend," No. 2, p. 16; and Stuart R. Schram, *The Political Thought of Mao Tse-tung*, enlarged and revised edition (Harmondsworth: Penguin Books, 1969), p. 54.

24.   Benjamin Schwartz, "The Legend of the 'Legend of "Maoism,"'" in *The China Quarterly*, No. 2 (April-June 1960), p. 35; and Lucien Bianco, *Origins of the Chinese Revolution, 1915-1949*, trans. by Muriel Bell (Stanford: Stanford University Press, 1971), pp. 73-81.

25.   Jerome Ch'en, *Mao and the Chinese Revolution* (New York: Oxford University Press, 1965), p. 139.

26.   William W. Whitson (with Ch'en-hsia Huang), *The Chinese High Command: A History of Communist Military Politics, 1927-71* (New York: Praeger Publishers, 1973), p. 29; and Bianco, *Origins*, p. 64.

27.   John E. Rue, *Mao Tse-tung in Opposition, 1927-1935* (Stanford: Stanford University Press, 1966), esp. pp. 265-72.

28.   Ch'en, *Mao*, pp. 114-15.

29.   Johnson, *Peasant Nationalism*, esp. pp. 1-70.

Cf. Kataoka, *Resistance and Revolution*, in which the
author argues that the Maoist strategy of "peasant
war" collapsed in 1934. Henceforth, the Chinese
Communists "turned toward the cities" (p. 9). They
appealed to the nationalism of "the urban middle
class and intellectuals" and compelled the Kuomintang
to abandon its effort to exterminate Communism in
China (p. 309).

30. "On New Democracy," in *Selected Works*, Vol.
II, pp. 339-84.

31. Fairbank, *United States*, pp. 277-78; and
Selden, *Yenan Way*, pp. 274, 275-76.

32. Mary C. Wright, "From Revolution to Restoration: The Transformation of Kuomintang Ideology,"
Far Eastern Quarterly, Vol. XIV, No. 4 (August 1955)
pp. 515-32.

Part 1
The Nationalists, 1927–1937:
A Case Study of
Revolutionary Failure

1

Factional Politics in Kuomintang China, 1928–1937: An Interpretation

Hung-mao Tien

This chapter seeks to analyze factionalism in the first ten years of the Kuomintang government prior to the outbreak of the Sino-Japanese War in 1937, a period commonly known as the Nanking decade. It attempts to show what factions existed, how they were organized, to what extent they operated to affect the political process of the time, and in what way they influenced the course of modern Chinese political development.

Factions as organized units of political conflicts appear in many arenas.[1] Studies by social anthropologists indicate that they exist in village, tribe, and other smaller social units.[2] Political scientists also document their existence in such larger political organizations as army, bureaucracy, party, state and national governments.[3] Traditional societies provide fertile grounds for factional conflicts, and so do some modern political systems. In Japan, for example, traditional social relations retain strong influence on political processes. As is evident from the existing literature, factionalism is not a special product of any particular culture or society. As a structure of conflicts, factional politics has been common in African and Indian tribes,

An earlier version of this chapter was presented at the annual conference of the American Historical Association in New Orleans, Louisiana, on December 27-30, 1972. I am grateful for the financial assistance provided by the University of Wisconsin Center System for the preparation of this article. I would also like to thank Andrew Nathan of Columbia University for his conceptual insight on factionalism.

in Thai bureaucracy, in the early republican government and the Communist Party of China, in Soviet
bureaucracy, in early American politics, and in contemporary Japanese political parties.

Factions are seldom durable. They lack the
lasting ingredients of party, kinship, clan, and some
other corporate bodies. Their basic organizational
feature is based on dyadic ties governed by interests,
friendship, or patron-client relationship. Although
some factions may remain in a political arena for a
relatively long period of time, their factional structure undergoes frequent changes, and political allegiance shifts among members.

Factions as a major form of organized political
conflicts emerged in Chinese political processes after
the collapse of the Ch'ing dynasty in 1912. Andrew
Nathan's study demonstrates that factionalism provided
the important structure of political conflicts in
the early republican government.[4] Jerome Ch'en likewise notes the existence of intriguing factional
alignments during the subsequent warlord period.[5]
Even under the Communist system in which impersonal
organizational principles and procedures supposedly replace ascriptive and particularistic social criteria, factions have continued to exist.[6] It thus
seems well-accepted among many students of modern
China that twentieth-century Chinese politics is characterized by pervasive factionalism.

The milieu in which the Kuomintang functioned
encouraged the continuous presence of factional politics within the party's power structure. The death
of Sun Yat-sen, the undisputed leader, created an
acute problem of succession. This resulted in the
diffusion of party authority into competing clusters
around several strong personalities who refused to be
subjugated by their comrades. The Kuomintang's
failure to institute a bureaucratic organizational
framework for policy formation and implementation was
symptomatic of its leadership crisis. This failure
weakened the institutional base of the party rule.
The succession crisis, coupled with the institutional
weaknesses, confronted the Nationalist regime with
years of instability and tedious legitimacy problems.
Meanwhile, the feudalization of political power at
a macroscopic level of all China further strengthened
factional alignments.

LEGACY OF SUCCESSION CRISIS

Faction-like group competitions had existed in
Kuomintang politics long before the Nanking government

was established in 1928. In the first half of the
1920s, group rivalries were tempered by Sun Yat-sen's
dominant position in the party. Following his death
in 1925, however, competitions sharpened along an
ideological line.[7]

Sun's collaboration with Chinese Communists and
the Kuomintang reorganization in 1924 on the Leninist
model generated severe group antagonism. The left-
right alignments among party leaders and their
rank-and-file supporters reflected a pro-and-con
stand on the Kuomintang-Communist rapprochement that
divided them right down to the lowest level of
party affairs.[8] Wang Ching-wei and Liao Chung-k'ai,
who led the left-wing group, took a reformist line in
favor of allying with the Communists.[9] On the other
hand, the right-wing party politicians, exemplified
by the Western Hills group, distrusted the Communists
and saw the changes of 1923-1924 as a major threat
to the survival of the Kuomintang.

In 1925-1927, these two groups, engulfed by their
ideological visions, exaggerated their mutual differences and became obsessed with doctrinalism.[10] As
the Kuomintang was involved in military maneuvers
in its sanctuary of Kwangtung, party leaders without
strong military background resorted to faction-like
alignments with local generals in order to consolidate
their positions. There was no leader in the Kuomintang who could stand above the troubled water to
perform a mediating role. Mutual distrust led to Liao
Chung-k'ai's assassination in August 1925.

From 1928 to 1937, Chiang Kai-shek, who had
earlier maintained a centrist position, steadily moved
to a commanding position in the Kuomintang regime.
Senior party leaders (Wang Ching-wei and Hu Han-min)
and many regional militarists (Feng Yü-hsiang, Li
Tsung-jen, Yen Hsi-shan, and Ch'en Chi-t'ang, among
others) challenged him. At times, they threatened to
destroy him with various coalitions of forces. The
anti-Chiang factions represented the legacy of the
pre-1928 intraparty rivalries that had flourished with
Sun Yat-sen's death. Wang and Hu never truly conceded to Chiang's leadership. Indeed, factional
strife intensified in the Kuomintang because of un-
resolved succession problems.

INSTITUTIONAL WEAKNESS

It is commonly asserted that institutional weakness reinforces, if not causes, factionalism in a
political arena. It constituted an important defi-
ciency in the developmental experiences of republican

China. The reasons for institutional weakness are complex and are beyond the scope of this study. Rigorous research is required to establish generalization. Observations, however, can be made to explain several plausible factors related to China's failure in institution-building.

The 1911 Revolution destroyed a legitimate governmental order already in decay. In the subsequent years, efforts to reverse the process were sluggish at best. Legitimacy crises, compounded by the steady erosion of civil authority, pushed the shaky governmental framework to the brink of total collapse. Prior to 1928, the warlords operated in a milieu of political decentralization. They relied mainly on military forces to foster a system of shifting alliances, and were unsuccessful in stabilizing the political situation. By the time the Kuomintang regime came into existence, China had been extremely chaotic for almost two decades.

The Nationalist government made some progress in institution-building. The organization of its army had a stronger institutional character than that of either its predecessors or its contemporary rival forces. Attempts were made to strengthen the party as a governing institution and to initiate administrative reconstruction at the center as well as in some provinces. Yet, the foundation of these institutions did not sufficiently demonstrate organizational vitality. Given the institutional needs of the Kuomintang regime at the time, the emerging political and administrative structive was functionally inadequate.

In spite of the Kuomintang's earlier adoption of the Leninist organizational framework, it did not build a broad-based apparatus for a national revolutionary party. Even after it came to power, party membership and organizational distribution continued to be limited to a narrow geographical area, principally in the lower Yangtze Valley provinces and Kwangtung; the latter was beyond the reach of central authority until 1936. Membership growth from 300,000 in 1930 to 496,000 in 1935 was unimpressive.[11] The party also lacked rigorous discipline and training programs, and organizational discipline required for an authoritarian political party was clearly absent. In the final analysis, organizational weakness prevented the Kuomintang from becoming an effective institutional instrument to integrate the heterogeneous political forces in China. It further set a limit on mass mobilization.

Moreover, within the party's power hierarchy,

designated decision-making organs were not institutionalized.[12] The Central Executive Committee,
the Political Council, and the Party Congress were
created on the Soviet model to provide legitimatizing
institutions for reaching decisions. Nevertheless,
rapid increase of membership in these organs severely
undercut their effectiveness. Influential party
leaders used them as patronage posts for their
military and political clients who sought such membership only to enhance their prestige and status.
Major decisions were often reached outside their
institutional arenas through informal dealings among
powerful leaders.

Although these organs served to legitimatize
decisions, policy made under their names could be con-
veniently abandoned by men of influence. Political
power belonged to those leaders who were able to
attract personal followers in positions to extract and
implement resource allocation, as well as to use
military and quasi-military forces upon which
the survival of the regime depended. Crippled by the
lack of institutional avenues to political power,
capable and prestigious party leaders resorted to the
cultivation of factional following.

This development in the Kuomintang was related
to the party's reliance on military power for its
survival. Party-building fell victim to the increasing militarization of the government. Chiang
Kai-shek's control of the army gave him enormous
authority. The weakness of the Kuomintang as a political institution facilitated the growth of military
apparatus. By the same token, the rising military
power under Chiang undercut the party's ability
to function as an effective political organization.

The apparent disregard of the military for
institutional development victimized the civilian
bureaucracy. The Nanking government under Chiang's
military control made little effort to build a
national administrative order based on rational and
routinized criteria. To obtain administrative
positions or to survive in them required factional affiliation and other particularistic relations. Unable to enforce objective rules in administrative
recruitment, the Kuomintang authorities depended on
the informal process of factional bargaining. Instead
of functioning as a formal implementation agency,
the administration became another areana of factional
interplay.

To sum up, the institutional weakness of the
Kuomintang regime encouraged the continuous existence
of factionalism. Since political conflicts could

not be structured within the formal and legitimate
institutions, factions retained their informal functions in politics.

PROVINCIALISM AND FEUDALIZATION OF POWER

To a certain extent, warlordism continued during
the Nanking decade. Although Chiang Kai-shek's
military effort and political maneuvers enabled him
to establish varying degrees of control over parts of
China, more than half of the provinces remained in
the hands of the militarists. In the north, Yen
Hsi-shan held Shansi, while Feng Yü-hsiang and his
protégés ruled Chahar, Suiyüan, Shantung, and Hopei.
Elsewhere, Li Tsung-jen and Pai Ch'ung-hsi controlled
Kwangsi, and Ch'en Chi-t'ang and Lung Yün dominated
Kwangtung and Yünnan respectively. Liu Hsiang and
other military leaders divided Szechwan. These major
militarists controlled their own territorial bases,
and they resisted Nanking's growing penetration. Many
feared that Chiang's power would expand at their
expense.

How did this feudalization of power affect the
organized political conflicts among rival leaders in
the Kuomintang? First, the territorial bases of
the militarists and their relative independence from
Nanking offered Chiang's factional opponents a
secure place for political retreat. These bases provided at least temporary sanctuary which, offered
by friendly provincial militarists, safeguarded the
survival of some factional leaders in Kuomintang
politics. Both Wang Ching-wei and Hu Han-min, for
example, enjoyed sanctuary with the Kwangtung
militarists.

Secondly, some provincial militarists became
natural allies of Wang and Hu in their opposition to
Chiang's authority. These militarists needed the
prestige and influence of the two Kuomintang leaders
who, in turn, benefited from the military strength and
territorial base of their allies. Thus, the alignments between Kuomintang leaders and provincial
militarists assured some degree of military-political
equilibrium in factional politics.

Even when Wang and Hu were not actually in alliance with the provincial militarists, such possibility alone seemed to strengthen their bargaining
power in dealing with Chiang. Factionalism within the
Kuomintang would not disappear as long as Wang and
Hu contended with Chiang. This permitted the
militarists to refuse to yield to Nanking's authority.
On the other hand, the fact that provincial mili-

tarism helped perpetuate factional rivalries within
the party gave Chiang an additional incentive to
rid China's politics of it.

CHIANG KAI-SHEK'S DOMINANT FACTION

Despite the ability of Wang and Hu to maintain
their rival factions, the Kuomintang regime was dominated by Chiang Kai-shek, whose loyal followers
had firm control over Nanking's financial resources,
the party machine, and, above all, the military
forces. Chiang's opponents had little chance to influence the fundamental policies of either the
party or the government. Only in decisions of minor
importance did factions headed by Wang and Hu participate as legitimate political groups in the party's
political process.

Nevertheless, while the positions of Chiang's
rivals on such significant issues as military policy,
financial extraction and allocation, and party
organization rarely carried much weight, the intraparty political conflicts required that their interests be accommodated and their policy preferences
be recognized. The complete alienation of Wang and Hu,
for instance, would destroy the already fragile consensus of the government.

Chiang's emergence as the leading political
figure of the Nanking regime resulted from his positions as commandant of the Whampoa Military Academy and, later, as commander-in-chief of the National
Revolutionary Army. As the survival of the Kuomintang
depended largely on the support of the military, he
could use his military power to bargain for political
influence. The presence of hostile warlords and
Chinese Communists in the provinces provided him with
a convincing justification for giving military affairs
top priority. As Japanese territorial ambitions in
China became evident after 1931, growing anti-Japanese
sentiment rendered him apparently indispensable.

Military power alone, however, was insufficient
to guarantee the Chiang faction its dominant status. The strength of the military forces depended on
the availability of financial support. This faction
maintained its authority as long as it was capable of
extracting revenue through heavy taxes, foreign
loans, or financial contributions from such wealthy
elites as industrialists, merchants, and bankers
of the major cities.

Chiang cultivated the backing of the financial
community in Shanghai, dominated by people from
Chekiang, his native province, and neighboring Kiangsu.

Strong support from the rich elites of the city enabled him to maintain his own forces, disregard factional compromise, and buy off provincial militarists. Since the establishment of the Nanking government, he had placed the control of government finances in the hands of his two reliable relatives, T. V. Soong and H. H. Kung, and other trusted industrialists and bankers from Chekiang and Kiangsu.

Both from Kwangtung, Wang Ching-wei and Hu Han-min had virtually no support from the Kiangsu-Chekiang elites. They lacked access to government positions that were related to finances. Without military forces in their command, they also could not depend on a general election to provide periodic changes of political power. Consequently, they had little bargaining power in Nanking. Since they were unable to reward their followers with public offices and lucrative resources, their factional machines had little room to grow. They could not use the existing formal organizations of the regime -- namely: the party, the military, and the administrative bureaucracy -- as institutional support to develop a strong and complex clientele-faction of their own.

When Wang Ching-wei was president of the Executive Yüan in 1932-1935, only a handful of important cabinet posts were awarded to his clients.[13] Even then, there was little evidence of a penetrating factional development. Thanks to his cool relations with Chiang Kai-shek, Hu Han-min was even less capable of using the formal organizations to back his factional followers. The occasional alignments of Wang and Hu with the sporadic anti-Chiang elements did not help to consolidate their factional strength. Within the Kuomintang government, the structure of conflicts was dominated by individuals associated with Chiang's faction.

STRUCTURES AND FUNCTIONS OF CHIANG KAI-SHEK'S DOMINANT
    FACTION

The Chiang faction was able to maintain its dominant position largely because of its complex system of stratification. It consisted of either individuals tied to him through personal connections or groups that served as supportive subcliques in the overall structure. Individuals like T. V. Soong and H. H. Kung, who attempted to modernize China's finances, performed a liaison function with the industrial-financial community and served as managers of the party government's financial apparatus.

Patron-client relations were also established with many provincial militarists who had shifted their allegiance for political and financial rewards. Ho Chien of Hunan and Han Fu-chü of Shantung were two obvious examples. But none of these leaders was able to develop a subclique of his own.

Three political groups that operated under Chiang's leadership, however, succeeded in developing "support structures," which functioned as the cornerstones of Chiang's complex faction.[14] They were the C. C. Clique, the Whampoa Clique (at times known as the Blue Shirts Society), and the Political Study Clique. As a means of "interest articulation," cliques were functionally differentiated from one another.[15] The formation of these three supportive cliques came at different times, yet they were functionally oriented from the beginning. They were created, maintained, and expanded by manipulating the prerogatives of state and party offices.

The C. C. Clique was led by two brothers, Ch'en Kuo-fu and Ch'en Li-fu, who took turns from 1926 to control the party's Bureau of Organization. Their major responsibility was to consolidate a party apparatus that would help Chiang maintain his dominant position in the Kuomintang. During the 1930s, the clique extended its activities to other areas. It developed a clandestine intelligence network and established major influence in education, culture, and media professions. In the formal administrative arena, the clique controlled the provincial and county governments in Kiangsu and, to a lesser extent, in Chekiang and Anhwei, as well as much of Shanghai's municipal government. In addition, it dominated Kiangsu's provincial Farmers Bank and had a strong influence in the National Farmers Bank of China.

These feats were accomplished by a reported membership of more than 10,000.[16] This number is misleading. Intellectuals, bureaucrats, and politicians, who were recruited by the Ch'en brothers, saw their affiliation with the clique as a critical avenue to personal advancement and wealth. The fact that the clique commanded institutional support in the party apparatus, the banking structure, and some provincial and city-county administrations offered ample attraction to those seeking political fortunes. The relatively small membership permitted close contacts between the Ch'en brothers and their followers. While serving the interests of both its leaders and members, the clique's octopus-like organization offered Chiang Kai-shek a "support structure" that was profitably used in his scramble for the leading position in the Nanking regime.

The Blue Shirts Society was the backbone of what is generally referred to as the Whampoa Clique. Founded in 1931 as a clandestine political group to uphold Chiang's personal power, the society drew its membership exclusively from the Whampoa cadets and a few instructors. Chiang was the first and only commandant of the Whampoa Military Academy. These cadets remained loyal to him without joining the Chinese Communist Party. They owed to him their steady rise in the military hierarchy during and after the Northern Expedition. To them, Chiang was not only a leader, but also a paternal patron.

Political developments in 1930-1931 were favorable to the creation of the Blue Shirts Society. The Chinese Communists led by Mao Tse-tung and Chu Teh had founded a soviet region in Kiangsi. In 1931, Chiang was temporarily forced to relinquish his presidential office as a result of combined pressures from his factional opponents. Meanwhile, Japan began to invade Manchuria. Chiang's Whampoa supporters felt that their common interests, as well as what they perceived as China's national interests, were severely threatened by these developments. They decided to create a political group on the Fascist model to mobilize and control the masses on Chiang's behalf.[17] They pronounced their determination to uphold Chiang's personal dictatorship.

In the following years, they developed an intelligence, espionage, and indoctrination apparatus in Nanking's military forces and some provincial police units. By the time the Sino-Japanese War broke out in 1937, they had developed political commissars and police in Chiang's military ranks and, through Tai Li's effort, had formed a police network encompassing the central and lower Yangtze Valley provinces.

The Political Study Clique was not so well organized as the other two groups. Yet, it put together a number of experienced politicians, militarists, bankers, and industrialists who saw great interest in their association with Chiang Kai-shek. It did not generally develop vertical organization apparatus. Neither did its leaders have a broad representation in the formal decision-making organs of either the party or the government. Nevertheless, they were all individually influential persons in their respective fields. Many occupied key positions in the financial world, and some were governors of such important provinces as Hupei, Kiangsi, and Chekiang. For example, Yang Yung-t'ai, a leading fig-

ure, also administered Chiang's powerful military
apparatus through his strategic position as secretary-
general in Chiang's anti-Communist field headquarters.

All three cliques were linked together by their
acceptance of Chiang's leadership. The political
fortunes of their members depended upon those of
Chiang. In Kuomintang politics, political competition
was confined to a narrow, somewhat homogeneous elite
group with few ideological differences. Consequently,
people in search of power and career advancement
frequently relied on personal alliances.

In the process of personal interaction, Chiang
stood out as the leader of the cliques; through
him clique conflicts were arbitrated, mediated, and
managed. All the members shared the common purpose of
seeking tangible gains and some symbolic values.
Their interests would be threatened by the ascendancy
of Chiang's factional opponents in the regime's
power structure. This complex pro-Chiang factional
system was the key to his success. The factions
of Wang Ching-wei and Hu Han-min did not have a "support structure" of comparable effectiveness. Political rivalries in the Kuomintang government can
therefore best be conceptualized within the framework
of a dominant factional system.

On what bases did Chiang foster his complex
support structure? To provide an answer to this question, it seems necessary to examine several types
of personal relations that may overlap and, at times,
reinforce each other. They are as follows:

1. Local affinity: Chiang had special affection
for his fellow provincials of Chekiang, and he trusted
those from neighboring Kiangsu. This feeling of
provincialism was perhaps strengthened by his early
experiences with Ch'en Ch'i-mei. During the first
decade after the 1911 Revolution, he spent most of his
time in Shanghai. Most of the friends he had in
this period later became his trusted lieutenants. They
included Chang Jen-chieh, Ch'en Kuo-fu, Ch'en Li-fu,
Tai Chi-t'ao, Huang Fu, and Chang Ch'ün. Among
his factional followers in the supportive cliques, he
was close to those from Chekiang. The Ch'en brothers, Tai Li, and Hu Tsung-nan were notable examples.

2. Family ties: Chiang's two main pillars in the
modernization of the financial and banking systems
-- T. V. Soong and H. H. Kung -- were his brothers-in-
law. Although Soong differed with Chiang on policies, he did not shift his loyalty to another faction.

3. School ties: The strong bonds between Chiang

and his factional followers resulted, at times, from their common experiences as classmates. There were also teacher-student and superior-subordinate relationships. Chiang's lasting friendship with Chang Ch'ün, for instance, had its origins at Japan's Shimbu Gakkō, where they were classmates. In this regard, perhaps the most outstanding example was Chiang's relations with the students and instructors of the Whampoa Military Academy, of which he was the commandant. Many graduates were loyally committed to Chiang; some of his staunch followers in the academy organized the Blue Shirts Society for the furtherance of his power. Ho Ying-ch'in, Ch'en Ch'eng, and Chang Chih-chung were Whampoa instructors, and they all occupied important positions in Chiang's factional structure.

4. Sworn brothers: Personal relations derived from sworn brotherhood frequently entailed self-imposed ethical obligations that required great sacrifice. While Chinese folklore is full of tales extolling the "virtuous" behavior of sworn brothers, this type of relationship was very popular in the 1920s among idealistic youth. They shared a common concern about the social and political ills of their time, and they were in search of similar solutions.

Chiang Kai-shek's sworn brotherhood with Chang Ch'ün and Huang Fu began when they served under Ch'en Ch'i-mei in Shanghai. This relationship later obligated Chang and Huang to secure for Chiang the desperately needed revenue for his military endeavors. They also recommended to him many experienced military and civilian leaders. During the Northern Expedition, Huang Fu helped to arrange a military payroll in Wuhan. Thanks to him and Chang Ch'ün, Chiang enlisted the support of Yang Yung-t'ai, who was to play a pivotal role in Chiang's anti-Communist campaigns.

As Chiang's political fortunes flourished, he awarded his two sworn brothers with positions of enormous importance. At different times, both served as the mayor of Shanghai. Chang Ch'ün was governor of Hupei and Huang Fu spent many years in Peiping as Nanking's special envoy, working as Chiang's liaison man with North China's military and political leaders. As Japanese territorial ambitions became evident in Manchuria and North China, Huang may have been in essence Chiang's watchdog in a region that was politically more and more troublesome for the Nationalist regime.

A similar relationship existed between Chiang and some influential leaders of Shanghai's secret socie-

ties. This became a significant political asset in
Chiang's decisive move to purge the Communists in the
city. It also helped to develop his factional
strength. Tu Yüeh-sheng, Yang Hu, and Ch'en Ch'ün,
among others, were his troubleshooters in his
successful attempt to gain complete control over that
nerve center of China's banking, commercial, and
industrial activities.

5. Patron-client relationship: In politics, this
allows an exchange of obligations and rewards. The
patron is usually more highly placed than his clients,
and the bond between them requires personal rather
than group loyalty. As James Scott notes, "A patron
develops a following of clients by virtue of his
unilateral control over resources the clients need."[18]
The patron's offerings are often concrete and tangible, in exchange for the clients' loyalty, political
support, and supply of information.[19]

Chiang's relations with his factional clients
involved a broad variety of ties not limited to the
needs of the time. Personal connections resulting
from similar provincial origins, family and educational backgrounds, as well as from sworn brotherhood,
formed the bases for his factional alignments. They
were the principal sources for the patron-client
relationship. Yet, besides these ascriptive and particularistic criteria, such utilitarian motives as
mutual profit also tied Chiang to other clients who
could claim no social connections with him.

Chiang's access to the wealth of the Shanghai
elites and the public resources of the Nanking government gave him exceedingly strong bargaining power.
In exchange for political rewards, many provincial militarists in strategic locations shifted their
allegiance to Chiang from their regional overlords.
Some were influential governors; among them were
Ho Chien of Hunan, Huang Shao-hung of Chekiang and
Hupei, Han Fu-chü of Shantung, and Liu Chen-hua
of Anhwei. Some industrialists and bankers also made
concrete political gains in return for their services. Chang Chia-ao received the portfolio of
the Ministry of Railways, while Wu Ting-ch'ang was
appointed to the governorship of Kweichow. Aside
from these tangible rewards, they, too, won security
for their business interests.

These bonds provided Chiang with a pervasive
network upon which his complex factional structure was
built. They enabled him to control the finances,
the military, the party apparatus, the provincial administration within Kuomintang jurisdiction,
and a network of liaison relations with various

regional overlords. They facilitated the penetration
of the provinces by the central authority and furnished contacts with the social groups that lay beyond
the reach of the superfluous formal institutions of
the government. While these bonds contained certain
nonutilitarian elements of commitment, political
support derived from them often transcended the needs
of the time. Those hungry for power and riches
offered their personal loyalty to Chiang, thus further
enhancing his authority.

The attainment of power on the basis of these
particularistic and ascriptive criteria had damaging
effects on the Kuomintang's development as China's
principal force of political integration. First,
it delayed if not prevented the Nanking regime from
establishing an institutionalized decision-making
structure upon which administrative legitimacy would
depend. So long as his factional strength prevailed, Chiang could manipulate public offices and
resources, in addition to bending government rules and
regulations to accommodate the needs of patronage.
Party programs were frequently sabotaged by the
resulting personal strife. Although the presence of
a dominant factional system permitted Chiang and
the Kuomintang to secure momentary control over
China's chaotic situation, it severely undermined the
party's chance to rule the country as an effective
and independent political institution.

Moreover, the politics of factionalism in the
1930s impeded the work of mass mobilization that was
essential to a revolutionary party. Factions may
have been convenient functional substitutes for
interest groups, but the exclusive reliance on the
informal and narrowly defined channels of communications precluded the development of an encompassing
formal framework that could rally mass support
for political purposes.

Finally, persistent control of the government's
strategic offices by a dominant faction alienated
other political elements. Lacking military-financial
resources and legitimate popular elections, the
opposition groups had little bargaining power. Only
with the use of coalition forces could they pose
some constraint on the dominant faction. While
allowing their opponents practically no room to grow,
Chiang and his followers possessed neither the
strength nor the will needed to exterminate them from
the political arena.

In the final analysis, Kuomintang politics during
the prewar decade represented a tragedy of leadership. As revolutionary fervor subsided, consen-

sus fragmented, and broad-based support never materialized, the party's dominant factional system
did much to alienate many talented Kuomintang leaders
without being able to recruit enough substitutes of
high quality. The party's failure to develop into an
effective instrument of political integration and
mobilization made it possible for its rival force, the
Chinese Communists, to emerge as an alternative to
foster China's political development toward a radical-
ly different course of action.

NOTES

1. To the extent that both factions and cliques
depend heavily on personalities and personal ties for
their survival, the two terms can be used inter-
changeably. The term "*p'ai-hsi*" in Chinese connotes
the meanings of both "faction" and "clique," although
"*p'ai*" alone spells more accurately the meaning of
"faction," while "*hsi*" implies a narrower scope
of group formation and activities that are best described by the term "clique." Thus, referring to
the Chiang Kai-shek faction and the C. C. Clique that
was attached to it, the Chinese equivalent expressions
should be Chiang *p'ai* and Ch'en *hsi* respectively.
Aside from such distinction, there is virtually no
conceptual difference in the use of the two terms in
this chapter. Insofar as such faction-like formations
permeated the structure of political conflicts, we
may speak of the Kuomintang politics in the decade of
1928-1937 as "factional politics."
2. See, for example, Michael Banton (ed.), *The
Social Anthropology of Complex Societies* (New
York: Barnes & Noble Books, 1966); Michael Banton
(ed.), *Political Systems and the Distribution of Power*
(New York: Barnes & Noble Books, 1968); Marc J.
Swartz (ed.), *Local-Level Politics: Social and Cultural Perspectives* (Chicago: Aldine Publishing Co.,
1968); and Marc J. Swartz, Victor W. Turner, and
Arthur Tuden (eds.), *Political Anthropology* (Chicago:
Aldine Publishing Co., 1966).
3. Some good examples are William W. Whitson,
"The Field Army in Chinese Communist Military
Politics," in *The China Quarterly*, No. 37 (January-
March 1969), pp. 1-30; Fred W. Riggs, "Interest
and Clientele Groups," in Joseph L. Sutton (ed.), *Prob-
lems of Politics and Administration in Thailand*
(Bloomington: Institute of Training for Public Service,
Department of Government, Indiana University, 1962),
pp. 153-92; Fred W. Riggs, *Thailand: The Modernization
of a Bureaucratic Polity* (Honolulu: University Press

of Hawaii, 1966); Robert A. Scalapino and Junnosuke
Masumi, *Parties and Politics in Contemporary Japan*
(Berkeley: University of California Press, 1962); Paul
R. Brass, *Factional Politics in an Indian State:
The Congress Party in Uttar Pradesh* (Berkeley:
University of California Press, 1965); and Andrew J.
Nathan, *Peking Politics, 1918-1923: Factionalism
and the Failure of Constitutionalism* (Berkeley:
University of California Press, 1976).

    4. Nathan, *Peking Politics*, *passim*.

    5. Jerome Ch'en, "Defining Chinese Warlords and
Their Factions," in *Bulletin of the School of Oriental
and African Studies*, University of London, Vol.
XXXI, Part 3 (1968), pp. 563-600. Cf. Hsi-sheng Ch'i,
Warlord Politics in China, 1916-1928 (Stanford:
Stanford University Press, 1976), esp. pp. 10-76.

    6. William Whitson suggests that political con-
flicts within the Chinese army followed factional
alignments centered on the five field armies created
during the civil war. See Whitson, "Field Army,"
pp. 1-30. Andrew Nathan also shows that factions have
existed at China's central government level. See
Nathan, "A Factionalism Model for CCP Politics," in
The China Quarterly, No. 53 (January-March 1973),
pp. 52-65.

    7. Group division and competition based on strong
ideological interests may not be the same as factional conflict. To the extent that a faction is an
odd assortment of temporary allies held together
by a series of dyadic ties and, in some instances,
supportive structures, its interests mainly lie
in acquiring and holding onto power, rather than in
establishing and maintaining an ideological position.
Grouping of rival Kuomintang elites on the basis
of their strong ideological orientation during 1923-
1927 differs from the usual definition of factionalism.
The end of the Kuomintang-Communist alliance in
1927, however, marked the beginning of a political
conflict structure that was not primarily dictated by
ideological interests, although ideological rhetoric
persisted. It is thus important to make some conceptual distinction between group competition within
the Kuomintang before and after 1927. I would
like to thank Professor James C. Scott for pointing
out this important conceptual distinction.

    8. For details, see James Shirley, "Control of the
Kuomintang after Sun Yat-sen's Death," in *Journal of
Asian Studies*, Vol. XXIV, No. 1 (November 1965),
pp. 69-82.

    9. The two good articles on the left-wing group
are: Jerome Ch'en, "The Left Wing Kuomintang -- A

Definition," in *Bulletin of the School of Oriental and African Studies*, Vol. XXV, Part 3 (1962), pp. 557-74; and James Shirley, "Factionalism and the Left Kuomintang," *Studies on Asia*, University of Nebraska at Lincoln, Vol. V (1965), pp. 97-104.

10. Andrew Nathan defines doctrinalism as "the couching of factional struggle for power in terms of abstract issues of ideology, honour, and fact." According to him, factions often "adopt rigid and minutely defined ideological positions, exaggerate small differences on abstract questions, and stress the purity of their own motives." See Nathan, "Factionalism Model," p. 49.

11. Hung-mao Tien, *Government and Politics in Kuomintang China, 1927-1937* (Stanford: Stanford University Press, 1972), p. 28. The figures do not include overseas branches and army members.

12. *Ibid.*, pp. 33-39.

13. The important appointments were Ch'en Kung-po as minister of industry, Ku Meng-yü, minister of railways, and Kan Nai-kuang, vice minister of interior.

14. "Support structures" as borrowed from Andrew Nathan refers to such power bases of a faction as clubs, parties, mobs, newspapers, banks, ministries, armies, and the like. See Nathan, "Factionalism Model," p. 40.

15. Ralph W. Nicholas, "Segmentary Factional Political Systems," in Swartz, Turner, and Tuden (eds.), *Political Anthropology*, p. 53.

16. Tien, *Government and Politics*, p. 50.

17. Lloyd Eastman argues that the Blue Shirts attempted to practice Fascism in China. See his "Fascism in Kuomintang China: The Blue Shirts," in *The China Quarterly*, No. 49 (January-March 1972), pp. 1-31.

18. James C. Scott, *Comparative Political Corruption* (Englewood Cliffs, N.J.: Prentice-Hall, 1972), p. 42.

19. Eric R. Wolf, "Kinship, Friendship, and Patron-Client Relations in Complex Societies," in Banton (ed.), *Social Anthropology*, pp. 16-18.

2 | The New Life Movement before the Sino-Japanese Conflict: A Reflection of Kuomintang Limitations in Thought and Action

Samuel C. Chu

In the long history of the Kuomintang, there have been times when it seemed doomed to extinction and other times when it seemed irrelevant or absurd. During the early 1970s, with the rapidly changing situation in Sino-American relations, the Kuomintang and its island government on Taiwan appeared to have entered into another state of siege. By mid-1979, however, the party and its grip on that part of China over which it still holds sway seemed stronger than ever. Its long-term future remains uncertain, but for the time being there appears no doubt that the Kuomintang will not only survive but will also flourish.

The passage of time has given historians of modern China a new perspective on the ideological dimensions of Kuomintang rule. Without outlooking the party's many shortcomings, or its eventual failure on the mainland, scholars today regard Kuomintang performance during the 1920s and 1930s as an essential component of China's tortuous modernization process.

The original version of this chapter, "The New Life Movement, 1934-1937," was published in John E. Lane (ed.), *Researches in the Social Sciences in China*, Columbia University East Asian Institute Studies No. 3 (New York: East Asian Institute, Columbia University, 1957), pp. 1-17. This revision includes references to important recent works by Lloyd Eastman, Pichon Loh, and Arif Dirlik, but the analysis and conclusions remain largely unchanged, having stood the test of time. I would like to thank the East Asian Institute of Columbia University for its gracious permission to reprint the revised chapter in this book.

37

And inasmuch as the Kuomintang on Taiwan still be-
trays palpable vestiges of its original characteristics, such as the "dynastic" succession from
Chiang Kai-shek to his son, Ching-kuo, and the continued commitment to one-party rule in a country
perceived to be under siege, a study of the party's
prewar record is of more than historical interest; it
also has implications for Taiwan's present and
future.

One of the most intriguing endeavors of the Kuomintang during its rule on the mainland was the New
Life Movement, which was designed to cope with the
"spiritlessness" of the country. It was unique
because nothing of comparable size, organization, and
method has ever been seen in China. Since the
beginning of the twentieth century, many currents
of thought and belief have risen and ebbed in China.
None, however, has received so much promotion, or
formed so large and visible an organization as did the
New Life Movement. Insofar as it was an integral
part of Kuomintang thinking of its time, it is worthy
of our attention.

CHINA UNDER KUOMINTANG RULE

In the summer of 1926, the Kuomintang initiated
the Northern Expedition, which by 1928 united the
nation under the party's auspices. Chiang Kai-shek
was the military leader, but the initial rapid success
of the expeditionary forces was due less to their
military prowess than to popular sentiment in favor
of national unity.[1] Until the mid-1930s, however,
effective Kuomintang control did not extend much
beyond the central and lower regions of the Yangtze
Valley. Various local warlords and regional commanders pledged and withdrew at will their allegiance
to the central government, depending on what was
politically expedient at the moment. Throughout the
early 1930s, open conflict broke out sporadically
between Nanking and such powerful warlords as Feng Yü-
hsiang and Yen Hsi-shan. Furthermore, government
control of such fringe provinces as Kwangtung,
Kwangsi, Szechwan, Shensi, and others, was nominal at
best. China was united only in the sense that it
had a central government in Nanking to represent the
nation at large; in reality, China was torn by
regional factionalism.

Among the antigovernment groups, one stood out.
This was the Communist Party. In 1922, it adopted
a policy of cooperation with the Kuomintang, believing
that a national revolution to unite the country was

a prerequisite to a proletarian revolution. To this
end, Communist leaders worked with the Kuomintang
to make the Northern Expedition a success. With the
occupation of the Yangtze Valley in 1927, however,
it became increasingly clear that a break was
unavoidable between the conservative and the moderate
elements of the Kuomintang on the one hand, and the
radical elements, including the Communists, on the
other. The Northern Expedition came to a virtual halt
in 1927 while conflict broke out between the two
factions. Chiang Kai-shek, supported by the right
wingers, succeeded in driving the Communists out
of their positions around the Wuhan cities. The Communists entrenched themselves in Kiangsi and set up
a soviet independent of the central government.
At first they did not represent a formidable threat,
but under the chaotic conditions of the time, they
steadily grew in number and strength until their
influence extended to the neighboring provinces of
Hupei, Hunan, Kwangtung, and Fukien.

Faced with internal unrest, China had also to
contend with outside pressure as Japan became its
greatest threat. Although Japan had returned Shantung
to China in conformity with the decisions made at the
Washington Conference in 1921-1922, it still considered that province as being within its special
sphere of influence. When the Northern Expedition
resumed in 1928, after the conservative and moderate
factions of the Kuomintang had consolidated their
control, Japan sent troops into Shantung under the
pretext of guarding its nationals. There were minor
clashes between Japanese troops and units of the
expeditionary forces in the environs of Tsinan, but
the Chinese avoided any serious hostile action,
realizing the folly of antagonizing Japan at this time.
Negotiations started for the withdrawal of Japanese
troops, but the situation in Shantung remained fluid
for some time.

Throughout this period there were Japanese who
openly advocated a policy of continental expansion,
notably a group of young officers in the Kwantung Army,
based on the Liaotung Peninsula. In 1931 they precipitated matters by occupying Manchuria. With this
fait accompli, Japan went on to defy the League of
Nations and set up the puppet state of Manchukuo,
taking in the province of Jehol as well. China was
powerless to apply effective countermeasures, and
popular indignation took the form of boycotting
Japanese goods. Having obtained Manchuria, Japan
turned its attention toward North China. The Japanese
threat to China's independence was very real from

this time onward.

As soon as Chiang Kai-shek felt himself strong enough, he devoted his energy to the problem of eradicating the Communists, certain that this step was the prerequisite to the unification of China and resistance to Japan. Four campaigns were launched against the Communists by the regional commanders in Kiangsi, Hunan, and Hupei. The lack of cooperation among the anti-Communist forces and the ability of the Communists to make full use of the hit-and-run tactics of guerrilla warfare thwarted all four attempts. In the spring of 1934, Chiang took charge of what was to be the final campaign against the Communists in Kiangsi. With the aid of German military advisers, he laid down a tight economic blockade around the entire Communist perimeter and constructed a series of fortified strong points in an even tightening circle. The Communists found themselves trapped in a smaller and smaller area of operation until late in 1934, when they abandoned Kiangsi altogether and made a break toward the west, starting out on what later became known as the Long March. It was in conjunction with this final campaign that Chiang initiated the New Life Movement in Nanchang. The movement was an outgrowth of the immediate problem of reconstructing and rehabilitating those areas in Kiangsi taken from the Communists, but it soon became a nationwide campaign.

The period from late 1934 to mid-1937 was marked by increasing friction with Japan, as Japan's designs in extending its sphere of influence in North China became more and more apparent. In 1935 Hopei and Chahar were loosely formed into a semi-autonomous unit under the authority of Sung Che-yüan, who professed allegiance to the central government while playing Nanking and Tokyo against each other.[2] In 1936, in Suiyüan, the troops of Governor Fu Tso-yi, in a series of engagements, defeated the forces of the Mongol Prince Teh, who was supported by Japanese troops and planes. Tension between China and Japan was near the danger point. In China, agitation among the people for resistance to Japan grew apace. Students, as well as the young, educated group as a whole, were in the vanguard of those demanding that Chiang stop appeasing the Japanese and take a firm stand. Meanwhile, an effective and prolonged campaign to boycott Japanese goods was carried on, a method of resistance that had been known to have had a definite effect on the Japanese economy.

The persistence of the demand to resist Japan demonstrated the strength of Chinese nationalism.

More than anything else, the loss of Manchuria in
1931, constantly harped upon in books and newspapers
as a disgraceful affront to the Chinese people,
made all thinking Chinese aware of their identifi-
cation with their country and their people. More substantial than this, however, was the work that had
been quietly accomplished by a number of able men
since 1928 in broadening the educational system; stabilizing the currency; constructing railroads, high-
ways, and other vital works; fostering the beginning of industrialization; and building up a national
army. As a result of the Sian Incident of December
1936, when Chiang Kai-shek was kidnapped by Chang
Hsüeh-liang, Chiang agreed to terminate his campaigns
against the Communists, who were now reestablished
in Shensi. Recognizing the internal pressures
for unity and national resurgence in China, Japan
precipitated matters. When armed conflict broke out
in July 1937 these same elements of nationalism
enabled China to survive the initial onslaught of
Japan and to continue its resistance.

The outbreak of general hostilities between China
and Japan marked the end of a distinct period and the
beginning of another in all phases of national life
in China. The New Life Movement was no exception.
In the face of a desperate struggle for survival,
there was no need to stress the need for self-
sacrifice and simplicity, as the movement had been
doing. It is a mistake, however, to assume that the
movement was quietly abandoned. On the contrary, the
machinery for promoting the movement was merely
readjusted to conform to wartime needs. And when
eventual victory seemed assured with the entry of the
United States into the general conflict in late
1941, Chiang Kai-shek once again stressed the importance of going back to the principles of the New
Life Movement in the future. Thus, the ideas embodied
in the movement should not be dismissed after 1937,
but since the war so drastically altered the movement,
and since events in the post-1945 years did not
permit a resumption of activities on the prewar scale,
the year 1937 is a suitable terminating point for
this chapter.

ORIGINS OF THE NEW LIFE MOVEMENT

On February 19, 1934, Chiang Kai-shek gave a
speech in Nanchang, Kiangsi, in which he for the first
time called for a "movement to achieve a new life."
Contrasting foreign strength with Chinese weakness, he
maintained that the foreigners were strong because

they had the proper way of life. Citing the examples
of Germany and Japan, he noted that Germany had
begun to reassert itself only sixteen years after
accepting an unjust peace at the conclusion of a disastrous war, and that Japan had grown from a backward country to a first-rate power in a little more
than half a century. Chiang contended that the single
greatest factor in the success of both nations was
the spirit of their people. To raise the Chinese
spirit to a comparable level would require the instil-
lation of discipline. Consequently, he proposed a
movement to "militarize the life of the people of the
entire country."[3] This speech launched the New Life
Movement. On February 21, two days later, the Nanchang New Life Movement Promotion Association was
established.

During the three weeks from March 5 to March 21,
Chiang clarified his ideas on the movement in four
speeches. Of the four cardinal virtues, he said, *li*
(regulated attitude) was the most important. Without
li there would be no other virtues. Hence any attempt
to instill spirit into the people had to start by
emphasizing the significance of understanding and re-
specting *li*. On March 11, he addressed a mass meeting
for the promotion of the New Life Movement. He
stressed the importance of strengthening oneself as
a prerequisite for strengthening one's country.
In subsequent speeches, he lashed out at uncleanli-
ness, lack of discipline, laziness, and weakness,
as manifested in bad eating habits, personal unclean-
liness, lack of good housekeeping, dispirited
appearance, and irregular daily schedules. To combat
these undesirable and unfortunate traits, he urged
the inculcation of six qualities: orderliness, cleanliness, simplicity, frugality, promptness, and
exactness. He placed no limit as to time, place, or
the type of persons in urging the people to develop
these qualities, but he warned against the danger of
going to extremes or of falling into the age-old habit
of "being enthusiastic for all of five minutes." He
further enjoined leaders in all walks of life to
set examples for the people, and called on everyone
to aim high but to start at the most practical level.[4]

When Chiang spoke of these matters he was ad-
dressing the whole nation. On March 17, the Central
Committee for Popular Movements, a Kuomintang body,
issued a proclamation urging the formation of New Life
Movement promotion associations throughout the country.[5] With the active promotion of the movement
by the Kuomintang, aided to some extent by popular
support, promotion associations were set up in various

parts of China. On March 16, Nanking, the capital,
was the first place outside Kiangsi to set up its
association. In rapid succession promotion associations were established in Fukien, Peiping, Honan,
Shantung, Chekiang, Anhwei, Shanghai, and elsewhere.
On May 5, a revised code of the movement, setting
forth the principles more systematically, was
published. And on July 1, the various promotion associations were reorganized into one nationwide organization, under the supervision of the Nanchang
New Life Promotion Association, which was renamed the
Central Association. They were divided into five
categories: provincial, metropolitan, railroad, *hsien*
(within Kiangsi), and overseas.

THE NEW LIFE MOVEMENT

The credit for initiating the New Life Movement
has been accorded to Chiang Kai-shek. Although
some have speculated that Madame Chiang may have had
more than a little to do with the inception of the
movement, the data seem to indicate that the credit
has been justly given. It was reported that Chiang,
while traveling through Fukien, had seen a boy of ten
smoking a cigarette. When he stopped to inquire how
his family could permit such misbehavior, he found
that the practice was not unusual in that section of
the country. This incident supposedly planted in
his mind the germ of the idea that became the New Life
Movement.[6] This story may nor may not be true, but
Chiang's claim as the founder of the movement rests on
a firmer basis. As early as 1927, he had established
the Officers' Moral Endeavor Corps in the army. Its
members were to forswear smoking, drinking, and in-
dulging in any luxurious habits. The corps also
stressed Confucian ethics. Although there is no evidence that the corps led directly to the founding
of the New Life Movement, their similarity suggests
that Chiang may have taken the precepts of the corps,
given it a broader basis for mass appeal, and launched
it as the movement. Robert Berkov credits Ch'en Li-
fu with supplying the Confucian philosophical basis of
the New Life Movement.[7] This claim, too, has not
been substantiated. There is no question, however,
that both Madame Chiang and Colonel Huang Jen-lin, who
was the first director of the movement, contributed
heavily to its operation, and may have had considerable
influence upon its establishment.
There is little doubt that the movement started as
a personal crusade of Chiang Kai-shek. As a young
man, Chiang had studied in Japan after it had emerged

victorious from the Russo-Japanese War. He could not
help but be influenced by Japan's example of transforming itself from a medieval country to a modern
power in less than half a century. Chiang had been a
military man since his early revolutionary days. He
had studied the Chinese classics and had absorbed
the tenets of Confucianism contained therein. Nonetheless, he had also been converted to Christianity when he married Soong Mei-ling and had accepted
its doctrines. His personal background and belief
were reflected in the principles and ideals of the New
Life Movement.

Chiang was, moreover, influenced by other foreign
movements. He looked to the examples of Japan, Germany, and Italy when he thought of strengthening
China, and perhaps he was not altogether unaware of
Soviet Russia either. The idea of starting a movement
under the auspices of the party was probably suggested by examples in other countries, but the principles and the manifestations of the New Life Movement
were unique. In contrast to similar movements, it
alone went back to an older school of philosophy for
inspiration and applied its principles by emphasizing
orderliness, cleanliness, and a cultural life. The
Three People's Principles Youth Corps, a later
outgrowth of the youth corps of the New Life Movement,
may have been directly influenced by such foreign
organizations as the Hitler Youth or the Communist
Youth League, but the movement itself was not.

The principles of the movement were Confucian-
oriented. The four virtues, *li, i, lien,* and *ch'ih,*
which formed the cornerstone upon which the movement rested, were taken bodily out of the Confucian
canon. Their meanings, as interpreted in Chiang's
Outline of the New Life Movement, were also primarily
Confucian, with modern trimmings added. In fact,
the whole philosophy behind the movement, that all the
ills of China would be cured if the heart and spirit
of the people were corrected, was derived from Confucianism. So was the idea that all efforts for
improvement had to begin with the individual. The
movement insisted that its aim was to restore the virtues of the ancients to the Chinese people. Therefore, it was not unnatural that Confucianism, long the
official philosophy, dominated the principles behind
the movement.

If Confucianism gave the movement its core of
ideas, Christianity also contributed its share. The
ideas of frugality and simplicity had no basis in
Confucianism. They were more akin to the teachings of
Christ, wherein the evils of concern with worldly

goods and ostentation are stressed. The movement
owed much of its application to the Christian emphasis on social work. Moreover, even if the principles
of the movement were based on Confucianism, they
were not opposed to Christian doctrine.

It has often been claimed that the movement was
launched with the aim of combatting the ideological
challenge of Marxism. This is only partially true.
In his earliest speeches on the movement, Chiang did
have Kiangsi particularly in mind. He wanted Kiangsi
to be a model province, the center of a movement
which would not only replace Marxism, but all other
"imported" doctrines as well. It was to be for
the Chinese what Marxism had come to be for the Russians, what Fascism was for the Italians, and what
liberalism was for the English and Americans.
The movement's all-embracing quality was stressed by
its proponents. This did not mean, however, that
it was to supersede Sun Yat-sen's Three Principles of
the People, but rather to implement them by focusing
on the problems confronting China at the time.

The avowed aim of the New Life Movement was to
revitalize the spirit of the nation so that the
Chinese would reach the same degree of social consciousness and patriotism as other peoples within a
relatively short time.[8] To do this, a return to the
virtues of the classical age was urged. In his
Outline of the New Life Movement, Chiang Kai-shek
stated that China, by virtue of its long history, vast
size, and large population, should by rights have
been at least on the par with the other major nations
of the world. Indeed, it had once been a great nation,
but because the people had drifted away from the
ancient precepts, China had fallen into its present
deplorable state. The remedy was a return to the four
ancient virtues of *li*, *i*, *lien*, and *ch'ih*.[9]

These four virtues were familiar to all who had
studied the classics, yet in order to apply them to
modern life, their meaning was redefined. *Li* stood for
regulated attitude, or etiquette in its broadest
sense, with the emphasis on the essential rightness
of a matter and not on its empty, ceremonial trappings.
I meant right conduct, or the visible manifestations
of *li*. It also had the meaning of justice. *Lien*
meant integrity, the ability to distinguish right from
wrong. *Ch'ih* stood for conscience, the sense of
shame when a wrong had been committed. These four
virtues were all interrelated. To attempt to live up
to them separately would lead only to pervasions.

In their practical application the four virtues
were to act upon the four essential elements of life:

food, clothing, shelter, and action. Since the first
three terms covered the basic material needs of life
and the last was used in its broadest sense to include
everything else, the four virtues were intended to
cover life in total.

Chiang foresaw the objections that critics would
raise and attempted to answer two of the more obvious ones. The first was that the four virtues dealt
only with morals and neglected knowledge and technology altogether. In response, it was maintained
that morals were of primary importance, since ability
without morals would only be abused for dishonorable
ends. The second criticism was that the four virtues
were confined to spiritual matters and had nothing
to do with the material aspects of life, upon which
life was based. This argument was refuted by the
assertion that the material ills of the nation had
first to be remedied through spiritual regeneration.
With the proper spirit, material hardships could
be overcome, whereas without the proper spirit, even
material abundance could not save China from chaos.

The main goal of the New Life Movement was to
lead the Chinese people to a more rational life with
three separate but interrelated facets: the cultural, the productive, and the militarized modes of
life. Through the cultural mode of life, it was hoped
that rudeness and vulgarity could be eliminated.
Through the productive mode of life, it was hoped that
more people would contribute to the material welfare
of the nation rather than rely on others. Through the
militarized mode of life, it was hoped that the people would become more disciplined and more able to
defend themselves, should they have to do so.

To make the New Life Movement more down to earth,
a list of ninety-six specific rules was issued at
the same time as the general principles.[18] These rules
dealt with the most minute aspects of daily life,
divided into the categories of food, clothing, shelter,
and action. All of them applied to individuals and
did not go much beyond habits. In the categories
of food and eating, the rules encouraged the Chinese
people to keep regular meal hours, to refrain from
making noise when eating, to learn correct posture, to
use native foodstuffs, and to abstain from smoking.
In clothing, a similar appeal was made to use only
native fabrics. In addition, shoes were to be worn
correctly, clothes were to be neatly buttoned, bodies
should not be exposed, and bed coverlets should be
washed regularly. In the matter of shelter (more correctly, living habits), such details as early rising,
proper care of nails and hair, proper disposal of fire

hazards and garbage, and the extermination of rats, flies, and mosquitoes, as well as respect for one's flag and country, were stressed. The use of native products was again emphasized. The category of action included rules that did not fit into the other three divisions. These were promptness, abstention from crowding and shoving at public places; refraining from sneezing, spitting, and urinating without regard to persons and places; and giving up gambling and prostitution. These ninety-six specific rules were to be the first step in self-improvement. From these, the movement was to move gradually into more substantial concerns.

The work of the movement was to be carried out in three stages. After investigation of the conditions and obstacles to be overcome came detailed planning of the steps to be followed, and then execution. At all times workers in the movement were to begin with the simple, inexpensive, and easy tasks and work up to the more complex, costly, and difficult jobs. Individuals should start with themselves before extending the movement to others. Civil servants should be exposed to the movement before the general public. For all these reasons, the movement should take effect in public places first, such as schools, offices, stations, parks, and the like.

The first order of business for the workers was to instruct the public about the aims and precepts of the New Life Movement, as well as its specific goals. After a campaign had been launched, the promotion association was to send out inspectors to check its results, with rewards given to the deserving. Above all else, three rules of operation were to be observed: (1) only superiors had the right to interfere in the daily life of others; friends could only advise one another; (2) the movement was to be carried on in leisure hours or vacation time and was not to interfere with regular duties; (3) funds for the operation of the movement were to be raised among the organizers or from local government, never from the general public.[11]

THE PROMOTION ASSOCIATIONS

Chiang Kai-shek wanted the New Life Movement to be a movement of the people, but he also wanted some kind of organization to give the movement impetus so that it would grow. His compromise was the promotion associations.[12] At first, the association in Nanchang had no direct connection with promotion associations in other places other than in an advisory

capacity, it being the original association and in
touch with Chiang. As the number of associations
mounted and a need to incorporate the various associations into a national organization was felt, both
for the purpose of promoting closer cooperation and
of insuring a standardized approach, the association
at Nanchang was made the Central Association on
July 1, 1934, with supervisory power over all other
regional associations. As the plan was set up, five
different types of promotion associations were
recognized: (1) the provincial associations, which in
turn supervised the various associations organized
on the *hsien* level within each province; (2) the
metropolitan associations, organized in large cities
that were political units independent of provincial
control; (3) associations organized along railway
lines, some of which extended through several provinces; (4) associations established in *hsien* in
Kiangsi; and (5) overseas associations.

In numbers alone the national organization of the
New Life Movement promotion associations was impressive. During the period 1934-1937, nineteen provincial associations were set up, with the majority
established within the first full year of the movement.
These nineteen provinces included all of China proper,
with the exception of Kwangtung and Kwangsi, plus
the outlying provinces of Sikang, Tsinghai, Suiyüan,
and Chahar. In addition, 1,300 *hsien* had sub-
associations under the provincial associations. In
a separate category were five metropolitan associations, located in the urban centers of Nanking, Shanghai, Peiping, Tientsin, and Tsingtao. Twelve railroad promotion associations, representing each of the
major national trunk lines, were established in the
first full year of the movement. Within Kiangsi,
sixty-eight *hsien* had promotion associations, directly
under the supervision of the Central Association at
Nanchang. Finally, as of January 1936, there were ten
overseas promotion associations: two in Japan (Naga-
saki and Osaka-Kobe); two in Korea (Wonsan and
Sinuiju); two in Southeast Asia (the Burmese and the
Indo-Chinese associations); two in Portuguese possessions (Macao and Timur); and two in the Western Hem-
isphere (Mexico City and Lima, Peru).[13] Later on,
the number increased to nineteen, most of them located
in the South Seas, but including one in Cleveland,
Ohio.[14] From the standpoint of numbers at least, the
New Life Movement was truly nationwide.

The reorganization plans of July 1, 1934, placing
the promotion associations on a national basis, provided for the following bodies to be represented among

the directing group of each of the five different
types of promotion associations:

Provincial, metropolitan, or *hsien*:-

The provincial (metropolitan or *hsien*) government
The provincial (metropolitan or *hsien*) Kuomin-
tang organization
The bureau of civil or social affairs
The bureau of education
The bureau of public safety
Local military authorities
Local civil groups

Railroad:-

The director of the railroad
The head of the police on the railroad
The Kuomintang organization of the railroad
Various organizations connected with the railroad

Overseas:-

Chinese consulate
Local Kuomintang branch
Chinese associations
Chinese schools
Chinese merchants guilds[15]

Since most of the positions on all levels of the governing bodies in China were then held by Kuomintang
members, the above stipulations insured Kuomintang
control of all promotion associations.

The Central Association had the responsibility of
supervising, coordinating, and inspecting all the
other associations to insure standardization in the
work of promoting the New Life Movement. It also
served as a central clearing house, keeping the statistics of the regional associations and stimulating
exchanges of ideas and suggestions concerning project
methods and approaches. The Central Association announced the timetable for the achievement of the movement's broader goals, leaving the practical details
of execution to be worked out by each local association, in accordance with local conditions. Teams
of inspectors were sent out periodically from Nanchang
to check on the work of local associations, to assess
local results, reactions, conditions, problems, ex-
penses, and methods, and to determine whether the
promotion had been sincere and thorough. Samples of
their findings were published from time to time in the
Central Association's monthly periodical, which also
published movement directives, important speeches,
articles, comments, and regional reports.

Since the various promotion associations were
no more than directing bodies, the actual work of such
campaigns as the antifly and the antirat movements
fell on the shoulders of such permanent organizations
as the military police, the regular police, and the
boy scouts. To aid these permanent bodies, and to
mobilize other types of people into the New Life Movement, various volunteer service groups were organized under the supervision of the promotion associations. Early in the movement, the Central Association
organized three separate groups to serve as models:
these were the Kiangsi Youth Vacation Service Corps,
the Merchants Service Membership, and the Women's
Civil Servants Service Corps.[16] Each was designed to
reach a different social group. The Kiangsi Youth
Vacation Service Corps was formed in June 1934 to take
advantage of the summer vacation. Membership was
divided into two sections, Nanchang and outside.
Between September 1 and November 1, the Nanchang membership jumped from 1,800 to 6,900. Outside membership increased on a more gradual scale from the
September figure of more than 5,000. During the summer, the students held exhibitions explaining the
New Life Movement to the general public, conducted fly
and rat extermination campaigns, and learned and
taught the acceptance of good hygiene. After school
began in the fall, students were asked to contribute their Sunday afternoons to such work as directing
traffic and urging others to conform to the rules of
the movement.

The Merchants Service Membership started in
August 1934, and by September counted 2,000 members.
Each shop appointed one member. Members were to help
observe the rules of the New Life Movement in their
shops and in the section of the street immediately
outside their shops.

Formation of the Women's Civil Servants Service
Corps was announced in August 1934 but was not organized until October, with a membership of 347
women. One of their duties was to help spread the New
Life Movement to their own homes, but they were also
asked to contribute their time and energy to public
service, particularly in the establishment of training
classes for other women.

These three Nanchang service groups were proto-
types for similar groups elsewhere. The idea of
organizing students to work for the movement caught on
rapidly, and most promotion associations had their
own youth vacation service corps. More significant,
however, was the organization of the Women's New Life
Movement Voluntary Service Corps on a nationwide

basis. Its branches were established as auxiliaries
of the promotion associations in thirteen provinces
and along two railroads. Madame Chiang was appointed
director. Members also worked on two levels: at
home they improved or encouraged such typically
women's interests as cooking, needlework, budgeting
and child care, while striving to make their homes
more in tune with the spirit of the movement. In
public, members organized classes for women in nursing,
working skills, reading, and writing. They also supported women's auxiliaries for promoting various
drives. This group was made a separate part of the
New Life Movement, in recognition of the fact that
Chinese women occupied an important but distinctly different place at home and in society from that of the
men.[17]

In a similar fashion, a New Life Movement Voluntary Service Corps was organized on a nationwide scale.
It aimed at using the energy of the younger able-
bodied men of the country. The scope of its activities ranged from physical labor, like road construction
and the repairing of dikes and ditches, to more
general campaigns, such as the promotion of science
and the encouragement of cooperation.[18]

Other service corps, aimed at specific groups,
were established under the auspices of the New Life
Movement. One was the Y.M.C.A. and Missionary Group
Service Corps, which aimed at enlisting those Christians who were willing to contribute to the movement.[19]

The character of the movement in Kiangsi was different from what it later became as a national movement. In Kiangsi, propagation went hand in hand with
the military campaign against the Communists and
the physical rehabilitation of the recovered territories. Outside Nanchang, it was pushed largely
in rural areas, towns, and villages. As the movement
spread outside of Kiangsi, it became more urbanized,
more detached from the idea of material reconstruction.
What had been a very practical and useful instrument
in combatting Communism in Kiangsi became less of
a part of an integrated policy and more of an all-
embracing movement, incorporating many separate drives
which had been in existence before the New Life Movement was launched.

THE MOVEMENT IN ACTION

It was decided, for the first year, to restrict
the operations of the New Life Movement to the achievement of two immediate goals: orderliness and clean-

liness. Accordingly, plans were devised in Nanchang
to conform to these two objectives. To promote
orderliness in Nanchang, public areas such as parks,
stations, and piers were to be supervised, streets
were to be improved in appearance, and office procedures were to be expedited. To insure cleanliness,
restaurants and bathhouses were to be regularly
inspected, with the results posted on a public display
board. To call attention to these activities, a
model section was to be set up within Nanchang to
publicize the New Life Movement. The results of thorough investigations of marriage and funeral cere-
monies, stevedore groups, factory workers, average
residential districts, theaters, restaurants, bathhouses, rice and noodle shops, hostel businesses, and
barber shops would be publicly announced.[20]

New Life Movement promotion associations all over
China carried out other specific projects in striving
toward the two immediate goals. To encourage orderliness, the Fukien association forbade mixed bathing
and the wearing of odd clothes by women; the Honan
association straightened out street stalls and encouraged promptness; the Hupei association also discouraged women from wearing odd apparel; while the Nanking
association supervised the correction of bad habits
among the people in the streets, in railroad stations,
and at various amusement places. To insure cleanliness, the Hupei association set aside a day for general cleanup; the Honan association increased the
number of garbage cans and killed stray dogs; the
Fukien association cleaned up public toilets and ban-
ned the dumping of garbage in the river.[21] The
Nanking-Shanghai-Hangchow Railroad set a particularly
good example for the other railroads. It appointed
a sanitation supervisor, cleaned its dining rooms and
rolling stock twice a month, forbade the sale of
unsanitary food, and in many other ways stressed cleanliness. To promote orderliness, the railroad adhered
to schedules, provided uniforms for all its personnel, and supervised the flow of passengers in getting
on and off trains and in buying tickets. Furthermore, the railroad stressed the health of its employees by encouraging medical checkups and innocula-
tions, and by sponsoring athletic teams.[22] Although
there is no reason to assume that other promotion
associations were as active as these few, at least the
work of the movement was concerned with much more
than mere planning.[23]

All the above activities involved the civilian
sector, but there was also an effective military phase
which showed what the movement was capable of when it

was applied on a limited yet concentrated scale. For
the task of recovering and rehabilitating those
areas of Kiangsi which were then under the Communists,
Chiang Kai-shek organized the Special Movement Force
out of youthful, promising officers. They were
sometimes called upon to work as undercover agents
within the Communist areas. When the Kuomintang
forces recovered an area from the Communists, members
of the Special Movement Force in that area then began the work of rehabilitation. They surveyed the
needs of the people, lent assistance to stricken families, organized local defenses, and maintained
order until a stable local government could be set
up. In addition, they instituted mass education,
rooted out corruption, and carried on morality
drives.[24] In short, they assumed positions of authority to insure order and security while disputed areas
in Kiangsi were being transferred from Communist to
Kuomintang control. The work of the Special Movement
Force contributed materially to the final pacification
of Kiangsi, after several years of inconclusive
fighting had severely worsened the already impoverished condition of the local peasantry.

The New Life Movement had its greatest period of
growth in its first full year of existence. Most of
the promotion associations were established in 1934,
and popular enthusiasm started the movement off auspi-
ciously. At the first anniversary celebrations
held in all parts of the country, highly optimistic
statements were made. Since the movement had no
target date for the achievement of its objectives, it
was hoped that, as more and more people came into
contact with it, the movement would "snowball" until
it had accomplished its aim of revitalizing the nation.
Accordingly, the Central Association issued a new
plan setting forth the details for achieving the first
step in the three desirable modes of life: militarized, productive, and cultural.[25] The two immediate
goals of the first year were not abandoned, but were
incorporated into the plan. Militarization for civil
servants included respect for the national and Kuomintang flags, obedience toward superiors, the wearing
of uniforms, promptness, and acquiring the habit of
taking cold baths. For teachers and students, it also
included obedience, the wearing of uniforms, military
training, participation in athletics, and the giving
up of smoking, drinking, and dancing. Militarization
for ordinary citizens between the ages of sixteen
and forty consisted of simple military training, air-
raid and first-aid training, respect for the law,
and development of the habit of regularity and clean-

liness. The productive mode of life was to be attained by reducing unnecessary expenditures, including
elaborate weddings and funerals, by developing the
habit of saving, by acquiring a spirit of cooperation,
by using all available time, including leisure hours,
by buying only native goods, and by learning to
respect public property. The cultural mode of life
was to be attained by being direct and temperate
in speech, friendly in attitude, thoughtful and ener-
getic in action, constantly improving in study, and
patriotic and self-reliant in belief. Toward others,
it was to mean fair treatment and helpfulness toward friends, and respect but not blind obedience toward leaders and superiors. This mode of life manifested in work was to include voluntary service
with no concern for reward, and the abandonment of
superstition. The plan outlined above was to go into
effect in the second year of the movement, with the
reservation that certain areas of China had responded
to the movement later than other sections and therefore had to proceed at a slower rate.

     As it turned out, the New Life Movement lost much
of its momentum in the second year. Growth slowed
to the addition of only three provincial associations,
two metropolitan associations, no railroad associations, and fifteen Kiangsi *hsien* associations, as compared to the figure of sixteen provincial, twelve
railroad, and fifty-three Kiangsi *hsien* promotion associations in 1934. The only gain was in overseas
associations, the number jumping from two to ten.
More significant than mere numbers, however, was the
indication of a general letdown throughout the country.
At the same time, the year 1934 saw only a limited
number of accomplishments. The movement continued to
be pushed actively on ship board and on all water
transporation. In Nanchang, standard time announce-
ments were instituted, an unemployment bureau was
established, and relief drives collected clothes and
money for the needy.[26] Beyond this, there was little
to report. Consequently, on February 19, 1936, at
the meeting celebrating the second anniversary of the
movement, the optimism that had characterized the
meetings of the first anniversary was absent. Ex-
pressing his disappointment on the occasion, Chiang
Kai-shek said, "This is very sad and shameful."[27]

     The Central Association's plans for the third
year of the movement stressed the importance of making
the movement even more of an organized drive.[28] The
reliance on mass enthusiasm was replaced by intensive
training of promotion association members and intensive development of inspection methods. Emphasis

was put on consolidating workers in the movement and
on the training of the general public. Aware of
disparities between the accomplishments of the different regions, the plan called for visible progress
in either orderliness, cleanliness, the three modes of
life, or the establishment of an active voluntary
service corps. In addition, the movement was to be
pushed in the rural areas. As an indication of
the closer link between the movement and the government, the Central Association was moved from Nanchang
to Nanking toward the end of 1935. Little work,
however, seems to have been accomplished in the following year. The pressure of other events made it
more difficult for Chiang to devote much time to the
movement.

On the third anniversary of the movement in 1937,
Madame Chiang, who by then had come to direct not
only the women's part of the movement, but to a large
degree the entire movement, made a radio broadcast
in which she stressed the need to solve China's economic problems and to broaden the mass education
movement. She reiterated that every intelligent individual should participate in the New Life Movement to insure its ultimate success.[29]

The Marco Polo Bridge Incident of July 7, 1937
pulled the curtain on the peacetime phases of the New
Life Movement. The events of 1937 and 1938, including
the mass movement of China's political and economic
centers from the coastal areas to the interior,
drastically changed the situation in China. The New
Life Movement became more of an adjunct of the Kuomintang. Resistance to the enemy and loyalty to the
party became more important than an orderly and cul-
tured life. Such organizations as the Three People's
Principles Youth Corps were a direct outgrowth of
the New Life Movement Youth Corps.[30] The women's auxiliary of the movement turned largely to war relief
work. A War Area Service Corps was organized under the auspices of the movement to serve the soldiers
at the front. Nevertheless, the civilian aspects of
the movement did not disappear altogether, as was
evidenced, for instance, in the establishment of a
modern cafeteria in Chungking in 1939.[31] The military
aspects of the movement became paramount, however,
as was to be expected in a nation engaged in a desperate struggle for survival.

During the pre-1937 years, the New Life Movement
achieved the greatest practical good and gained its
strongest support through directing the work of four
campaigns: the antiopium drive, the use of national
goods, public health, and civics. While the antiopium

campaign was essentially a separate movement, opium smoking came naturally under the headings of items to be corrected by the New Life Movement. The campaign for the use of Chinese goods went hand in hand with the anti-Japanese boycotts, yet it also fitted in neatly with the New Life Movement's stress on simplicity, since Chinese manufactures were not so elaborate as foreign wares. As for public health and civics, they were not so much drives as they were part of the educational process. Students in primary schools were already taking courses in hygiene and civics that emphasized cleanliness and orderliness. The New Life Movement extended these efforts to reach the adult population or those who had had no opportunity to come into contact with these ideals in the schools.

The New Life Movement gave these four campaigns added impetus and manpower. All of them received much publicity through the movement, and public health in particular had the benefit of the various service corps to carry out large-scale projects, such as anti-fly and antimosquito campaigns. Through the movement, several centers were set up for the treatment of opium addicts. These concrete results brought much credit to the movement. People realized that concentrated efforts and practical demonstrations could produce results more quickly than could education alone.

Nonetheless, the movement had some grave defects. One of its weakest points was its basic assumption that a movement of this kind had to be promoted by the Kuomintang. The whole concept of the promotion associations, with the compulsory inclusion on every level of government officials and party heads, suggested an artificial rather than a spontaneous movement. It was a movement from above. As such it suffered from the weakness of all spiritual movements not genuinely derived from the people. It could not aspire to compete with any religion, because in the minds of the people the movement was inextricably bound with the Kuomintang. This was especially true for the intellectuals, most of whom were not attracted by the movement because they did not regard its philosophical basis as profound. To some it seemed incongruous for the Kuomintang to assume leadership of a movement that was intended to be spiritual.

Moreover, the use of the police and the boy scouts to insure conformity with the rules of the movement was obnoxious to some and annoying to many. Perhaps there was no alternative to the promotion of such a movement other than by the Kuomintang. The

party was founded on the belief that it could lead
the nation on all levels, including the spiritual, but
it was neither efficient nor dedicated enough to
crush all opposition, as the Communists had succeeded
in doing in Russia, and as the Nazi Party was to do
in Germany. Moreover, the movement's Confucian stress
on individual self-improvement and its Christian-
derived preference for persuasion rather than coercion
had two disadvantages. On the one hand, the movement
failed to appeal to the people; on the other, it was
unable to assert itself forcefully. Its rapid growth
in the numbers of promotion associations was illu-
sory. The movement looked good on paper, but in the
process of expansion, all kinds of people were
taken into the group responsible for the promotion
of the movement. Kuomintang officials, whether they
were dedicated or not, occupied responsible positions
in the promotion associations because it was politic
to do so. Some opportunistic and hypocritical people
were given the task of promoting a movement which
they either did not believe in or could not live up
to.

Consequently, when the public found out that its
leaders were voicing platitudes without conviction,
the movement lost its vitality. The Chinese Communists have been successful in inculcating their ideas
exactly where the Kuomintang failed, not because
Communism holds any more intrinsic appeal than the
tenets of the New Life Movement, but because they have
skillfully combined the most effective methods of
persuasion with a systematic application of coercion
in all its ramifications.

Another unfortunate aspect of the movement was
its plan of procedure. Logically speaking, it seemed
correct that the movement should proceed from the
simple to the complex, but, as it too often worked out,
the movement concentrated on symptoms of a problem
rather than on eliminating the underlying causes. The
New Life Movement thereby gained a deserved reputa-
tion for superficiality. In too many places, it
involved no more than a periodic cleanup before an
inspection, after which everything was allowed to
lapse back to its original condition.

Furthermore, the original plan of the movement
required civil servants to be the first group affected.
As was evident from the reports of the promotion associations, nearly all efforts from the start were
directed toward the general public. It almost seemed
as if the officials and public servants were exempt
from the movement.

The above defects emerged as the movement progressed. What was more serious was the basic assumption that its implementation required no concrete plan for the material improvement of China. A People's Economic Reconstruction Movement was finally established on April 1, 1935. It was to be the other half of a two-pronged program, together with the New Life Movement, for the improvement of China.[32] This movement, instituted more than a year after the start of the New Life Movement, seems to have been a concession on the part of Chiang Kai-shek that the New Life Movement alone could not solve China's problems. Nothing in his earlier speeches showed that he had originally planned to have a second campaign following the New Life Movement. As late as February 1935, the emphasis continued to fall on the revitalization of the spirit, with the tacit understanding that material troubles would be alleviated as a matter of course afterward. This line of reasoning was not only fallacious, but was also unfortunate, because it led certain elements (the young students, for example) to expect too much of the movement. When they had supported it for some time and still could not see any noticeable improvement in the condition of the country, they lost hope altogether.

Another weakness of the movement was its neglect of the rural population. With the exception of Kiangsi, where the movement achieved a measure of success because it was integrated into the larger plan of reconstruction and rehabilitation, it was active primarily in the cities and along the railroads and had little effect on the rural population. In fact, its whole practical program was geared to upgrade the appearance of urban areas to resemble the cities of other nations. Chiang forgot that other nations like Germany, Italy, and Japan, which he thought of as models for China, had already achieved varying degrees of industrialization. China was still principally agricultural; the neglect of the rural population foredoomed the movement to failure.

DOMESTIC AND FOREIGN REACTIONS TO THE MOVEMENT

For so ambitious a movement, the New Life Movement caused surprisingly little public reaction in China. Far more space in Chinese newspapers and periodicals was devoted to international affairs. On national topics, such magazines as *Kuo-wen chou-pao* /̲ National News Weekly_/ reported the more important events and published a few pictures of the movement. Other publications, *Hua-nien* /̲ The Young_/ for example, commented on the movement in short editorials.

Only in a few periodicals, notably *Shih-tai kung-lun*
/ Contemporary Forum / and *Hsin she-hui* / New Society /, can there be found more than one relevant
article on the movement. Only one magazine, *Ta-hsüeh*
/ Great Learning /, devoted an entire issue to the
subject. This poor coverage indicated either a lack
of interest on the part of the reading public, or,
more likely still, for some a lack of interest and for
others a prudent silence. By 1934, the Kuomintang
had already consolidated its power to the extent that,
wherever its influence could be felt, it was wiser
not to antagonize the party. Among potential critics,
the political climate gave pause to many writers
and intimidated the cautious ones.

The existing newspaper editorials and magazine
articles, however, do convey some idea of Chinese
reactions to the movement. Most of the commentators
favorable to the movement reiterated what Chiang
Kai-shek had said. They felt that the people were
eager to find a way out of the predicaments of 1934,
and they cited the rapid growth of the New Life
Movement in that year as proof. They saw the movement
as an absolute necessity, because education alone
could not raise the Chinese to the same level as the
great powers.[33] They argued that, although many
people in China were seeking a way out of the difficulties facing their country, they usually committed one of four errors: some concluded that there
was no way out; some embraced Marxism; others believed
that the wholesale introduction of technology would
be the solution; still others looked to political
reforms as the panacea. None of these was the answer.
The real obstacle to the improvement of China's
conditions was the lack of popular will. Material[34]
progress alone could not overcome China's ills.
Pro-movement commentators further deplored any rejection of the movement on the grounds that it was new
and untried and criticized those who gave way to
despair, thinking that the movement was too utopian
to succeed.[35] For the good of the country, they
urged, the work of the movement must not be affected
by these pernicious influences.

In contrast, those who criticized the movement
were more specific and raised more points in their
objections. There were two distinct groups among the
detractors: those who thought that China should seek
other improvements first, and those who approved
of the idea of the movement but thought its emphasis
was misplaced.

Most writers of the first group regarded material
benefits -- economic self-sufficiency, the improve-

ment of communications, rural rehabilitation, and the amelioration of the effects of natural disasters -- as more urgent than any other aims. As Hu Shih contended, life was based on material wellbeing and many of the ills plaguing China were caused by insufficient food and goods for all and the resultant low standard of living.[36] Hu and others believed that the New Life Movement was merely attacking the symptoms without changing the basic causes. Still others of this group listed national independence and education as two of China's more pressing needs. Tu Ming-yi proposed still a different thesis. According to him, everyone went through three stages of education: family, school, and society. Since habits were formed early in life, each stage was less important than the preceding one. The New Life Movement belonged primarily to the third stage and was hence of less value as an educational instrument than the family training of the child.[37]

Among the second group of critics who approved of the movement but thought that its emphasis was misplaced, several believed that the initial emphasis should have been on the civil servants, intimating that this group needed moral uplifting more than the general public. Others bracketed civil servants with the military and the students, maintaining that the youth of the latter group made it especially suitable for improvement. Still others argued that since peasants constituted around 80 percent of China's population, any movement that was truly national in scope had to deal with the problems of the rural masses.[38]

Among critics of the movement, several provided conflicting suggestions. In an article in *Hsin she-hui*, a writer advocated that the emphasis of the movement be placed on society rather than on individuals. In contrast, an editorial in the same magazine a month later suggested that the movement stress the individual, deeming that such things as meetings and parades were unnecessary.[39] Another disagreement centered on the question of whether principles of the movement or practical application should be emphasized.[40]

Still another group, led by Hu Shih, believed that the movement should be solely educational. This, of course, was contrary to Chiang Kai-shek's contention that education alone could not remedy China's ills rapidly enough. Hu Shih also argued that the New Life Movement was of less benefit to the people than material improvements. He pointed out that even those who lived up to all the principles and rules

of the movement would not be contributing anything
positive to the good of China. The movement was
preparatory in nature. In order to contribute to the
national welfare, one had to go beyond the standards
of the movement.[41]

　　With the passage of time, there were new suggestions. The most frequent warnings centered on the
role of the leaders, who should set good examples
for others to follow. If any stain of hypocricy was
detected, the movement would collapse.[42] Apparently this fear was not groundless. On the occasion of
the first anniversary of the movement, an editorial in
the *Ta-kung pao* ∠ L'impartial_/ complained that the
unfortunate personal morals of some of the leaders
were undermining the movement. An editorial in the
Chung-hua jih-pao ∠ China Daily_/ on the same occasion
warned of the danger of allowing politics to become
involved in the movement.[43] More relevant suggestions
urged (1) a realization that the movement could not
survive without popular acceptance and enthusiasm; (2)
a drive for construction and increased productivity;
(3) an emphasis on wiping out all gambling; and (4)
efforts to combat official dishonesty.[44]

　　One noteworthy article dealt with a specific instrument of the movement, the police. Noting that
policemen were vital in making sure that the movement
was more than empty words and therefore merited
public respect, the author pointed out that over-
zealous police work was as harmful to the movement as
inaction. The police should be trained never to
invade the private life of an individual, to use persuasion and direction instead of force, and to use
force only when absolutely necessary, and then in conformity with legal procedure.[45]

　　The Christian attitude toward the New Life Movement was generally favorable with some reservations.
The Catholic church was not completely in favor of it,
although officially it endorsed all efforts to improve the lot of the Chinese people. A number
of Chinese and foreign Protestants were more outspoken
in their support. They saw the movement as striving
to modernize ancient teachings. They commended its
process of building new elements upon old and looked
on it as a social revolution that deserved the support
of all Christians.[46] Some Christians, however, deplored the stress on militarization, seeing it as contrary to the Christian goal of peace. Others feared
that the "purity drive" within the movement would
go beyond combatting indecency and seek to put women
back into the old mold.[47] Nonetheless, it was argued that Christians should recognize the good that

was in the movement and should strive to bring its
aims closer to the Christian ideal. For instance,
some charged that the movement lacked a central personality to provide the spiritual driving force
needed to realize its ideals. Christianity would give
the movement the personality of Jesus Christ, for
human efforts needed the backing of divine guidance.[48]

In general, Christians were willing to endorse
the New Life Movement because none of its principles
was contrary to Christian doctrine, and because
they approved of its calls for inward and outward
cleanliness, the beautification of public places, and
honesty. Christians thought that they could contribute much to the movement, especially in the field
of social service.[49] The fact that Chiang Kai-shek,
the founder of the movement, was a Christian pre-
disposed other Christians to favor the movement. R.
Y. Lo, the editor of the *China Christian Advocate*,
went so far as to claim that "the New Life Movement
was based upon the fundamentals of the Christian
religion."[50] An editorial in the *Missionary Review*
concurred, arguing that "the elements of truth and
strength" in the movement came from "the roots of true
spiritual life," instead of from "Chinese history and
ethics."[51]

THE MOVEMENT IN PERSPECTIVE

It is appropriate, in conclusion, to return to a
number of questions implicit in this chapter. To
what extent did the New Life Movement reflect the ideology of the Kuomintang? In what ways did the shortcomings of the movement mirror the party's failure
in general? The answers are obvious. With its
curious blend of Confucian values and Christian social
gospel activism, the movement epitomized some central
aspects of Kuomintang ideology. In consequence, its
deficiencies were symptomatic of the Kuomintang
failure as a whole.

One of the most serious weaknesses of the New Life
Movement, one that was not lost upon some of its con-
temporaries, was its almost exclusive concern with the
urban sector of China. The rural masses did not benefit much from the movement; nor did Chiang Kai-shek
and his associates regard them as a primary target.
From the very beginning of the movement, when one of
the main considerations was the reconstruction of
Kiangsi after the Communist withdrawal, the Kuomintang
was more interested in Nanchang and other urban
areas, while paying some attention to the large landlord class in the rural sector. Somewhat reminis-

cent of the leaders of the T'ung-chih Restoration who
sought to put the country together again after the
Taiping devastation, the Kuomintang leadership placed
primary emphasis on restoring law and order, reopening schools and libraries, repairing the transportation network, and of course, tax relief and aid
to the economy of the region. After its initial
success in Kiangsi, the New Life Movement did not
change its urban emphasis throughout its early years
of operation. Its goals and procedures expressed
the civic and moral values of the upper leisure class
in cities and towns. Its promotion associations
were all established in urban centers, and so were
the few professional organs. And in that the movement
was closely tied to the modernized (and often Christian) sectors of the population, the very ethos of the
movement smacked of urban orientation.

It is perhaps ironic that the Confucian element
of the movement, which dominated the Christian-
modernized elements, did not move the New Life leaders
closer to the concerns of the rural masses. One
reason for the longevity of the Confucian system was
its remarkable ability to transcend urban-rural
differences in Chinese life and to become relevant
in both sectors. Most Confucian scholar-gentry lived
in cities and towns scattered throughout the country, but they were found in every *hsien*, and their activities ranged from scholarship and teaching to
land reclamation, famine control, and water conser-
vancy. The late nineteenth and early twentieth century, however, as recent works by David Buck, Daniel
Bays, and Joseph Esherick have shown, witnessed the increasing alienation of the modernized sector from the
rural population.[52] In the premodern era, for example, sons in peasant families (admittedly the
wealthier ones) had been able to obtain schooling
and compete in civil service examinations from the
countryside level upward. With the establishment of
modern schools, however, they had to live within
traveling distance of towns, since the modern schools
were, almost without exception, founded in towns
and cities. This and other changes increased the
cleavage between cities and countryside.

The Kuomintang was a product of this situation,
for it represented the modernized urban elites.
Inspired by the examples of other late developing
nations (Japan and Turkey, for instance), it naturally
and unconsciously concentrated its attention on the
urban sector. Its leader, Chiang Kai-shek, reflected
not only the indigenous Confucian tradition; his
career was also consistent with those of Kemal Ataturk

and the Meiji oligarchs. They were all products of
their times, when the "creative minority" found
largely in the cities was successful in transforming
the late developing nations. In this sense, Chiang
may be regarded as the last of the late nineteenth-
century reformers, a man as much a victim of the times
as of his own weaknesses. To the extent that the
New Life Movement was personally tied to Chiang's visions and commitments, it was clearly symptomatic
of his failures to deal with China's agrarian problems,
a failure attributable to the entire Kuomintang,
going all the way back to founder Sun Yat-sen himself.

The second weakness of the New Life Movement,
which also reflected Kuomintang failures, was its emphasis on appearance over substance. Again and
again the leaders worried about what appeared to be
rather than what was, thereby discrediting the
movement in the eyes of the Chinese people, who saw
it as a sham rather than as a genuine movement of
moral regeneration. Why was this so?

Those who espoused the ideals of the movement
were caught in a dilemma of their own making, one that
went to the roots of the movement. Since the founding of the party, there had always been a certain
superficiality in Kuomintang ideology. Sun Yat-sen's
Three Principles of the People, which were presumed
to be superior to capitalistic or Marxian values, were
nothing but a pastiche of borrowed ideals. They
neither attracted the populace nor convinced the intellectuals. The infusion of Confucian values
into Kuomintang ideology in the 1930s added certain
Confucian dichotomies to the intrinsic weaknesses
of Sun's Three Principles.

Confucianism had always placed a premium on rites
and ceremonials, preaching that external action was
evidence of internal grace. Nevertheless, Confucius
had also warned of the danger of confusing appearance
with substance. One of the basic Confucian values
was sincerity: nothing really counted unless it was a
genuine expression of the heart. Yet, just as the
nineteenth-century Confucian literati, notably
the Mongol scholar-official Wo-jen, increasingly sub-
stituted verbiage for action, so Chiang Kai-shek
and the supporters of the New Life Movement replaced
performance with exhortation. Rites and rituals were
encouraged for their own sake.

In partial defense of the Kuomintang, one may
argue that at no time in the 1930s did the party have
effective political or fiscal control of the nation,
and that the twin threats of internal Communism
and Japanese incursions forced the Kuomintang to resort

to half-way measures as expedients rather than as
stated policy. But such arguments are not totally
convincing. Throughout the 1930s, there was a genuine
wave of patriotism in China, with the students becoming an increasingly potent force waiting for
mobilization. The Kuomintang could neither harness
nor cope with this powerful force, as much because of
its basic failure to separate appearance from reality, as because of its distrust of the young and
the radical. Ultimately, the message became the substance, and the Kuomintang had to pay a high price
for this weakness.

Thirdly, the New Life Movement in microcosm
reflected the party's penchant for paternalism.
Everything was done from the top down. The people
could not be trusted. Like ignorant children, they
were to be taught to distinguish right from wrong and
led by the nose to do what was good for them, regardless of whether they agreed or not. This tendency, marked throughout Kuomintang history, became
even stronger when Chiang Kai-shek, under the influence of the Ch'en brothers (Li-fu and Kuo-fu), turned
increasingly to the right in ideology. Such paternalism was again consistent with Confucian values,
which stressed the moral obligation of the elites to
rescue the uncultured masses from their plight. There
was a strong sense of *noblesse oblige* in Confucian
tradition, and the New Life Movement mirrored that
same tendency in the Kuomintang. Moreover, the
modernized foreign-educated students who cooperated
closely with the party were themselves elitist in
origins and conviction. When they coalesced with the
Kuomintang, they reinforced the party's elitist
orientation.

This paternalistic trend was not a uniquely
Chinese phenomenon; it was part of the ethos of the
times in which the Kuomintang was operating. Germany
and Japan, for example, which had managed to catch
up with the dominant powers of England and France,
were centralized elitist states. Nevertheless, even
if the Kuomintang could not be faulted for being
elitist and paternalistic in that era, it can
be criticized for its failure to carry out its best
intentions, elitist or otherwise. The Kuomintang was
unable to recognize that there was a basic contra-
diction between the nature of a mass movement (which
is what the Kuomintang was trying to forge) and the
paternalistic and elitist methods that the Kuomintang
used to promote it. Insofar as the Kuomintang
failed to recognize this basic weakness, its leaders
were unsuccessful not only in the New Life Movement,

but also in almost everything else they tried to accomplish.

In short, the Kuomintang failed not only because of what it was, but also because of what it tried to be. It had before it the models of Japan and other nations. In later years, the Chinese Communist Party, in its social and hygienic programs, did much of what the Kuomintang had attempted to do in the New Life Movement. There were, of course, vast differences between Kuomintang and Communist operations. Thanks to the foresight of Mao Tse-tung, the Chinese Communists perceived the efficacy of tying their fortunes to the peasants. They strove for both substance and appearance, and they moderated their own paternalistic and elitist tendencies in their successful mobilization of the masses. Essentially there were no deficiencies in the content of the New Life Movement's aspirations or programs that another leader or another party could not have overcome. In this, the New Life Movement closely resembled its parent Kuomintang. The failure of the movement thus provides an excellent case study of the larger failure of the Kuomintang itself.

NOTES

1. Cf. Donald Jordan, *The Northern Expedition: China's National Revolution of 1926-1928* (Honolulu: University Press of Hawaii, 1976).
2. Cf. Li Yün-han, *Sung Che-yüan yü ch'i-ch'i k'ang-chan* / Sung Che-yüan and the July 7 War of Resistance / (Taipei, 1973).
3. *Min-kuo erh-shih-san nien hsing sheng-huo yün-tung tsung pao-kao* / Complete Report of the New Life Movement in 1934 / (Nanchang, 1935), hereafter cited as *Report*, p. 66.
4. *Ibid.*, pp. 56-105.
5. *Ibid.*, pp. 116-18.
6. Hollington K. Tong, *Chiang Kai-shek: Soldier and Statesman* (Shanghai: China Publishing Co., 1937), Vol. II, p. 544.
7. Robert Berkov, *Strong Man of China* (Boston: Houghton Mifflin, 1938), p. xii.
8. Chiang Kai-shek, *Outline of the New Life Movement*, trans. by Madame Chiang (Nanchang: Association for the Promotion of the New Life Movement, 1934), pp. 5-9, 11-12.
9. For details, see Arif Dirlik, "The Ideological Foundations of the New Life Movement: A Study in Counterrevolution," in *Journal of Asian Studies*, Vol. XXXIV, No. 4 (August 1975), pp. 945-80.

10.   *Hsing sheng-huo yün-tung shou-ts'e* ⎾ New Life Movement Handbook⏌ (Nanchang, 1935), hereafter cited as *Handbook*, pp. 53-57.

11.   Chiang, *Outline*, pp. 10-11.

12.   The following materials on the promotion associations are largely drawn from *Handbook*, pp. 12-13; and *Report*, pp. 204-208.

13.   *Hui-k'an* ⎿ New Life Movement Association Periodical⏌, published by Hsin sheng-huo yün-tung ts'u-chin tsung-hui, Vol. XXXII (January 1936), p. 23.

14.   Personal notes of Professor John E. Orchard, based on talks with Colonel Huang Jen-lin, April 24, 1939.

15.   *Report*, p. 129.

16.   *Ibid.*, pp. 242-71.

17.   *Hui-k'an*, Vol. XXXII (January 1936), pp. 12-16.

18.   *Handbook*, pp. 75-77.

19.   *Hui-k'an*, Vol. XVIII (March 1935), p. 165.

20.   *Report*, pp. 221-42.

21.   *Ibid.*, pp. 290-383.

22.   *Ibid.*, pp. 284-390.

23.   For the accomplishments of the movement, see *ibid.*, pp. 290-429.

24.   Chiang Soong Mei-ling (Madame Chiang Kai-shek), "New Life in China," in *Forum*, Vol. XCIII (June 1935), p. 359.

25.   *Hui-k'an*, Vol. XVIII (March 1935), pp. 10-33.

26.   *Ibid.*, Vol. XXXII (January 1936), pp. 27-28 and 34-42.

27.   *Ibid.*, Vol. XXXIII (March 1936), pp. 1-2.

28.   *Ibid.*, p. iii.

29.   Tong, *Chiang Kai-shek*, Vol. II, p. 577; and Chiang Soong Mei-ling, "Interpretation of the New Life Movement," originally published in *People's Tribune*, reprinted in *Missionary Review*, Vol. LX (July 1937), pp. 361-62.

30.   Hsiung Shih-i, *The Life of Chiang Kai-shek* (London: P. Davis, 1948), p. 339.

31.   Orchard notes.

32.   Tong, *Chiang Kai-shek*, Vol. II, p. 563.

33.   *Hsin she-hui* ⎿ New Society⏌, Vol. VII (August 16, 1934), p. 92.

34.   *Ibid.*, Vol. VII (September 1, 1934), p. 118; and *Shih-tai kung-lun* ⎿ Contemporary Forum⏌, Vol. III (April 13, 1934), p. 10.

35.   *Hsin she-hui*, Vol. VII (October 1, 1934), p. 224; and *Shih-tai kung-lun*, Vol. III (June 8, 1934), p. 9.

36.   *Tu-li p'ing-lun* ⎾Independent Review⏌, Vol. CXV (April 8, 1934), pp. 17, 20; and *I-shih pao* ⎿ Pub-

lic Welfare_/, February 19, 1936, reprinted in *Hui-k'an*, Vol. XXXIII (March 1936), p. 54.

37. *Hui-k'an*, Vol. XXXIII, pp. 38-41.

38. *Shih-tai kung-lun*, Vol. III (April 13, 1934), p. 11; *Hsin she-hui*, Vol. VII (October 1, 1934), p. 224; and *Hui-k'an*, Vol. XVIII (March 1935), pp. 47-49.

39. *Hsin she-hui*, Vol. VII (September 1, 1934), p. 119; and Vol. VII (October 1, 1934), p. 224.

40. *Hui-k'an*, Vol. XVIII (March 1935), p. 91.

41. *Tu-li p'ing-lun*, Vol. CXV (April 8, 1934), pp. 18, 19.

42. *Hua-nien* /_The Young_/, Vol. III (March 24, 1934), p. 2; and *Hui-k'an*, Vol. XVIII (March 1935), p. 96.

43. *Hui-k'an*, Vol. XVIII, pp. 86-87, 95-96.

44. *Ibid.*, pp. 55-57; Vol. XXXIII (March 1936), pp. 56-57; *Kuo-wen chou-pao* /_National News Weekly_/, Vol. XI (April 16, 1934), p. 3; and *Hua-nien*, Vol. III (March 31, 1934), p. 2.

45. *Hsin she-hui*, Vol. VII (August 16, 1934), pp. 92-95.

46. "China's Revival Movement," *Chinese Recorder* (hereafter abbreviated CR), Vol. LXV (October 1934), pp. 609-10; and R. Y. Lo, "Christians! Support the New Life Movement," CR, Vol. LXVIII (May 1937), p. 286.

47. E. S. Yu, "What Can Christian Cooperation Add to the New Life Movement?" (symposium), CR, Vol. LXVIII (May 1937), p. 296; and "China's Revival Movement," pp. 609-10.

48. See E. S. Yu's article in CR, Vol. LXVIII (May 1937), p. 294.

49. George W. Shepherd, "Cooperation with the New Life Movement," CR, Vol. LXVIII (May 1937), p. 287; and George W. Shepherd, "Church and New Life Movement," CR, Vol. LXVIII, p. 282.

50. Shepherd, "Church and New Life Movement," pp. 285-86.

51. "The New Life Movement in China," in *Missionary Review*, Vol. LVII (June 1934), p. 325.

52. David D. Buck, *Urban Change in China: Politics and Development in Tsinan, Shantung, 1890-1949* (Madison: University of Wisconsin Press, 1978); Daniel H. Bays, *China Enters the Twentieth Century: Chang Chih-tung and the Issues of a New Age, 1895-1909* (Ann Arbor: University of Michigan Press, 1978); and Joseph W. Esherick, *Reform and Revolution in China: The 1911 Revolution in Hunan and Hubei* (Berkeley: University of California Press, 1976).

3

Agrarian Reform in Nationalist China: The Case of Rent Reduction in Chekiang, 1927–1937

Noel R. Miner

On April 12, 1927, brutal attacks on Communist unions in Shanghai by Kuomintang troops and affiliated underground gangs brought the first united front between the Nationalists and the Chinese Communists to a bloody conclusion. More than just a political defeat for the Communists, the purge necessitated a change in revolutionary strategy by indicating the frailty of Communist organization in the urban areas. The cities, as bastions of Chinese and foreign wealth and power, did not offer a safe haven for labor unions, regardless of Marxian dictates which required the proletariat to serve as engine of the future revolution.

Although the Communist policy of the post-1927 years vacillated between concern for the all-important proletariat and rejection of urban China, it is evident in retrospect that events on April 12 had spelled the end of total concentration on the cities. Communist leaders, notably Mao Tse-tung, began to move from urban to rural China, and from organizational work with the proletariat to agrarian revolution with the peasantry. Increasingly from 1927 to 1935, Mao offered land reform and social organization of the countryside as key ingredients of a successful Communist strategy. Kuomintang-Communist rivalries did not pit city dwellers against urban inhabitants of another class; instead, they set poor rural peasants in opposition to the more comfortable upper class in rural and urban China. As the Communist strategy became more rural-oriented and the Nationalist policy more elitist, the two contenders for national power found themselves sharply divided on developmental policies. Nevertheless, in 1927, the tension between urban and rural China did not yet appear so divisive as the northern expeditionary forces captured provinces

along the eastern coast of China, such as Chekiang,
the native province of Chiang Kai-shek.

According to contemporary Nationalist leaders,
the capture of Hangchow in 1927 by the troops of the
Northern Expedition was a watershed in Chekiang
history. To them, the military victory marked an end
of the warlord era distinguished by political disunity, social oppression, and economic decay. It also
signaled the beginning of an orderly and prosperous
rule by the Nationalists. Conservative government
based on personal power and military force was to give
way to progressive rule by political leaders es-
pousing a positive ideology. Unabashed by the magni-
tude of the task of modifying Chekiang politics and
society, the Nationalists launched into their work
with enthusiasm. After so many years of abortive revolutions, they had finally won an opportunity to
implement their program.

Politically, the Nationalists in Chekiang inherited a province in which the institutions of local
government were powerless and disorganized. Most
of the essential documents of the county governments
-- land records, population tables, and tax registers
-- had disappeared during previous decades when the
province was shuffled from one warlord faction to
another. Without these minimum statistics, the new
provincial government had only a superficial knowledge
of the current political and economic conditions in
the various counties. In fact, the economy was in a
state of stagnation.

Dependent largely on traditional techniques and
ingredients, agriculture constituted the dominant
sector of the economy in terms of capital investment
and production. Industry held only a meager foothold
even in the major urban areas of the province. Floods,
droughts, or plant diseases annually depressed crop
production levels. Land distribution was very inequitable, with large numbers of peasants handing over
a sizable portion of the harvest to their landlords.
Except for a few private roads around Hangchow and the
incomplete Shanghai-Hangchow-Ningpo railway, the province had no network of modern internal communications. Given the impoverished state of politics and
economy in Chekiang, there was ample room for
reform and construction.

As the initial excitement of victory began to
wane in the calmer weeks following the capture of
Hangchow, the Nationalist authorities in Chekiang became increasingly aware of the complex social, economic, and political problems that would resist
positive reform. It was obvious that some of these

inherited problems would impede constructive action;
it was far simpler to proclaim the dawn of a new
era than to generate fundamental change. The encouraging force of ideology and a sincere desire to
strengthen China might not be enough to sustain reform
and construction in the heated atmosphere of political pressures.

IDEOLOGY AND AGRARIAN REFORM

The ideological handbook of the Nationalists, Sun
Yat-sen's *San-min chu-i* (Three Principles of the
People), espoused a comprehensive policy dependent
on the joint application of agrarian reform and infra-
structure development policies. Aside from calling
for the construction of roads, railways, and cooperatives, Sun demonstrated his concern for the
plight of the peasants by advocating a program of land
reform, exemplified by his slogan of "land to the
tiller." These ideological guidelines served in the
Nationalist period of rule as the main fountainhead of
government policy; the first Kuomintang program for
the rural areas thus mirrored the directives of
the party founder.
The objective of this chapter is to examine the
Nationalist efforts in agrarian reform, as implemented
in the province of Chekiang. The program consisted
of a rent reduction campaign, which constituted
the Kuomintang's principal attempt at basic structural
change in the socio-economic relationships of the
countryside. By reducing the amount of rent paid by
the tenants, the government hoped to increase their
annual income and ultimately raise their standard of
living. This program aimed at guaranteeing that
production increases generated by either agricultural
research and extension or other crop improvement
efforts would filter down to the peasant cultivators.
Chronologically, the chapter concentrates on
the Nanking decade from 1927 to 1937. During this
time span the Nationalists had the best opportunity to
execute their policies. Although much of China maintained a loose or even autonomous relationship with
the central government in Nanking in this decade,
Chekiang was controlled by men directly loyal to
Chiang Kai-shek.[1] Furthermore, many programs carried
out in Chekiang were considered experimental proto-
types for other provinces, as most Nationalist leaders
viewed Chekiang as a "model province." Because of
the combination of local political power buttressed by
central support and the avowed desire of the Nationalists to experiment in Chekiang, the political and

economic policies implemented in the province could
be treated as integral components of an overall
Nationalist plan to reform Chinese society.

In addition to having substantial authority
behind its political institutions, the provincial government in Chekiang could operate in a political
arena essentially free of foreign invasion and domestic insurrection. Even the small number of Communist forays into the southwest corner of the province
near Kiangsi did little to disturb the general tran-
quility in military affairs. By focusing on the rent
reduction campaign, this chapter studies the degree
to which Nationalist policies affected the rural
tenants and part-tenants. If successful, the campaign
would improve the living standard of the peasants and
gain political support for the Nationalists; otherwise, the adverse conditions of tenant life would
remain unchanged, and the peasants would be suscepti-
ble to Communist programs of land reform. Moreover,
since a very inequitable system of land distribution existed throughout the province, the people affected by agrarian reform represented a substantial portion of the provincial population.

Estimates vary slightly on the proportion of
owners and tenants in the province.[2] According to
a provincial survey conducted by the Ministry of
Industries, 35 percent of the farmers in Chekiang were
full tenants, 33 percent part-tenants, 24 percent
owners, and 8 percent laborers with no land. Another
survey of thirty-five *hsien* (counties) over a four-
year period was published by the Bureau of Economics in
Nanking. The cumulative results were as follows:

	Tenants	Part-owners	Owners
1931	48%	31%	21%
1932	48%	31%	21%
1933	45%	33%	22%
1934	47%	33%	20%

According to both surveys, full owners comprised
less than one quarter of the farming population, while
those who rented some or all of their land constituted the absolute majority. The discrepancy between
the two estimates of the number of tenants is probably
due to the fact that rural laborers were included in
the survey of the Bureau of Economics. Regardless
of the slight variations in figures, the statistics
demonstrate that a major proportion of the population
could profit from rent reduction. By translating a
pledge of social reform into action, the Nationalists
could garner the active support of a more prosperous

population.

The land-tenant ratio varied according to geographical regions. The more fertile coastal plains had larger numbers of tenants and part-tenants, while the unproductive mountainous areas sustained a higher level of personal ownership. On the northern plain, the counties of Pinghu and Wuhsing had more tenants than average. The survey of the Ministry of Industries notes that 79 percent of the farmers in Pinghu were tenants, while only 9 percent owned some land in Wuhsing.[3] On the eastern coast, John Lossing Buck surveyed Chenhai County and discovered that 76 percent of the cultivators under examination were tenants.[4] Not all of the counties in the province, however, maintained such high levels of tenancy.

The most striking differences occurred in the mountainous counties of the northeast near Ningpo. In Fenghua, 50 percent of the farmers owned land, and 70 percent cultivated land of their own in T'ient'ai. The highest ratio of owners was recorded along the provincial border with Kiangsi. In Shunan *hsien*, 91 percent of the farmers held titles to their land.[5] Owing to this great diversity in the pattern of land distribution, county authorities required a generous degree of local initiative to adjust the rent reduction campaign to regional landlord-tenant relations.

Even those who had ownership title did not possess a sizable amount of land: the majority owned less than ten *mou* per person. A survey conducted by the Construction Commission in March 1934 revealed that 88 percent of the landlords in Yuyao had less than ten *mou*. In Linan County, 48 percent possessed less than ten *mou*, with another 40 percent owning less than fifty *mou*. In Wuyi County in 1934, 34 percent of the landowners held less than ten *mou*, while 23 percent controlled between ten and twenty *mou*.[6] A cursory examination of the data suggests that land concentration in Chekiang had reached a high level. Moreover, most of the holdings described in the survey were not single contiguous parcels of land, but small scattered plots.

With only a small number of farmers in possession of ownership titles, the land was concentrated in the hands of relatively few people. A survey team dispatched by the Executive Yüan reported that a small group of men owned large sections of land in five counties. In Lungyu County above Lanhsi, 7 percent of the population in the villages under survey owned 72 percent of the land, while in Tsungteh on the northern plain near Hangchow, 2 percent of the people were in possession of 22 percent of the land. In the southern coast county of Yungchia, 1 percent of the population in those villages covered by the survey controlled 28 percent of the land.[7] Other survey results supported the data presented by the Executive Yüan. In Pinghu County on the northern coast, 66 landlords controlled 40 percent of the land farmed by more than one thousand families. In Yiwu located in central Chekiang, landlords who represented only 3 percent of the population controlled 40 percent of the land.[8]

For many years, scholars have contended that there was a tendency toward increasingly smaller land holdings, with landownership slowly but consistently coming into the hands of fewer and fewer people. The study of the Executive Yüan conducted by Ch'en Han-sheng (probably the most rigorous spokesman among these scholars) confirms this contention. Included in the study were charts detailing the changes in landownership between 1928 and 1933; they purported to defend the view of gradual concentration of land. More recent studies have called into question this widely held belief by pointing out that landownership in some areas of North China remained steady throughout the early decades of the twentieth century.[9] Despite the lack of detailed statistics to clarify the broader pattern of changes in landownership, the available data support the proposition that landownership of most of Chekiang's agricultural fields was concentrated in the hands of a few individuals during 1927-1937.

To complicate further the existing socio-economic relationships, there were myriad types of tenure arrangements under the general classification of tenancy. No single contract system governed the economic relations between landlords and tenants throughout the province. History and local customs had so diversified the contract system that many localities had a blend of several different tenancy agreements. The variety of contract agreements encompassed a spectrum from permanent tenancy to limited tenure dependent on cash or kind payments with sharecropping as another alternative. Within each category was a wide variation in contract provisions.

Permanent tenancy was the most stable arrangement since the renter secured unrestricted control over the land. By dividing the land into topsoil and subsoil, the landlord and his tenant distributed legal rights to the land for the sake of tenancy.[10] The tenant received absolute control of the topsoil in exchange for a set deposit and an annual percentage

of the crop. The landlord retained the ownership of
the subsoil and responsibility for paying the
taxes. As permanent lessee of the topsoil, the tenant
could sublease any portion of the land as long as he
-- the primary tenant -- insured the annual payment
of rent to the landlord.

The size of the deposit, paid only once at the
time of leasing, depended on the quality of the soil.
To rent excellent soil, a tenant usually paid a
deposit of 7-9 yüan per *mou*, while poorer soil could
be rented with a deposit of merely 3-5 yüan per *mou*.
In both cases, the deposit corresponded to approximately 13 percent of the land value. There were, however, extreme examples in which the deposit could
reach an excessive height of 30 yüan a *mou*.[11] After
paying the deposit, the annual rent on land would
be slightly reduced. According to the conventional
rules of the permanent tenancy system, a landlord
could not evict a tenant unless his delinquent rent
payment reached a sum equivalent to the value of the
topsoil. Although the system had no legal guaran-
tees, the force of local customs generally restrained
a landlord from arbitrarily evicting his tenant.

Permanent tenancy offered substantial benefits to
both the tenant and his landlord. The landlord could
avoid the anxieties of finding enterprising tenants,
because the customary relationship based on fixed rent
and standard arrangements reduced the disagreements
which normally arose between landlords and tenants.
On the other hand, permanent tenancy insured the
tenant that he would reap the fruits of his effort to
improve the quality of the agricultural enterprise.
The stable agreement thus gave the peasant an incentive
to invest in the agricultural process. It also freed
him from the constant interference of the landlord,
provided that he paid his annual rent on time. Especially common on the fertile coastal plains where
the size of harvests was more standard than elsewhere
in the province, the system of permanent tenancy
provided a degree of security of occupancy.

Besides the system of permanent tenancy, many
tenants rented land according to a complex variety of
contract arrangements in which no one system prevailed.[12] Some of them secured written contracts
clearly defining the financial responsibility of each
party, while the majority settled the terms of tenancy
on a verbal agreement with their landlords. In the
latter case, there might be no exact limit to the rent;
sometimes the landlords would use their superior
economic position to impose higher rents on the tenants. Written leases commonly specified an exact

period of occupancy, whereas the verbal agreements
usually left the terms of tenancy undefined. In the
latter case, a landlord could confiscate the land
at any time by simply claiming that his tenant had not
observed the agreement. He could then rent the land
to another prospective cultivator. Without a written
contract, the tenant could only depend on the uncertain weight of customs, which did not always restrain the local elite.

The form and the size of payment varied according
to both the crop and the quality of the land. In the
agricultural areas that grew grain crops with a harvest value of 12-14 yüan per *mou*, tenants paid rent in
kind with a portion of their harvest equivalent to
about 7-9 yüan per *mou*. Tenants with poorer land, as
well as those who cultivated the mountainous fields
that produced a harvest value of 8-10 yüan, paid rent
of 3-5 yüan per *mou*.[13] Tenants in areas suitable
for double-cropping paid rent twice a year at each
harvest season, but farmers in the more mountainous
areas paid only once a year. Some landlords required
their tenants to pay the rent before the harvest,
forcing the tenants to take loans on their future income at high rates of interest.

Deposits were commonly required on land rented
without the right of permanent tenancy on either verbal or written contracts. Customarily, the landlord returned the deposit upon the termination of the
rental contract. Upon paying the rent, a tenant
offered in tribute such supplemental gifts to the
landlord as a chicken, a piglet, or an auspicious dish
of food, and the landlord was expected to prepare a
small feast in return. In periods of drought or
flood, landlords and tenants usually decided to lower
the rent to compensate for the effect of natural
disasters.

Land owned by temples, schools, or clans was often
rented through an agent, who also collected rent and
supervised the tenancy obligations. On the northern plain, some absentee landlords pooled their land
in bursaries, which managed the collection of rent and
policed the land.[14] Much of the oppressive nature
of the tenancy system arose in these indirect relationships, because the rental agents usually exacted an
extra fee from the tenants ostensibly to cover the cost
of collection. Local ecological conditions determined
the choice of crop for most farmers; in some cases,
the landlords or their agents directly instructed the
tenants which crop to grow.

The most irregular form of tenancy was sharecropping. According to this arrangement, the landlord

provided not only the land, but also a share of the
capital to cover the operation of the farm. In
return, the tenant paid a major portion of the harvest
to the landlord, usually 60-80 percent.[15] This system did not appeal to the landlord, because it necessitated too large an investment. In less fertile
land, however, a landlord often had to help a tenant
with money to improve the fertility of the soil,
thus making it suitable for intensive cultivation.

Within the geographical boundaries of one province and even a county, tenants rented land under
many variations of the tenancy system. In fact, the
term "tenancy system" conceals more than it reveals,
because it implies a certain uniformity among contract
agreements. The different contract systems in the
province frequently carried with them the unconscious
power of tradition and customs; any program to
streamline the system would have to overcome the
habits of generations.

To this complex society, the Nationalists came
as a diverse assortment of individuals with different
educational experiences and plans for the future.
The loose coalition of people who presented themselves
as Nationalists included semitraditional military
officers, foreign-trained students, urban businessmen,
and rural landlords. Inexperienced in administration and guided only by a sometimes vague set of
ideological principles conceived by Sun Yat-sen, they
joined in support of rent reduction and such infra-
structure construction as roads, railroads, and
cooperative lending societies. With such ill-defined
parameters to ideology, all policies with a promise
to strengthen Chekiang could be equally applied.
There were auspicious hopes for the future of Chekiang's agriculture and rural society.

THE RENT REDUCTION CAMPAIGN IN OPERATION

Interest in the rent reduction campaign began in
1927 when Shen Ting-yi, a respected local politician
and a member of the Chekiang branch of the Central
Political Council, began to draft a series of rent reduction laws with the help of other provincial party
leaders. Shen and his fellow workers modeled the
Chekiang laws on the recommendations of the Kuomintang
Central Executive Committee in 1925, which encouraged
a program of rent reduction by 25 percent. By November 1927, the provincial rent reduction law had
been formally promulgated after being approved by both
the party and the government. Agrarian reform in
the form of rent reduction was thus set in operation.

According to the provisions of the 1927 law, the rent ceiling on a main crop was to be 50 percent of the total annual production. Furthermore, all rents were to be reduced additionally by 25 percent, leaving 37.5 percent as the highest annual rent.[16] The law also stipulated that deposits on land, pre-harvest payment, and demands for extra gifts at payment time were to be discontinued. Tenants were forbidden to water their harvested rice to increase its weight.

In an effort to formulate a simple law that could be understood by all tenants and landlords, the drafters created instead a simplistic law that failed to recognize the complexities of agrarian society. Many questions arose to complicate the execution of the rent reduction campaign. What exactly constituted the "main crop"? Were all rent contracts -- including permanent tenancy, cash rents, and sharecropping -- to be affected by the law? If payment of a deposit insured a lower rent, could the deposit already paid to the landlord be refunded and the rent raised?

In early 1928, instead of increasing the amount of money kept by the tenants, the ambiguous rent reduction law only increased the number of disputes between landlords and tenants. It was indeed so vague that it did little to force the landlords to change their natural reluctance to support any kind of reform, with the result that most of them interpreted the law to their own advantage. When the tenants asked for a reduction of rents and an end to deposits and early payments, many landlords disregarded their demands. Hence, the first steps toward agrarian reform had only fomented new problems, especially on the rich northern plain.

The first revision of the law came in the summer of 1928 when stricter provisions concerning infractions of the law were added. A mediation committee composed of party, government, and peasant association members was also established in each county to arbitrate disagreements about the meaning of the statutes. After 1928, any landlord who demanded more than the legal 37.5 percent would suffer the loss of all rent; a landlord who confiscated land would have to justify his action to the mediation committee. On the other hand, tenants who continued to water their rice would be heavily punished. Yet, in spite of these amendments, the party and government discovered within six months that the enactment of the reduction law was neither easy nor universally supported.

The effort to curtail the rural turmoil that the

rent reduction campaign engendered by revising the
law and increasing the penalties did not end the disputes. While many tenants who misunderstood the
law refused to pay any rent, some landlords simply
evicted an obstreperous tenant who asked for a reduction. In the area surrounding the provincial capital of Hangchow where statistics were recorded, arguments developed between 190 tenants and 93 landlords
over more than 5,000 *mou* of land.[17] Tenants brought
most of the cases before the mediation committee.
Their charges included failure to reduce rent (22
percent) and the confiscation of land either to rent
to new tenants (39 percent) or to cultivate themselves (33 percent). The statistics demonstrated that
when a tenant demanded rent reduction, many landlords
relied on the traditional procedure of evicting
troublemakers.

Since minor revisions of the law had not succeeded in calming rural tensions, the representatives
of the ruling committees of both the government and
the party met in a series of joint meetings in 1929 to
revise and update the rent reduction statutes. From
these meetings, the joint committee was able to write
a better and more flexible set of rent reduction
laws. Because many landlords had ignored the rent
ceiling of 50 percent when reducing their rent, the
new law stated forthrightly that 37.5 percent of the
harvest was the highest annual rent. The main crop
classification was clarified to include any that
constituted the major product of the area, whether it
be rice, wheat, silk, barley, or cotton. Other
statutes stated that all rented land was to be covered
by the law, and this included temple, clan, and
school land, which had been considered by many landlords to be outside the purview of the campaign. The
new law also recognized the force of local customs
by stipulating that deposits would be allowed if they
enabled the tenants to secure lower rents.

By 1932, the quality of the rent reduction laws
had been greatly improved by clarification of ambiguities and relaxation of the inflexibility of the
earlier laws. The appreciation of former mistakes enabled the provincial authorities in charge of the
Chekiang rent reduction campaign to develop a set of
more workable laws. When the number of disputes began
to subside in 1930-1933, the revision and clarification efforts of both the party and the government
appeared to have succeeded in fostering social
calm. In fact, the improvement of the law had little
to do with the reduction in the number of disputes.
Political pressures rather than law revision had a more

telling effect on the course of the campaign.

Just as the quality of the law improved, political support of government leaders for the campaign
evaporated, leaving few administrators willing to
enforce the revised statutes. In 1927, both party and
government figures had supported rent reduction following the ideological precepts of their leaders.
This early consensus, however, had begun to collapse
by 1928 and early 1929 when tensions in the countryside started to affect government programs. Local
mediation committees could not resolve many of the
disputes in Hangchow, and higher authorities had to
be involved in their settlement. This often expended
excessive time and energy and curbed the efforts of
government officials on behalf of other programs.

More important than the excessive expenditure
of time and energy in resolving tense civil disputes
was the increasingly vocal and active opposition
of the landlords. Both publicly and privately, they
began to lobby with government officials in order
to persuade them to curtail the entire reduction campaign. Governor Chang Jen-chieh, member of a large
landowning family in Wuhsing County, was receptive
toward the opposition of the landlords who resented
both the campaign and the resultant social turmoil
generated by the rent reduction programs. In an
effort to put their verbal opposition in action, many
landlords withheld their land taxes as a protest
against the campaign.[18]

In 1929, many party and government officials were
learning more about their base of power. Rent reduction might have to be reconsidered in light of the
objection of the landlord class. The government
began to perceive that the economic power of the landlords, who constituted one segment of the Nationalist coalition, outweighed their limited numbers.

In contrast to verbal protest, which could be
tempered or ignored, nonpayment of land taxes -- the
main source of government income -- was a direct
attack on government operations. It was clear by
early 1929 that the rent reduction campaign would not
only continue to roil the countryside, it would also
cripple government activities by drying up the flow
of income. In addition, Chang Jen-chieh and other
leaders hoped to persuade wealthy landlords to
subscribe to the construction bonds that would finance ambitious programs of railway and road development. With the problems created by rent reduction,
many landlords would no longer be willing to purchase
bonds. By 1929, the Nationalists in Chekiang had
found that agrarian reform was not compatible with

road, railway, and cooperative construction, since
structural modification threatened to jeopardize the
intrastructure development so highly valued by
government leaders.

On its own initiative, the provincial government,
with the approval of Chang Jen-chieh, abolished the
rent reduction campaign in April 1929 to regain
the political and financial support of the landlords.[19] The government announced that it had decided
to discontinue the entire rent reduction law, since
the campaign had had little salutory effect on the
rural areas except for creating new tensions.

Immediately, the Party Political Council in
Hangchow -- separate from government control and dependent on Nanking rather than Hangchow officials
-- reacted to the provincial government's action by
strenuously objecting to the termination of the
campaign. In private meetings with Chang Jen-chieh
and in *Min-kuo jih-pao*, the party newspaper in
Hangchow, the Nationalists berated the government for
failing to live up to the ideology of Sun Yat-sen.
For one month, the heat of political pressure
increased as the party continued to protest the abandonment of agrarian reform.

Repeatedly embarrassed by the attacks of party
committee members and anxious to avoid further opposition, the provincial government quashed all criticisms by arresting the editor of the party newspaper
and suspending its publication. This blunt act of
suppression quickly galvanized antipathies between the
two local political institutions and rendered further
negotiations impossible. With political paralysis
evident in Hangchow, the party committee appealed to
its allies in Nanking to secure the release of the
newspaper editor and to settle the political crisis.
To defuse the tension in Chekiang, central authorities
liberated the editor and transferred him out of the
province. They also ordered the continuance of
the rent reduction campaign. Finally, they delegated
Tai Chi-t'ao, a former party activist in Chekiang,
to act as a mediator between the two political
institutions in the province and to develop a new set
of rent reduction laws.

Out of the joint mediation committee of party and
government officials came the revised rent reduction
laws of 1929. By the end of 1929, some of the political tensions had been calmed by compromise. The
party was to be placated by the work of the joint
revision committee and the reinstitution of the rent
reduction law. The provincial government was to
be satisfied by receiving the sole responsibility for

implementation of the law, without the review of any
other political institution. The full meaning of
the compromise did not become clear until 1930 when
the government quietly ceased concerted implementation of rent reduction. Most of the legal revisions were essentially face-saving moves for
the party; the government, by a policy of nonaction,
had decided to allow the agrarian reform to die
an easy death. After 1929, provincial officials
devoted their energy to their own programs of economic
development in transportation and scientific agricultural research.

Concurrent with the settlement of the political
crisis and the demise of agrarian reform came the
assassination of Shen Ting-yi, the early advocate of
rent reduction and an active leader in self-
government experiments for peasants.[20] As an activist for the Nationalists in Chekiang and a well-
known proponent of reform policies, Shen had become
the embodiment of structural reform and of peasant
involvement in the political process. His murder
dampened the support for any kind of reform and served
as a warning to those who still advocated such
measures. Although the assassin escaped capture, the
coterminous death of rent reduction and the leading
spokesman for political and economic changes left
no doubt about the future of agrarian reform in
Chekiang. Political pressures had simply outweighed
the command of ideology and undermined the support
for agrarian reform from government leaders who were
not strongly motivated reformers in the first place.
This lack of political commitment -- instead of
the improved reduction laws -- brought about the
decrease in rural turmoil, and the decline of political support affected the results of the short-lived
campaign.

IMPACT OF RENT REDUCTION

The geographical extent of the campaign was
limited to the northern Chekiang plain, especially
Hsiaoshan where Shen Ting-yi was active and Hangchow
County surrounding the capital, as well as a few
other counties with strong party organizations capable of goading the county government into action.[21]
In some counties, the campaign had no effect at
all, as rent collectors and landlords continued to
levy high rents. In mountainous counties, traditional social organizations and widespread illiteracy
left most peasants ignorant of rent reduction. In
an interview in Taiwan, a knowledgeable observer of

the entire campaign confirmed the narrow geographical
limits of rent reduction by stating that he knew of
only a few counties that had experienced any kind
of reform.

Even the Party Political Council of Chekiang
tacitly admitted that the campaign had been something
less than a crowning achievement. A pamphlet entitled "Why 25 Percent Rent Reduction Cannot Be Applied Extensively" noted in 1933 that most tenants in
the province had not received any benefit during the
six years during which the rent reduction laws were
in effect.[22] According to the party description
of the campaign, in counties where rent reduction was
in operation, only a few *ch'ü* (districts) supported
the effort, and only a few *hsiang* (townships) in these
ch'ü truly implemented rent reduction for tenants.
Another salient admission of failure was made in 1937
when the Construction Commission published a special
edition of *Che-kiang sheng chien-she yüeh-k'an*
/ Monthly Journal of the Chekiang Construction Commission / to commemorate construction achievements of
the first decade of the Nationalist rule.[23] The
absence of any article on the rent reduction campaign
was an obvious indication that the laws had not been
very successful. Even the drop in land value,
which the Nationalists often mentioned as a proof
of the effectiveness of the campaign, stemmed more
from the sharp reduction in agricultural prices
brought about by the worldwide depression than from
the tentative effort in agrarian reform.

Many reasons accounted for the poor performance
in agrarian reform. The inexperience of the Nationalist leaders who misunderstood the complexities of
rural society damaged the initial endeavors to control
the social composition of an agrarian community. The
rent reduction law was too simplistic in its early
versions to direct a peaceful reform campaign untrou-
bled by confusion and political opposition. The
government and party officials had to learn that they
could not govern by simple fiat -- regardless of
their admirable intentions -- and expect everyone to
follow the laws obediently, especially when the
provincial government lacked the power to enforce implementation or quell opposition.

Additionally, many government leaders, especially Chang Jen-chieh, had construction projects of
their own which they favored over structural reform.
When rent reduction was applied concurrently with
their projects, they were willing to support it; when
it became clear that agrarian reform would force the
cancellation of their pet ideas and probably even

bankrupt the government, Chang and other leaders
halted the disruptive campaign. The government simply
did not have a sustained commitment to agrarian
reform, whatever the ideological justification for
such changes. As the political opposition intensified,
the leaders concluded that it was easier to terminate
the campaign than to lose the political and economic
support of the landlord class.

Admittedly, neither the government nor the Kuomintang was servile handmaidens of the landlord
At first, the leaders of both institutions helped to
initiate policies that were detrimental to landlord
interests. When the end to agrarian reform came, it
was the result of a combination of inexperience,
alternative government projects, and political weaknesses, as well as strong landlord opposition. Moreover, the death of rent reduction in 1929 did not
come either easily or quietly. Party leaders fought
hard for the campaign and continued to harbor
resentment against government officials, even to
the extreme of publishing an indictment of provincial
implementation of rent reduction in 1933. As late
as 1971, many former party officials still spoke with
apparent dislike for Chang Jen-chieh and other government figures associated with him.[24] Not everyone
in Chekiang accepted the abandonment of rent reduction
with equanimity, but those who objected had no way
to redress their grievances against a coalition
of government and landlord forces. The true outlines
of the Nationalist coalition in Chekiang had become
crystal clear with its more ideological-minded members
being forceably pushed to the side.

In summary, even a superficial agrarian reform
-- the reduction of rents -- had failed in Chekiang.
After the abandonment of the campaign, the provincial
government never experimented with any other land
reform as suggested in the motto of "land to the
tiller." Interpretations of Nationalist endeavors in
agrarian reform vary between two extremes. The
Nationalists in Taiwan proudly declare that Chekiang
had a most successful rent reduction campaign that
provided substantial benefits to the people.[25] This
contention is clearly an overstatement. The contrasting interpretation of the Chinese Communists
claims that the Nationalists "subjected the peasantry
to an economic exploitation ... more ruthless than
ever before."[26] This indictment also appears
exaggerated, since there is no evidence to support
the argument that conditions of the peasantry deteriorated greatly under the Nationalist rule. A more
accurate interpretation lies between the two con-

flicting poles. When ideology reigned supreme as the
main source of action, both the party and the government followed the ideological dictates. It
was only when ideology was put to the hot test of
political tensions that the government retreated from
agrarian reform and failed to improve the living
standards of the peasants.

   After 1929, the government turned to the policies
of economic development that neither improved nor
threatened the existing social and economic relationships of the rural countryside.[27]   Similarly, these
policies did not greatly affect the general distribution of wealth. Both the party and the government would continue to swear allegiance to Sun Yat-
sen's Three Principles of the People, yet henceforth
programs dealing with infrastructural construction
and production increases rather than with land
distribution would be implemented in the rural areas.
The proclamation of the national land law in 1930
had a hollow ring for the populace of Chekiang since
this land law reflected the rent reduction statutes
that had so recently been abandoned. Simple pro-
mulgations of national laws could not reverse
the reality that experiments in agrarian reform had
ended for the Nationalists in Chekiang. Despite the
initial enthusiasm for the 1926 social reform, the
Chekiang government decided to ignore the unequal
socio-economic relations of the rural areas.

   Some Nationalist officials from Chekiang now in
residence in Taiwan argue that the unimpressive
performance in the countryside during the first decade
of the Kuomintang rule can be explained by the threat
of war with Japan, which was then looming over
China. The money intended for economic construction
projects had to be diverted to the military to
strengthen national defenses. While military considerations doubtless commanded much attention in the
1930s, the political decisions concerning agrarian
reform were made far in advance of the Japanese takeover of Manchuria in 1931. The main determinant
for the success or failure of agrarian reform was not
the threat of war; it was rather the political concern of the Nationalists over their elitist base
of support.

THE SIGNIFICANCE OF AGRARIAN REFORM FAILURE: A HYPO-
   THESIS

   In every discipline or area study, certain important theories and events capture the interest
of many scholars and become centers of academic con-

troversy. The argument over the causes and effects
of World War I has achieved such stature in modern
European history. In modern Chinese studies, two
historical developments have stimulated similar interest among Western scholars. They are, namely, the
challenge of the West for traditional China in the
nineteenth century and the Communist victory of 1949.
For those who study twentieth-century China, the
factors leading to Communist success have become a
key focus of analysis.

A number of different and, at times, conflicting
interpretations explain the political, military,
social, and economic reasons for the successful establishment of the People's Republic of China. Lionel
M. Chassin emphasizes the military factors in his
analysis of the Communist victory over the Kuomintang.[28] Chalmers A. Johnson, however, directs his
attention mainly to the impact of Japanese aggression in China. It transformed the Chinese Communists
from peripheral revolutionaries into national leaders protecting the peasants from foreign enemies.[29]
Mark Selden suggests that the social, political, and
economic policies developed in Yenan -- known as
"new democracy" and "mass line" -- helped the Communists to build a strong base of support among the
peasantry. According to this interpretation, the
Japanese invasion did not drive the peasants into the
arms of the Communists. Rather, the Chinese Communist Party won peasant support on its own with efficient local organization and with the implementation
of progressive rural reform programs.[30]

It seems a plausible hypothesis to relate the
failure of the agrarian reform analyzed in this
chapter to the Nationalist defeat in 1949. A discussion of the direct relationship between positive
and negative poles -- the social and economic success
of the "Yenan Way" versus the Kuomintang failure to
implement agrarian reform in Chekiang -- may shed
light on the debate about the Communist victory in
1949. The Nationalists in Chekiang abandoned the
peasantry because of the concerted opposition of the
landlords. This left a political vacuum in the
rural areas, which was later filled by the Communists,
thanks to their revolutionary programs of land reform and their advocacy of the mass line as developed
in Yenan. Mostly because the Kuomintang had ignored
the interests of the peasants, they rallied to the
Communist banner. Ironically, because of their
successful opposition to gradual reform, many landlords lost their properties and political rights
in the post-1949 years. By suppressing even the most

superficial reform efforts, they left the peasants
with no alternative except revolution and full
expropriation of landlord property.

Even though rent reduction is its central subject, this chapter does not suggest that the Nationalist failure in agrarian reform is the only explanation for the victory of the Chinese Communist Party in
1949. There are too many non-Communist societies
with unequal land distribution to claim that inequitable landholdings can alone generate revolution.
Even Mark Selden denies that the single factor of unequal distribution of land could have been enough
to bring about Communist success.[31] The effects of
the Sino-Japanese War, Communist techniques of
organization embodied in the mass line and new democracy, and the relative weakness of Kuomintang political, economic, or military leadership helped to
determine the outcome of the civil war in 1949.
Nevertheless, Nationalist ineptitude in rural reform
did provide a setting for successful Communist
activities. Inequitable land distribution and the
oppressive socio-economic relationships it engendered
helped provide the tinder that organized revolutionaries sparked into fire.

NOTES

1. Robert A. Kapp, "Provincial Independence vs.
National Rule: A Case Study of Szechwan in the
1920s and 1930s," in *Journal of Asian Studies*, Vol.
XXX, No. 3 (May 1971), pp. 535-49.
2. Kuo-chi mao-i tsu (Bureau of Foreign Trade),
ed., *Chung-kuo shih-yeh chih: Che-kiang sheng* / Survey
of China's Industry: Chekiang Province / (Shanghai,
1933), Vol. I, p. 36; and "Classification of Farmers
by Percentages," *Chinese Economic and Statistical
Review*, Vol. II, No. 9 (September 1935), p. 9.
3. *Chung-kuo shih-yeh chih*, Vol. I, p. 32.
4. John Lossing Buck, *Land Utilization in China*
(New York: Council on Economic and Cultural Affairs,
1956), p. 146.
5. *Chung-kuo shih-yeh chih*, Vol. I, p. 34.
6. Ying Mo-ju, "Che-kiang Yu-yao te nung-min
sheng-huo" / Farmers' Lives in Yuyao County,
Chekiang /, *Chung-kuo nung-ts'un* / China's Agricultural Villages /, Vol. I, No. 5, p. 62; Statistical Department of Chekiang Economics Institute, *Chekiang Lin-an hsien nung-ts'un tiao-ch'a* / Survey
of Agricultural Villages of Linan County, Chekiang /
(Hangchow, 1931), p. 85.
7. Hsing-cheng-yüan nung-ts'un fu-hsing wei-

88

yüan-hui (Rural Rehabilitation Commission, Executive
Yüan), ed., *Che-kiang nung-ts'un tiao-cha* / Survey
of Agricultural Villages in Chekiang/ (Shanghai,
1934), p. 7 and p. 8.

8. Chien Chen-jui, "Land Holding in Pinghu,"
Statistical Monthly, Vol. I, No. 3 (1929), p. 3.

9. Ramon H. Myers, *The Chinese Peasant Economy:
Agricultural Development in Hopei and Shantung,
1890-1949* (Cambridge, Mass.: Harvard University Press,
1970), pp. 212-94.

10. Fei Hsiao-t'ung, *Peasant Life in China: A
Field Study of Country Life in the Yangtze Valley* (New York: Dutton, 1939), pp. 184-87.

11. Ch'en Cheng-mo, *Chung-kuo ko-sheng te ti-tsu*
/ Land Rents in China's Provinces/ (Shanghai,
1936), pp. 20, 61.

12. *Chung-kuo shih-yeh chih*, Vol. I, p. 22; and
Buck, *Land Utilization*, pp. 147-49.

13. Rent figures in Feng Ho-fa, *Chung-kuo nung-
ts'un ching-chi tzu-liao* / Source Materials on
China's Agricultural Economy/ (Shanghai, 1935), p.
582; and harvest values in Ch'en, *Chung-kuo*, p. 20.

14. Yuji Muramatsu, "A Documentary Study of
Chinese Landlordism in Late Ch'ing and Early Republican Kiangnan," in *Bulletin of the School of
Oriental and African Studies*, Vol. XXIX, No. 3 (1966),
pp. 566-99. Both the source materials and the
interviews suggest that such bursaries were limited
to only a few counties on the northern Yangtze plain,
especially Wuhsing, Pinghu, and Shaohsing. Clan
and temple land rent to tenant farmers in an impersonal rental system was far more common throughout the province.

15. *Che-kiang nung-ts'un tiao-cha*, p. 52.

16. Cheng Chen-yu, "Chung-kuo chih tien-keng chih-
tu yü tien-nung pao-chang" / China's Leasing Systems
and Safeguards for Farmers/, in *Ti-cheng Yüeh-
k'an* / Land Administration Monthly/, Vol. I, No. 4
(1933), pp. 470-90; and Chekiang Party Political
Council, *Erh-wu chien-tsu fa-kuei chi ch'i-t'a* /25
Percent Rent Reduction Laws and Other Materials/
(Hangchow, 1932), pp. 1-124.

17. Ts'ai Pin-hsien, "Che-kiang tien-yeh chiu-fen
an-chien t'ung-chi chih shih-pien" / A Record of
Statistics on Disputes Between Chekiang Farmers and
Landlords/, in *Che-kiang chien-she yüeh-k'an*,
Vol. IV, No. 4 (1930), *t'ung-chih*, pp. 46-58.

18. *Shih-shih hsin-pao* / The China Times/, April
27, 1929, p. 7.

19. *Ibid.*, May 3, 1929; and August 9, 1929, p. 5.

20. K'ung Hsüeh-hsiung, *Chung-kuo chin-jih chih*

nung-ts̲'un yün-tung ∠⁻The Rural Movement in China Today_/ (Shanghai, 1934), pp. 329-400.

21. *Shih-shih hsin-pao*, August 30, 1932, p. 4.

22. Chekiang Party Political Council, *Che-kiang sheng tien-nung erh-wu chien-tsu fa-kuei shih-li* ∠ A Record of Chekiang's 25 Percent Rent Reduction Laws_/ (Hangchow, 1933), p. 12 and p. 13.

23. "Shih-nien-lai chih Che-kiang chien-she" ∠⁻Ten Years of Chekiang Construction_/, in *Che-kiang sheng_ chien-she yüeh-k'an* ∠ Chekiang Construction Monthly_/, Vol. X, No. 11 (1937).

24. Interviews with author in Taipei, Taiwan, in January-March 1971.

25. Kao Yüeh-t'ien, "Shen Ting-yi hsien-sheng te i-sheng" ∠ The Life of Mr. Shen Ting-yi_/, in *Chekiang Monthly*, Vol. IV, No. 4 (May 1972), pp. 15-20.

26. Mao Tse-tung, *Selected Works of Mao Tse-tung* (Peking: Foreign Languages Press, 1965), Vol. I, p. 63.

27. *Che-kiang cheng-fu kung-pao* ∠ Chekiang Government Gazette_/, No. 720 (October 3, 1929), p. 14.

28. Lionel M. Chassin, *The Communist Conquest of China: A History of the Civil War, 1945-1949* (Cambridge, Mass.: Harvard University Press, 1965), pp. 1-45.

29. Chalmers A. Johnson, *Peasant Nationalism and Communist Power: The Emergence of Revolutionary China, 1937-1945* (Stanford: Stanford University Press, 1962), pp. 1-70.

30. Mark Selden, *The Yenan Way in Revolutionary China* (Cambridge, Mass.: Harvard University Press, 1971), pp. 121-276.

31. *Ibid.*, p. 34.

4

China's Vulnerability to Japanese Imperialism: The Anti-Japanese Boycott of 1931–1932

Donald A. Jordan

In retrospect, the 1931-1932 Chinese boycott of Japanese goods seems eclipsed by the cannonade in¹ Manchuria between Chinese and Japanese forces. But this boycott, the eighth one since 1915, did at least represent the *potential* for national action that was rising within the Chinese people. Even more significant for history was the boycott's revelation of the persistent divisions in the Chinese body politic and the weakness of the modern sector of the Chinese economy.

Decentralized political and military power frustrated Chinese attempts to resist the much more effective military and economic imperialism of Japan both in Manchuria and in China proper. The boycott of 1931-1932 may be viewed as an act of governmental and collective desperation. In the midst of the world depression, China struggled to compete with the masterfully efficient and government-subsidized Japanese export industries. To overcome basic economic and political weaknesses, Chinese commercial and industrial leaders in Shanghai collaborated with the Kuomintang leadership in Nanking to mobilize the Chinese people in another boycott. Financially involved in apparently futile civil wars, Chiang Kai-shek and the Nanking government had been unable to bring together the capital and expertise that might have quickened China's industrial modernization. Despite the urban and commercial orientation of much of the Kuomintang constituency, Nanking was far from meeting the Japanese industrial and commercial challenge. Although disconcerting, the boycott of Japanese goods and services was, likewise, not a successful means of blocking Japanese imperialism.

Although historians have been distracted from this particular anti-Japanese movement in 1931 by the rising tumult in Manchuria, contemporary Japanese diplomats and generals gave it much more serious attention. Less than a month after the September 18 invasion of Manchuria in 1931, Japan's minister to China insisted that this outbreak of hostilities was "nothing but the outcome of reported anti-Japanese feeling in China." He complained particularly about the boycott, which he described as the "so-called severance of economic relations with Japan." Later in the year, Foreign Minister Shidehara Kijūrō demanded that any Japanese military evacuation from Manchuria would have to be preceded by the "discontinuance of government sanction of boycotts ... or other economic action."

Sympathetic to China's vulnerability, American Secretary of State Henry L. Stimson described the boycott as China's best weapon but later noted that Japan's military intervention in Shanghai in 1932 was mainly undertaken "to kill the boycott."[1] As tensions built toward full-scale warfare, what part did the anti-Japanese boycott of 1931-1932 play? Was it solely a means to defend China? Or was it, as some Japanese charged, a form of economic warfare waged by China's ambitious capitalists?

This most intensive of the nine anti-Japanese boycotts in the twentieth century began with Sino-Japanese rivalries in Manchuria. Festering there was the competition between Japan's South Manchurian Railroad and the newly constructed Chinese lines. Newly revised Chinese tariffs also hurt the Japanese shipments from the Kwantung outlets to the Chinese markets. Violence erupted in early July 1931 in the village of Wanpaoshan near Changchun, Manchuria, over irrigation rights between Chinese farmers and Korean emigrants. It brought the Japanese railway police to the rescue of the Koreans, as subjects of the Japanese emperor. In response to the skirmish, anti-Chinese riots broke out in Korea and killed more than one hundred Chinese merchants and workers. Many Chinese accused the Japanese of having promoted these outbursts through the press. If the sensationalistic accounts of Wanpaoshan in the Japanese-controlled press did not trigger the "massacre" in Korea, they certainly provided stimulus.

Allegations of such a conspiracy abounded at the Kuomintang headquarters in Nanking, only in its fourth year as China's new national capital. Significantly, the more immediate and active response to the killing of the Chinese in Korea came from the merchants and industrialists of Shanghai. By 1931, the themes of conflicting Chinese and Japanese nationalism and

competing Chinese and Japanese capitalism had become
intertwined. While the response from China's weak,
disintegrated military was muted, the patriotic
outcry from China's capitalists was loud and clear,
and they were encouraged by some Kuomintang elements.

Since the Chinese Revolution of 1911, Japan
had enjoyed an expanding, favorable trade with China
and was its leading trade partner by the 1920s.
Interrupting the steady increase in Japanese imports
and in Japan's trade surpluses were periodic anti-
Japanese boycotts, but these were of short duration
and were often followed by dramatic upsurges in
Japanese sales in China. Furthermore, by the late
1920s, Japanese ownership of Chinese factories
outranked the British, the leading foreign contenders.

By 1931, however, there were some signs that
Japan's domination of the China market had already
peaked. Chinese purchases of the products of Japan's
leading modern industry, cotton textiles, were on
the wane. Domestic manufactures of cotton yarn and,
to a lesser extent, cloth weavers were taking an
increasingly greater share of the sales. Cheaper
coarse Chinese yarn had taken over much of the vast
market of Chinese peasants who, though continuing
to weave their own cloth in winter, had begun to buy
factory-spun Chinese yarn. In general, the infant
industrial sector of China's basically agrarian
economy was struggling to compete with the well-
developed giant operations of neighboring Japan, as
well as with the Japanese mills in China sheltered by
the "unequal" treaties and the foreign concessions.

The urban business elites of Shanghai were
anxious to check what they considered the oppression
of fellow Chinese merchants in Korea and Manchuria,
and it was not surprising that they should choose boycott as their weapon. Their participation in the
previous eight anti-Japanese boycotts had been fairly
successful; besides, all of their endeavors had cut
into Japanese sales.[2] It was also fitting that
Shanghai should witness the organization of the 1931
effort, since the metropolis was not only a great
entrepot of Japanese imports, but also the location of
most of the Japanese factories in China. Its financial support of the Nationalist government guaranteed
the Shanghai business world direct and indirect
backing from Nanking.

During the Northern Expedition, Chinese businessmen had taken part in the boycotts of 1927 and 1928
to protest against the Japanese military intervention
in Shantung. Those endeavors had speeded both the
downfall of the Tanaka cabinet in Tokyo and the

removal of Japanese troops from Shantung. After
Chiang Kai-shek's split with the Communists in 1927,
he had attracted support from many of the merchants, bankers, and industrialists on whom China's
modern economic reconstruction would depend. In
its resistance to Japanese dominance in China and Manchuria, the anti-Japanese boycott of 1931 signaled
cooperation between the business community and
the government. They shared some common objectives.
Both wanted the abolition of extraterritorial
rights enjoyed by the Japanese and other foreigners,
as well as the "unequal" treaties that protected
the Japanese factories in the treaty ports. In these
ports, the Japanese took advantage of the supply of
willing Chinese workers who were paid less than half
of the wages received by the workers in Japan. The
Nanking leaders and their business allies in Shanghai
saw the boycott as the most effective means to
resist Japan, in the absence of adequate military
power and political unity.

In Japan, the expanding industrial sector had
become increasingly dependent on export surpluses to
pay for the raw materials that its modern factories
devoured. For the past decade, China had been Japan's
largest market for a wide range of manufactures and
for services provided by the Japanese steamers plying
the busy Yangtze and Chinese coastal waters. The
China market produced the biggest export surpluses for
Japan.

By 1931, Chinese industrialists were eager to
promote industrial expansion at the expense of Japan.
They were attracted by the exciting prospect of
forcing the Japanese military to reassess the cost
of aggression against China. In addition, they hoped
that the boycott would turn Chinese purchasers away
from Japanese products and attract them to native
manufactures.

The proponents of boycott were aware that the
159 Japanese factories and 28,000 nationals in
Shanghai were protected by the imperial Japanese navy
with its long-range cannons and marines.[3] On the
other hand, these superior forces could not compel
Chinese businessmen and consumers to buy Japanese
goods and services, in spite of the privileges of the
"unequal" treaties. While a boycott would hurt
those merchants who dealt in Japanese wares, such
damages would probably be counterbalanced by the expansion of Chinese industry and its related commerce. If Shanghai's International Settlement
provided shelter to Japanese salesmen and factories,
so did it protect the masses of Chinese customers

and businessmen who lived and worked there.

The idea of an anti-Japanese boycott emanated in the second week of July from the business elites of Shanghai. While the earlier eight boycotts had been strongly influenced by Kuomintang activists and students, this attempt to resist Japan was initially dominated by the Chinese Chamber of Commerce. Shanghai not only had the largest branch of the chamber, but was also the location for both the head-quarters of its loose national federation and an important Kuomintang branch headquarters.

On July 13, 1931, many citizens met in the building of the Chinese General Chamber of Commerce with the delegates of those organizations favoring active response to the Korean killings. The head of the Chamber of Commerce presided over this open mass meeting of some eight hundred participants, rep-resenting more than one hundred economic guilds, associations, and unions. Also in attendance were local Kuomintang officials and some members of the Chinese Ratepayers Association (for those paying taxes in the International Settlement).

The meeting resolved to organize a boycott association and to commence planning and implementa-tion. Anxious to keep themselves away from the Whangpoo River, which bristled with the fire-power of Japanese warships, the conferees decided to move their boycott headquarters across the street to the large compound of the Temple of the Goddess of Heaven. It had been designated by the Shanghai Municipal Council as a religious institution and was thus off-bounds to the police of either the International Settlement or the various consulates.[4]

In response to the news that had reached Shang-hai, the spokesmen at the meeting denounced the riots in Korea as the conspiratorial work of the Jap-anese who released the inflamatory press reports on Wanpaoshan and unleashed the ensuing "spontaneous" mobs in the Korean cities. In deference to the "martyrs" in Korea, the initial organization was named the Oppose Japan and Support Overseas Chinese Society (Fan-Jih yüan-ch'iao hui).[5] The pangs of patriotic indignation felt by the participating business leaders were reinforced by their longstanding goal of domes-tic industrial expansion and by the discouraging status of the economy. With the world market for Chinese goods in its depressed state, the boy-cott might give Chinese producers a larger share of sales in their home market.[6]

In this expression of resistance to Japan, what role did the Kuomintang and its government play?

In the 1928 conflict with the Japanese military in
Tsinan, Chiang Kai-shek and the Nanking faction
of the party had steered clear of a full-scale confrontation. In 1931, after four years of consolidating its national power, Nanking was still too
insecure to risk a war with Japan. This was particularly so because of the rise of the Cantonese sep-
aratists. Moreover, Chiang was militarily distracted by his campaign against the Communists in
Kiangsi. The Kuomintang was thus in a position
of weakness, and its support of the boycott had to be
indirect and obscured. Nonetheless, some of the
party leaders probably saw the boycott as a means to
thwart the Cantonese attempts to establish separate
relations with the Japanese government.

Disunity seemed endemic within the Kuomintang.
In early 1931, Chiang Kai-shek and Wang Ching-wei, the
two leading party rivals, had shared some degree of
optimism about their prospect of improving China's
relations with Japan. In the middle of the year,
however, they again found themselves in two hostile
camps. In Canton, the pro-Wang faction refused
to accept the leadership of Nanking and was apparently
mobilizing for a military duel with Chiang's forces.

Similarly, among the Chinese capitalists in
Shanghai, the Cantonese bankers were at odds with
their Ningpo colleagues, and they had supported the
separatist movement in Canton by dumping their government bonds on the money market. This hurt the value
of the bonds which, in turn, hindered military expansion that depended on the bonds for funding. While
the Shanghai merchants, especially the dominant group
from nearby Ningpo, promoted the boycott in mid-
July, Wang Ching-wei spoke publicly in Canton of cul-
tivating closer relations with Japan. He imposed
a local ban on the boycott and sent off Eugene Ch'en
to Tokyo for private conference with Shidehara Kijūrō
and the military. It was not until after the Mukden
Incident in September 1931 that the Cantonese
backed Nanking's form of resistance. Another bloc
that did not support the early phase of the anti-
Japanese boycott was the Manchurians under
Chang Hsüeh-liang, who negotiated directly with
Japanese diplomats and the Kwantung Army.

In July, the Foreign Ministry in Nanking launched
a diplomatic offensive against the Japanese encroachment in Manchuria and the "massacres" in Korea. A
series of notes of protest blasted Tokyo for its use
of armed forces at Wanpaoshan and for the lack of
protection for Chinese nationals on the Korean
peninsula. The Chinese minister to Japan traveled in

person to survey the devastated shops and homes and to assess the continuing danger to Chinese nationals. In Manchuria, agents of Nanking and Mukden likewise protested to the local Japanese diplomats against the high-handed actions of their police.

The Kuomintang government, however, concluded that Japanese leaders of the Kwantung Army were seeking pretexts to use force; its approach to the July incidents was therefore one of caution and restraint. Then busy with his "antibandit" campaign against the Communists in Kiangsi, Chiang Kai-shek reminded his colleagues in Nanking and Chang Hsüeh-liang in Peiping that "any national movement against the Japanese at this time" would be used by the Communists "for their own interests." It would "also further complicate relations between Chinese and Japanese government officials." He thus requested "the people at large ... to refrain from such action and to wait patiently for the final outcome."[7]

Nevertheless, there were many -- both within and outside the Kuomintang -- who wanted united action against Japan. Lacking political consensus and party unity, Nanking adopted an ambiguous multilevel approach to the Japanese problem. On the official level, Chiang and the Foreign Ministry ordered restraint of the anti-Japanese efforts, while allowing indirect promotion of the boycott through the party branch network. Within the government were leaders close to business circles in Shanghai who saw an opportunity to promote Chinese industry through the boycott. This ambiguous policy gave Japan some justification for accusing Nanking of "insincerity" in its endeavor to reach a peaceful settlement.

The interaction between boycotts and industrial expansion had been noticeable in the two earlier experiences of 1915 and 1928. In 1928-1929, there was a surge in Chinese factory construction and a corresponding increase in production, especially of cotton yarn. As the boycott subsided in 1929, the organization in charge of the anti-Japanese activities had been transformed into the Domestic Product Protection Society. Its representatives met with Nanking's Ministries of Industry, Finance, and Foreign Affairs in April 1931 to discuss means to support Chinese industries in their competition with Japan.[8]

Three months prior to the Wanpaoshan Incident, these enterprising industrialists had petitioned Nanking to: (1) check the construction of new foreign factories in China; (2) raise the duties on foreign imports; (3) tax foreign factories; (4) require the labeling of manufactures of foreign mills either abroad or in China; and (5) lower the taxes on domestic commodities.[9] When the boycott movement emerged in Shanghai in July, Japanese observers in the city viewed it as an economic attack launched by Chinese businessmen. As the Anti-Japanese National Salvation Association (AJNSA) coalesced, one of its highly visible member organizations was the Domestic Product Protection Society.

In mid-July, while AJNSA promoters discussed boycott objectives and regulations, agitators aroused the public with demands for the retaliatory killing of Japanese and Koreans in Shanghai and for the creation of firing squads to execute boycott violators.[10] This rhetoric may have been useful for those Chinese diplomats urging the Japanese to work toward a peaceful settlement of the conflict.[11] On July 17, the AJNSA Executive Committee asked the delegates from the many member organizations for approval of the rules of the boycott. Although the Kuomintang was represented, the Nanking officials insisted that the boycott was not a government project. Party members were only involved in the movement as individuals. Moreover, the government had no legal rights to interfere with voluntary contractual arrangements between private organizations and their members headquartered within the International Settlement.[12]

The first boycott regulations were not publicized through Kuomintang branches. Instead, the Shanghai headquarters of the Chinese Chamber of Commerce sent a circular telegram to the branches of the federation in all major cities throughout China.[13] The July 17 rules required the Chinese to: (1) cease the purchase of any Japanese goods; (2) stop the sale of Japanese goods from warehouse stocks and shops; and (3) register the stocks of all Japanese goods held by Chinese merchants before the prohibition on sale went into effect on July 24.

In anticipation of a long boycott, an immediate boom commenced in the clearance of Japanese goods. Japanese shipments were speeded up so that one million yüan worth of Japanese goods were quickly offloaded along Shanghai's bund. In Central China, the hinterland of Shanghai, the import of Japanese products jumped up about 1.6 million yüan in July to the peak for 1931.[14] From the July 24 deadline on, the associations of Chinese dock workers and customs employees agreed not to handle any Japanese imports.[15]

Upon registration, the AJNSA transported to the warehouses it acquired the Japanese goods stocked

by Chinese dealers. A system of accounting for the
goods sealed in the warehouses evolved. As with
the anti-British boycott of 1925-1926 at Canton, a
staff of inspectors and pickets roamed the miles of
the wharfs and railroad depots searching out con-
traband goods, and the AJNSA rivercraft and trucks
transported such goods back to the warehouses. Boycott violators would be detained in the headquarters at the Temple of the Goddess of Heaven.[16] The
AJNSA treasury in the temple held the fines levied on
the violators, the proceeds on auctioned confiscated
goods, and the import fees paid on particular Japanese
goods judged vital to Chinese industry. To admin-
ister the proliferating organization, the AJNSA set
up committees for planning, for investigating the
origin of goods, and for promoting Chinese manufactures.[17] In the first general meeting, one of
Shanghai's leading financial magnates and head of the
Chamber of Commerce spoke out in support of the
efforts of the Fund Raising Committee.

Known respectfully as the "barefoot god of
wealth," Yü Hsia-ch'ing enjoyed status and wealth
accrued during a long career that had brought him from
the proximity of Ningpo, origin of most of Shanghai's
merchants and bankers, to youthful Shanghai as an
apprentice. He rose rapidly in the city and expanded
from comprador to steamship owner to financier. His
economic power allowed him access to political influence. He had gained eminence raising funds for the
Commerical Exhibit of 1910, then for the anti-Manchu
rebels in 1911, and most recently for Chiang Kai-
shek's new regime in 1927.[18] As Chiang's financial
patron, Yü was in a good position to elicit support from the government in nearby Nanking. In mid-
1931, the boycott campaign contributions for which Yü
appealed were initially used to aid the beleaguered
Chinese in Korea but they were later shifted to
the support of industrial expansion.

To facilitate fund-raising and to publicize the
boycott and its regulations, July 23 -- the day before
the regulations were to go into effect -- was set
aside to honor the Chinese killed in Korea. In line
with the Kuomintang practice of designating days
of "national humiliation," shops and firms, particularly those in the Shanghai area, closed their
doors in mourning. Significantly, the memorial service was held in the Chinese Chamber of Commerce headquarters in the International Settlement.[19] From
July to mid-September, the AJNSA expanded its organization and enjoyed sporadic results.

The anti-Japanese boycott required the support of

the large conglomeration of national and local commercial, manufacturing, and labor guilds and associations, as well as noneconomic social, educational,
and political organs. Among the first to endorse the
AJNSA resolutions was the Chinese Manufacturers and
Dealers in Cotton Yarn and Textiles. Given the
overwhelmingly agrarian nature of the Chinese economy
and the weakness of its industrial sector, textiles
were in the vanguard of China's industrial expansion.
In spite of their generally low standard of living,
the hundreds of millions of Chinese presented a
vast market for cheap cotton textiles and yarn. On
the other hand, powerful Chinese merchants specialized
in Japanese imports and they suffered economically
from the boycott. Yü Hsia-ch'ing was frustrated by
the complaints from these merchant groups and the lack
of promotion from Nanking. In late July, he criticized his fellow Chinese for not supporting the
boycott voluntarily the way the Japanese would back a
national boycott effort.[20]

In order to placate those Chinese interests
dependent on the Japanese trade, the AJNSA exempted a
list of items -- mainly goods not available from
either Chinese or other non-Japanese foreign sources
-- from the boycott on the grounds of critical need
by Chinese manufacturers. Upon importation of the
exempted goods, Chinese dealers had to pay a fee to
the AJNSA fund for the expansion of Chinese industries.
The Fund Raising Committee also tried to collect
money to support Chinese workers in Japanese firms
should they go out on strike. In the Japanese cottons
mills of Shanghai alone, there were some 61,000
laborers but the AJNSA was frustrated in its attempts
to finance an anti-Japanese strike.[21] The activists
hoped to emulate the anti-British Canton-Hong Kong
strike of 1925-1926, which had been funded by the Kuomintang and its government in Canton, and led by the
Chinese Communist Party. The British firms had
consequently been deprived not only of their Chinese
customers, but also of their Chinese laborers.

The AJNSA came under immediate attack from Japanese diplomats in Shanghai and Nanking. Its seizure
of Japanese goods was considered a hostile act,
especially when the pickets confiscated goods being
delivered from Japanese agents to their Chinese
patrons. With the support of their marines in Shanghai, the Japanese demanded that such seizures be
halted. The AJNSA yielded and warned its pickets
against antagonizing the Japanese firms by limiting
their actions to Chinese offenders. To stop rumors of
bribe-taking and profiteering, the association began

in August to have more careful regulation and supervision of boycott enforcement procedures. Goods
suspected of being Japanese imports could not
be seized until an authorized investigation team could
be called in to verify the allegation. Proven Japanese goods had to be more elaborately accounted for
both en route to the AJNSA warehouses and after
being locked up by the Custody Committee.[22] With the
increase in confiscations in early August, Japanese
sales began to drop, especially in Shanghai, from
their peak in July.

Although the AJNSA had been forced to make concessions to particular Chinese vested interests and to
the Japanese, it tried to maintain the momentum of
the boycott movement by dealing more severely
with violators. It forced offenders to wear a sign
reading "traitor" around their necks, paraded them in
the streets of Shanghai, and then fined and impris-
oned them either in log cages or in the AJNSA
headquarters. Chinese were under pressure from their
guilds and associations to adhere to the rules. Few
were apparently bold enough to appeal the seizure
of their goods or their punishments before Chinese
courts under the Kuomintang. The AJNSA efforts gained
the attention of the Japanese cotton interests at
their Osaka headquarters where trade analysts estimated Japanese trade losses in August at 1 million yen.
The analysis was complicated by the devastation of
the Yangtze basin by summer floods and the advantage
of silver-based Chinese prices, which spurred the
rising sales of cheaper Chinese cloth and cotton
yarn.[23]

Sino-Japanese relations deteriorated steadily
during the month prior to the Mukden Incident of
September 18, 1931, and the boycott centered in Shanghai was both a cause and an effect. Mutual antagonism arose between the ubiquitous AJNSA pickets ready
to seize alleged Japanese goods and the equally
zealous Japanese marines off the many warships on the
Whangpoo River and on guard in the International
Settlement. The Japanese consulate was strategically
located on the waterfront, or bund, at the conflu-
ence of the busy Soochow Creek and the Whangpoo
where the boycott pickets were most active. There
was a Japanese warship tied up at the wharf of
the consulate so that the marines could be quickly
mobilized for sudden sorties in and out of the International Settlement. Upon notification from a
Japanese firm, marines could rush to the scene where
pickets were confiscating Japanese goods. The
movement of the marines was eased by swift armored

cars and motor launches. Their effectiveness was
proven in August when marines recaptured seized goods
for return to Japanese owners. A succession of
skirmishes erupted between the Japanese marines and
the AJNSA pickets in the International Settlement.
Along with the notes of protest that flew back
and forth between Tokyo and Nanking were rumors that
the Japanese navy was prepared to land a full-scale
intervention to break the boycott at its Shanghai
source and along the lower Yangtze.[24]

The response of the navy at Shanghai should not
be interpreted merely as the typical direct action
of Japanese military. Japanese residents there and in
other treaty ports had been stirred to band together
for self-defense. The Minseitō cabinet in Tokyo
authorized the navy to take appropriate action should
the AJNSA pickets threaten the lives and property
of Japanese nationals residing in Shanghai and other
ports.[25]

In mid-August, a coalition of Japanese organizations in Shanghai petitioned Tokyo to send more warships to protect shipments of Japanese goods and
to stand off the mouth of the Whangpoo River at
Woosung. This would block the AJNSA investigators on
launches from checking steamships entering the
Shanghai area.[26] When Shigemitsu Mamoru, Japanese
minister to China, cautioned against the landing of
Japanese marines, a delegation of Japanese cotton
cloth merchants confronted him with demands that
stronger means be used with the Nanking government for
the immediate dissolution of the AJNSA. Simultaneously, the Japanese Chamber of Commerce in Shanghai
dispatched a similar demand to the Foreign Ministry
in Tokyo, the political parties, and the Diet,
claiming that the boycott amounted to an "act of
war."[27]

Among Japanese residents in Shanghai, Tsingtao,
and Tientsin were groups of dozens of young Japanese civilian vigilantes, nicknamed rōnin (warriors
without lords in the samurai tradition) who sought
out Chinese boycott pickets. According to some
knowledgeable Chinese, the Japanese Residents Association, which struck a militant pose in August, was an
official organization commonly created in sizable
Japanese communities abroad.[28]

The activities of this association and the armed
rōnin were characteristic of the escalation toward
military operations in Manchuria and China in
1931. Similar skirmishes between the Chinese and the
Japanese took place in Tsingtao and, later, Tientsin, as well as in Shanghai. The anxiety over the

military threat and the steady Japanese diplomatic offensive forced Nanking to restrain some aspects of the anti-Japanese boycott. A weak China did not feel free to choose from a wide range of responses to foreign powers, especially Japan.

As Nanking walked a tightrope in its relationship with Japan, its diplomats tried to exploit the sympathy of Western powers doing business in Shanghai. When the International Settlement prohibited the seizure of Japanese goods within its boundaries,[29] the Nationalist government made concessions. In mid-August, rumors circulated that Chiang Kai-shek had personally ordered that the seizure of Japanese goods be stopped, that the AJNSA be restrained, and that confiscated goods be returned.[30]

The curtailment of the pickets and, in late August, the return of confiscated goods to Japanese dealers would, it was hoped, remove the threat of large-scale retaliation by the Japanese marines. Such a military conflict would disrupt the trade of the Westerners as well as the Chinese in the Shanghai and Yangtze area. As the boycott movement ebbed, the Japanese news agencies in Shanghai attributed the decline to the suffering of the many Chinese merchants who were dependent on the profits of the Sino-Japanese trade.[31] This seemed likely to account for the AJNSA concession to the Chinese Shipping Brokers Association, permitting its members to ship Chinese goods to Korea on Japanese vessels.[32]

In the first month and a half of the boycott, the AJNSA pressed for massive immediate results. Yet, by late August, it had developed a long-range comprehensive plan, calling for a five-year boycott. This would minimize the disruption of Chinese trade and enterprise. At the same time, the plan would encourage the expansion of Chinese manufacturing to replace what was still needed from Japan. A new list of Japanese products was exempted from the boycott to ease the pinch felt by some Chinese firms. These vital imports would be charged a 10 percent fee. The fees collected by the AJNSA would be placed in Chinese banks and kept under careful watch while they gathered interest during the five-year period. The capital this produced was to go toward replacing Japanese imports with home goods. Thus, on shipments of special Japanese cotton yarn, there was to be a fee of 7.5 taels per unit plus a handling charge; both would be deposited in a specific account to be used later for the expansion of the Chinese facilities needed to produce that particular quality of yarn.

Although the AJNSA had to stop the seizure

of Japanese goods from Chinese violators, it promoted
more volunteerism in boycott enforcement and education of Chinese consumers. Even in Peiping where
Chang Hsüeh-liang had restricted the boycott, the local AJNSA branch publicized the five-year boycott
in August and organized merchant volunteers into
teams of forty men who would watch for incoming Japanese goods at thirteen check points.[33] Under the
threat of Japanese military intervention, the boycott
slowed in momentum in August but expanded into long-
range planning. Not even the Japanese marines
could force Chinese consumers to buy Japanese products, provided there were suitable substitutes.

The boycott movement was further sapped by the
fears arising from the publicity that Japan gave
on August 17 to its story of the atrocious "murder"
of Captain Nakamura Shintarō, an intelligence officer,
in Inner Mongolia. The warlike response of the
Japanese press and the toughening stance of Japanese
diplomats disillusioned some Chinese as to the effectiveness of their boycott. In early September, a
commercial attaché at the Japanese consulate in
Shanghai optimistically insisted that the anti-
Japanese boycott had already run its course. The
goods seized earlier from Japanese firms had been returned, and Japanese imports were again selling on
the Shanghai market. While Japanese representatives
in Nanking and Mukden made conciliatory gestures
to the Chinese, consular diplomats in Shanghai claimed
that the "direct action" of the Japanese marines had
been proved effective by the rising trade in late
August.[34]

Nevertheless, Japanese hopes for a return to
trade normalcy seemed premature, as the news from
North China reported that the AJNSA branches had expanded their boycott to include Chinese exports
to Japan.[35] Tensions again escalated on September 7
when Chiang Kai-shek criticized Japan, among other
things, for "secretly aiding the Canton government and
conducting various intrigues." According to him,
"Japan has no claim to be a civilized country." The
Japanese military branded this speech a provocative
act that breached international faith and could
not be tolerated.[36] The build-up of Sino-Japanese
tensions orchestrated by the Kwantung Army and its supporters broke through into armed operations in Manchuria on September 18. The desire for national unity
in China took an immense upsurge and, for many,
feelings focused on the anti-Japanese boycott.

From mid-July to September, the boycott had been
regional and merchant oriented. It spread like wild

fire after September 18 into a much more national
movement with wider social -- albeit primarily urban
-- representation. Shanghai again witnessed the
recurrence of mass meetings and plenary sessions at
the AJNSA headquarters. More than one thousand
delegates from diverse organizations pledged renewed
support. They pressed Nanking to strengthen its
diplomatic action with Tokyo, to publicize Japan's
wrongs to the world community, and to use this
opportunity to unify the warring Kuomintang factions
and various Chinese armies against the Japanese in
Manchuria.[37]

On September 25, the Kuomintang headquarters in
Nanking responded to the public uproar by ordering
party branches to cooperate with the AJNSA in the
creation of boycott offices throughout China. Still
attempting to keep the popular movement in check,
the directives insisted that there should be no
provocative attacks against Japanese nationals and
their property, which could be exploited by the war-
readied Japanese military. In appearance, the
AJNSA came close to being a quasi-official organ of
the Nanking regime.[38]

Following a period of divisive conflict between
the regional autonomists and the new Nationalist
government, and within the Kuomintang leadership,
which had been buffeted by one civil war after another
since 1929, the Mukden Incident brought a conver-
gence of Chinese opinion against Japan and pressure
for a total boycott. In early October, Shao Li-
tzu, a Kuomintang leader, declared that "this time
the spirit of the people shows that we are no longer
scattered sand." He further maintained:

> China's hope of survival lies in our perse-
> verance in the economic boycott ... Japan
> will be forced to change its stand in less
> than half a year.[39]

Thousands of zealous students carried boycott banners
into the streets of China's cities and even towns.
By late September, anti-Japanese boycott efforts were
evident from Peiping to Chungking deep in China's
vast interior. In Yünnan, the boycotters destroyed
Japanese shops.

In Canton, where the local Kuomintang had suppressed the boycott, the movement played a part during
October in the reconciliation between the Nanking
regime and the Canton faction. Although gaping
antagonism remained among the leaders, the two contending camps turned their attention from fac-

tional rivalries to the defense against Japan. Canton joined in the nationwide boycott. By September 26, Japanese residents had withdrawn from their enterprises in that city into Shameen's foreign concession. When Chinese depositors set off a bank run, Japanese banks closed after the coffers had been emptied. From the decks of the slick but empty Japanese steamers anchored on the muddy Pearl River, loafing seamen gazed down on the once bustling Japanese godowns, or warehouses, which showed no signs of life.[40] By excluding Japanese goods and services from the markets of Canton and other treaty ports, the anti-Japanese boycott began to approach total effectiveness in October.

By September 25, in response to a plea from Chiang Kai-shek to settle their political differences, Cantonese Sun Fo replied that Canton would join with Nanking in its resistance to Japan in Manchuria. Furthermore, Sun indicated that the Canton faction would disband its rival government and collaborate in a truly national government if Chiang would only relinquish his political leadership in Nanking.[41] Yet, when Chiang finally turned over the political reins to the Canton faction in December, he was responding to more than the pressure from the Cantonese politicians.

By November, Chinese students involved in the boycott and the general anti-Japanese movement turned against the Nanking government in frustration. Earlier in September, the Kuomintang had acquiesced to the point of allowing the cadets of Nanking's Central Military Academy to indulge in spreading propaganda. The National Salvation Corps was similarly useful in channeling students' zeal, as well as in preparing them for possible military operations. Some eight thousand students from secondary and higher educational institutions were kept preoccupied in drill and military techniques during the tense autumn.[42] Thousands of other students volunteered their time to the AJNSA branches. Across China and overseas from Berlin to Seattle, Chinese students prowled the streets in support of the boycott. Many became politicized by the succession of anti-Japanese demonstrations and parades.

The bitter feelings were obvious in AJNSA wall posters that urged the Chinese not to buy or sell Japanese goods, not to supply any sort of goods to the Japanese, and not to ship cargoes on Japanese vessels. They should also withdraw all their deposits from Japanese bankers and reject Japanese checks and bills of exchange. The posters insisted:

No exception should be made, even of Japan's
diplomatic representatives. Those who vi-
olate these instructions shall be shot
to death after due trial by the disciplinary
committee. They shall be shot to death
after being exposed to the public view.[43]

Popular with the students and faculties at the universities in Nanking, and receiving what must have been
at least tacit approval from the Ministry of Education, was the following oath for boycotters:

By the blue sky that watches over me, by the
bright sun that shines on me, by the mountains and rivers of my ancestors, I swear with
warm blood and with utter sincerity that for
the rest of my life I shall never use Japanese goods. May heaven punish me should I
retract my decision or change my mind![44]

As thousands of students gathered in mass meetings, those from Shanghai were in the vanguard.
In that city, the strong desire to "do something"
to recover Manchuria was manipulated into demands on
Nanking. The students soon turned from pressing
the government to take action in Manchuria to
attacking Kuomintang leadership. Many in Shanghai and
Nanking dropped out of schools to devote their attention to the anti-Japanese and anti-Kuomintang efforts. The activists demonstrated against Shanghai's
mayor and severely beat the foreign minister in
Nanking, accusing both of them of being "too conciliatory" toward Japan.[45]
    T. V. Soong tried to urge Japan to move toward
a negotiated settlement. As he argued:

At this juncture the demand for direct action
against Japan is everywhere increasing. As
an example, the boycott of Japanese goods,
which is everywhere complete, is a direct result of popular feeling. It has not been
inspired by the government; but no government
which attempted to prevent it could remain
in power for a day.

His words in October were prophetic of the disorders
of December when Nanking faced incoming trainloads
of student protesters from Shanghai, Peiping, and Tientsin. Students became increasingly violent in the
capital. By December 12, they had ransacked the Kuomintang headquarters in Nanking, the party's *Cen-*

tral Daily News, and the Foreign Ministry, and had
triggered the resignations of the mayors of Shanghai
and Tientsin, two foreign ministers, and ultimately
Chiang Kai-shek.

This highly emotional state intensified the
effectiveness of the boycott. Compared with the record a year earlier, Japan's sales to China of cotton cloth for October 1931 -- 6 million dozen pieces
-- represented a drop of 5,114,000 yen. Wheat
flour exports had likewise declined by 1,331,000
yen. Only a mere 261,000 yen of hosiery was sold over
the same period, and this represented a sharp drop
of 99 percent. Similarly, paper and coal had
each suffered a decline in sales of 1 million yen.

By October 19, ten cotton mills in Japan
had closed owing to the loss of their Chinese markets,
as had the refineries of the Meiji Sugar Company.
Meiji had been dependent on the China market and, in
closing, had joined with nearly one hundred large and
small factories, which had produced, for example,
glass, hats, mosquito nets, iron, and steel primarily
for Chinese consumers. Chinese analysts in Shanghai
estimated that the Japanese had lost 34 million yen
from the beginning of the boycott through the end of
October.[47]

There was a stiffening in the stance of the
Japanese business circles both at home and in China
toward the boycott and the anti-Japanese movement.
Rather than supporting their diplomats as they struggled to negotiate, the exporting producers and factory
owners in China abandoned their earlier policy of
watchful waiting for the expected loss of Chinese interest in the boycott, and shifted to a tough line.
As the boycott expanded in September, Osaka's Chamber
of Commerce, representing the Japanese cloth dealers
of Shanghai, supported the "defensive" operations
of the Kwantung Army in Manchuria and urged the adoption of a more "fundamental solution" to Sino-Japanese
differences in that region. While the vast market
in Central China might be lost as a result, the economic gains in Manchuria, as expected by the Osaka
textile leaders, would be worth the sacrifice. Within
days, the National Chamber of Commerce in Tokyo
backed the action of the Kwantung Army and condemned
the Chinese boycott as a hostile act against international peace. In late September, the business
delegates in Tokyo proclaimed that it was "the duty of
every Japanese to be united at any cost and urge the
fundamental solution of the Sino-Japanese troubles."[48]

The first week of October witnessed the emergence of cooperation among business, diplomatic, and

military circles against the Chinese. In what was
seemingly a pattern, the Japanese Chamber of Commerce
first petitioned from Shanghai its Tokyo headquarters, the political parties, the press, and Foreign
Minister Shidehara for action to end the Chinese
boycott. The Tokyo Chamber of Commerce endorsed the
petition and attacked the boycott as an "act of
war" aided by the Kuomintang government.[49] Next, the
Japanese diplomat in Nanking threatened to resort to
forcible measures should the boycott continue.[50]
The prospect of military confrontation materialized
on October 6 when the cabinet authorized Naval
Minister Abo Kiyokazu to decide when warships and
marines should be dispatched to Shanghai's International Settlement for the protection of the Japanese
nationals.[51]

During the remaining days of October and November, the Japanese marines repeatedly interceded on
behalf of their nationals against the AJNSA pickets
and crowds of Chinese student activists. Angry
confrontations between marines and demonstrators outside Japanese mills were common, and they helped to
justify the navy's requests for reinforcement. Again,
when the Japanese cotton exporters sent off a plea
to the League of Nations to end the "injustice" of the
boycott, Consul Murai in Shanghai warned that the
imperial navy was prepared to take "decisive measures"
to protect Japanese properties in Shanghai's International Settlement.[52] Such saber-rattling rhetoric
was effective with the settlement, which prohibited
the seizure of Japanese goods, as well as with Nanking
where fear became crippling.

In December, the boycott enforced the nonsale of
necessities to Japanese nationals and military in
China. This, however, did not weaken the Japanese
resolve. Civilian opinion in Japan increasingly supported the military's demands for direct action to
safeguard Japanese rights in Manchuria and China. The
issue of the anti-Japanese boycott was used tellingly
by the opposition to Minseitō's Wakatsuki cabinet.
When the 3 million members of the association of Japanese military reservists pressed the cabinet to
solve the China problem, the civilian press was on
the whole supportive.[53] The battered Wakatsuki
cabinet fell on December 12, strangely simultaneous
with Chiang Kai-shek's resignation, and with this
doomed the "conciliatory" policy of the Shidehara Foreign Ministry. Immediately voting funds to
support the military, Seiyūkai's Inukai cabinet
bolstered the navy in its pursuit of a more independent approach to the anti-Japanese movement in

China.

In January 1932, the military in Shanghai shifted from its policy of protests and threats against the boycotters to a conspiracy to provide pretexts for armed intervention. A series of minor incidents featured assaults on Japanese nationals and their property, as well as on the honor of the Japanese emperor. Japanese diplomats and military in China seized on some Chinese editorials that expressed sympathy for an unsuccessful Korean assassin who had tried to bomb the Japanese emperor in Tokyo. The Japanese military used this assassination attempt to attack the civilian cabinet for its failure to protect the emperor and in order to force the closure of several newspapers in China. The newspapers had either to apologize and remain closed for a period or to provoke the landing of Japanese marines in Shanghai and a few other treaty ports.

An assault staged against Japanese monks in Shanghai brought about a violent mobbing by Japanese "rōnin." Both the Japanese consul and the local naval commander in Shanghai accused the Chinese of making bombing and arson attempts on the consulate and the residence of the absent minister to China. Their ultimatums demanded that AJNSA operations be disbanded. This returned attention to the real issue, which was the anti-Japanese boycott.

While the civilian support to the Japanese military increased, the temporary reconciliation of the different Kuomintang factions was again falling apart. Japanese ultimatums came while Nanking was struggling with the resignations of key Cantonese from the coalition. With little help from the divided Nationalist government, Shanghai's mayor was forced to concede to the demands in the presence of Japan's superior naval firepower on the Yangtze. The response of Mayor Wu T'ieh-ch'eng, a military man himself, satisfied the Japanese consul on the afternoon of January 28, when Wu declared that since "all AJNSA have gone beyond their proper limits, the Chinese authorities have issued orders that they be forewith dissolved." Nevertheless, Admiral Shiozawa, commander of Japan's Yangtze patrol squadron, mistrusted the mayor's concessions, and he dispatched troops into the Chapei section of Chinese Shanghai "to enforce law and order."[54] This marked the beginning of the Shanghai Incident of 1932, with the Japanese navy and, ultimately, the army engaged in full-scale warfare in the heartland of Kuomintang territory.

Instead of halting differences with China, Japanese military activities in 1932 only aggravated the

Chinese who in turn became even more determined in the boycott of the Japanese products in China. The war in Shanghai during February and March spread out past the suburbs toward Nanking and disrupted virtually all international trade that passed through China's chief seaport. How effective, then, had the boycott been as an instrument of China's international relations? Lacking real military capacity, had the economic leverage of the boycott succeeded in deterring Japanese ambitions in Manchuria and China?

To weigh the impact of the boycott of 1931-1932, it is necessary to assess trade between China and Japan prior to the boycott. A key indicator in that trade was Japan's cotton textile industry, which led the nation's modern industrial sector and provided the leading export items to China. Through the 1920s, Japan's favorable trade balance with China was due mainly to the burgeoning market for Japanese cottons and cotton yarn. Japan had earlier edged British competitors out of the market. But, partly because of an anti-Japanese boycott, the importation of many types of Japanese cottons to China had begun to decline in 1928. In spite of this setback, Japan still managed to capture 66 percent of the Chinese market for foreign cottons, an impressive accomplishment if compared with its prewar share of 18 percent. In 1931, while suffering from slight residual effects of the 1928-1929 boycott and, more seriously, from the depressed world economy, Japan sold 38 percent of its total cotton products to China.[55]

By mid-1931, however, sales of Japanese cottons in China showed a sharp decline. This was caused not only by the economic depression and the devastation of floods along the Yangtze, but also by the competition with cheaper cottons from the Chinese factories. Chinese textiles benefited from low labor costs. The slump in the international demand for silver, the Chinese monetary base, also made Japanese goods more expensive in China. The tariffs imposed in January 1931 by the Nationalist government further elevated the price of Japanese goods. As a result, Japanese cotton textile exports to China dropped 40 percent in early 1931.[56] Against this background of slipping sales, the anti-Japanese boycott broke out in July.

The growth rate of China's cotton textile industry was outpacing that of Japan's more mature industry and the rate had speeded up through the 1920s. By 1931, China had 2.4 million spindles for its cotton yarn production, compared with 7

million in Japan, and 1.6 million in the Japanese
mills in China.[57] Chinese producers catered to the
domestic demand for cheap coarse cloth, and to peasant
households which now purchased ready-made cotton yarn
for their home weaving. On the other hand, Chinese
production was slowed by what the Chinese themselves
admitted to be nepotism in management, inexperience,
obsolete technology and equipment, and lack of capital
to meet production needs and expansion.[58] Despite
the low cost of labor, some mills went bankrupt in the
absence of enough capital to purchase large quantities of needed raw materials. By 1931, Chinese industrialists were hoping for increased capitalization, which would bring expansion and improved
manufactures.

The tariff increase of 1931 was but one sign of
collaboration between the Nationalist government
and Chinese industry. The Kuomintang was aware of the
debt owed to the modern urban business circles.
Aside from the burden of military expansion, the party
focused much of its remaining economic resources on
the modern industrial sector in the cities, which
seemed to be the vanguard of China's modernization.
Rural China in its vastness required reform and
investment that were beyond the political and economic
capacity of the Kuomintang.

In April 1931, a Shanghai municipal order had
prohibited the sale of a local Chinese textile mill to
a Japanese bidder or any other foreign buyer. Nanking followed this precedent by extending the prohibition to a national level. If necessary, the
Ministry of Industry and Commerce would provide credits to Chinese industrialists. It would even take
over the bankrupt mills instead of allowing them to be
bought by foreigners.[59] The boycott in July was
therefore an escalation of the effort of Nanking and
the Chinese capitalists to end the era of Japanese
economic domination over China.

Shortly after the beginning of the boycott, a
group of Kiangsu and Chekiang promoters solicited public investment to finance a new cotton yarn factory
to meet the expanding demand for Chinese yarn. As the
AJNSA coffers expanded through auctions and fees,
its treasury was convenient not only to the commerce
of Shanghai, but also to the concentration of more
than half of China's spindles and looms in factories
in the metropolitan area and in surrounding Kiangsu.

By November 1931, the Foreign Ministry in Nanking
had connected the promotion of home industries with
improving relations with Great Britain. The British

agreed to use a portion of their share of the Boxer
indemnity as guarantee for Chinese purchases of
British textile machinery on credit. They would deliver at least 10 percent of the 600,000 spindles
ordered by the Chinese prior to the end of 1931. The
devaluation of the British pound also eased the sale
of fine count yarn and cloth to China as an alternative to the boycotted Japanese goods.[60] The exclu-
sion of the Japanese from the Chinese textile market and the importation of British machinery combined
to allow, by December, the reopening of several
Chinese spinning mills in Shanghai.[61]

The drop in Japanese sales of cottons accelerated
after the Mukden Incident. They declined throughout China from 5 million yüan in the slow month
of August to a depressing low of 1,763,000 yüan in
September.[62] A few modest upturns in late 1931 did
not alter the gloomy picture of Japanese losses. Did
the boycott deal the cotton textile industry in
Japan a serious blow?

Prior to the boycott in early 1931, the industry
had exhibited a remarkable resiliency in marketing.
With the depression, the Japanese had suffered a
loss of more than 3.5 million yen in the second half
of 1930. Nevertheless, as a testament to the expertise of Japanese banking and exporting cartels that
arranged for expanded sales in new markets, the first
half of 1931 produced for the industry a profit of
nearly 22 million yen.[63] Efficient management
retooled the mills and streamlined labor input, cut-
ting the number of Japanese workers from 35 per thousand spindles in 1928 to 29 by late 1930, and from
719 per thousand looms to 619.[64] Japan was also able
to reduce its prices through the purchase of large
volumes of American raw cotton, which became cheaper
in 1930 and 1931. Japanese cotton cloth and yarn
expanded rapidly into the markets of India, the Dutch
East Indies, and the Middle East. By mid-1931,
Japan's textile industry was recovering from the earlier blows of the world depression. In 1931 and
1932, despite the British effort to devalue the pound
sterling and raise tariffs on foreign cloth, Japanese cottons remained competitive.[65]

The Chinese boycott affected this Japanese recovery, as evidenced by the drop in cottons exports in
August and the sharper decline after the Mukden Incident of September. The setbacks, however, were
halted when Tokyo devalued its yen in late 1931. By
early December, Japan's vital cotton cloth exports
had surged upward on the world market, in spite of the
Chinese boycott which was extended to overseas Chi-

nese merchants in Southeast Asia. The dramatic upsurge expanded throughout the period of Japanese
intervention in Shanghai and most of 1932. If the
boycott did not disrupt the key Japanese textile industry at home, what were its effects on the Japanese
mills in China, especially in Shanghai?

Japanese textile and financial interests had
invested heavily -- some 232 million yen -- in forty
cotton yarn and cloth producing factories operated
by fifteen Japanese firms. The Japanese mills
exploited the low wages in China, less than half of
what was paid in Japan, and yielded one-fifth of
the production at home. Prior to World War I, the
British had had equal production capacity in
China. But, by 1931, the Japanese had forced most
British textile operations out of China and controlled
90 percent of the foreign spindles and looms there.
Of the total cotton yarn produced in China, Japanese
mills spun more than 30 percent and wove 55 percent
of the total cotton cloth.[66] Since about 75 percent of these mills were located in Shanghai, their
owners were concerned about the boycott headquartered
in the city. The largest of the Japanese firms was
the Nagai Cotton Company. It had opened its first
Chinese mill in 1911 and, by 1931, had 90 percent of
its spindles in China, with the remainder at its Osaka
head office.[67] Since the anti-Japanese boycott
affected goods from Japanese mills in China, these
companies, too, suffered losses on the China market.

The first phase of the boycott, from July to
September, isolated the local Japanese mills from some
of their Chinese customers. Nonetheless, most of the
cotton cloth and yarn mills were located within the
concessions in Shanghai, Tsingtao, Hankow and Tientsin
and were thus protected by foreign military units.
They were free to operate as long as their Chinese
workers stayed on the job, and were free to ship their
yarn and cloth to outside markets on Japanese
steamers. As sales slowed in China, the Japanese
mills began to increase their shipments to the markets
in Japan, India, the Dutch East Indies, and, later,
Manchuria. Until the September 18 invasion of
Manchuria, when the boycott became truly nationwide,
these mills retained their customers in those parts of
China that had not joined the boycott, and they continued to make sizable profits. As late as September
11, the Nagai Cotton Company in China had decided
to double its capital by selling its stocks in order
to expand with the booming market.[68] To demonstrate the healthy state of their business, the Nagai
leaders added a 10 percent dividend to the usual 12

percent annual dividend.[69] In September, cotton yarn
from the Japanese and Chinese mills in China together outsold the yarn from Japan on the Dutch East
Indian market.[70]

As the boycott became more comprehensive later
in September, some of the smaller Japanese factories
were forced to close, and the Association of Japanese
Cotton Manufacturers of Shanghai resolved to cut
back its operations to 30 percent of full capacity.
The mills were dependent on their Chinese workers.
From October to January, the Shanghai mills repeatedly
warned that they would all close if strikes should
erupt. These rumors of closure coincided with
the AJNSA efforts to accumulate a strike fund sufficient to maintain the 60,000 to 70,000 Chinese who
worked in Shanghai's Japanese textile mills. The
AJNSA pledged to organize an anti-Japanese strike in
October.[71] Yet, it did not receive adequate financial
support from the Nationalist government and the concentration of its limited funds on the program of
industrial expansion diverted the money from the
strike.

In early November, a few more of the smaller
Japanese mills located outside the International Settlement closed; the rest agreed to voluntary curtailment of production. The larger firms managed to
ride out the worst period of the declining Chinese
market. By shifting their sales to Manchuria, India,
and Hong Kong, they were able, in late November,
to restore their production schedules to 50 percent of
their capacity. Most Japanese textile firms in China
were confident that their Chinese workers, with many
obligations to meet at the end of the year, would
not dare to strike. Although analysts in Shanghai
concluded that local Japanese textile firms had lost
2 million taels per month since the Mukden Incident, the Japanese were certain that the worst of the
boycott had passed and prosperity was returning.[72]

Public support given by the Japanese mills for
the tough line of the military proved to be coun-
terproductive. It hurt their recovery from the boycott, and they ultimately had to close down once
the naval intervention began in Shanghai on the night
of January 28, 1932. It resulted in a strike by the
Chinese workers on the following day, and many stayed
away from work until May. Nevertheless, even during the period of open warfare in February and March,
not all Japanese mills ceased to function. Within
the protective sanctuary of the concessions of
Tsingtao and Tientsin, most Japanese factories continued production.[73]

While the boycott reduced the dwindling local sales of textile goods of the Japanese factories in China, their foreign sales expanded. To meet the demand abroad, Japanese mills increased their share of the total spindles in China from about 32 percent at the time of the boycott to 42 percent in 1936. After the Japanese mills reopened in Shanghai in April 1932, their cloth production surged ahead. They soon recovered their former level of sales and, by 1933, yielded 53 percent of China's total cotton cloth production. This was further expanded to 61 percent in 1935.[74]

The boycott failed to deprive Japanese textile factories in China of their dominant position. Despite the efforts of the AJNSA, the Japanese mills survived within the guarded foreign concessions and then prospered. With neither the financial support of the Nanking regime nor the promise of new job openings in Chinese mills, the workers could not afford to strike against the Japanese firms in China. While some Japanese factories closed, the endeavor of Chinese textile producers to expand at the expense of the local Japanese operators failed. The Chinese industrialists could not muster the necessary capital from either the Nanking government or other private sources during the boycott to sustain their program of expansion.

The anti-Japanese boycott of 1931-1932 was the most comprehensive economic weapon used by the Chinese thus far. It cut into Japan's vital exports. Its promotion by the national network of the Chinese Chamber of Commerce was, as much as indirect government support, responsible for the expansion of the movement. To the organizational apparatus of the AJNSA was added the zeal of student volunteers. As was the case with the previous anti-Japanese movements, this boycott caused temporary setbacks to Japanese economic recovery from the world depression.

Between the 1911 Revolution and the end of 1930, Chinese imports of Japanese goods had tripled. While Japan enjoyed the favorable balance of trade, the Chinese export of agricultural products and raw materials to Japan had also increased more than three times over the same period. As Japanese industry built up in the 1920s, Japan suffered from trade deficits on the international market. Yet, China had remained a bright spot until the boycott of 1931-1932. Japan generally enjoyed good to huge export surpluses in the Sino-Japanese trade. These ranged from the peaks of 110 million yen in 1917 and 120 million yen in 1926 down to low surpluses dur-

ing some of the anti-Japanese boycotts. For example,
the 1915 surplus represented a decline of 20 million yen from that of the previous year. Japan
suffered even more serious setbacks in 1919, 1921,
1923, 1927, and 1931. These were all years when anti-
Japanese boycotts broke out in China.[75]

Between September 1931 and March 1932, when the
boycott became most damaging, there was even a
trade *deficit* for Japan. In November 1931, Japanese
sales were down 75 percent from those of November
1930, and the Chinese developed an export surplus of
more than 5.5 million yen. In December 1931, Japanese
exports to China likewsie showed a decline of 80
percent from those of December 1930.[76] Given Japan's
need for raw materials and food imports, it was
difficult to cut back on its purchases from China.
Chinese export surpluses continued until the boycott
began to wane in March 1932. By then, the forced
disbandment of the AJNSA and the Japanese reconstruction of the Manchurian economy helped to lessen the
damaging effect of the boycott.

In certain regions of China, the boycott was
exceptionally effective. Although Japanese Foreign
Ministry figures showed a 51 percent drop in Japanese
trade throughout China from September 1931 through
February 1932, the decline in the Yangtze basin was 75
percent when compared with the same months in 1930-
1931. In this heartland of the boycott, the low
point in Japanese sales was reached in February 1932,
when there was a 95 percent fall from the sales of
February 1931. While the Canton faction of the
Kuomintang suppressed the boycott in July-September
1931, the period from September 1931 through March
1932 witnessed an overall decline of 90 percent from
the same months in 1930-1931; the drop in sales
was 97 percent for the months of January through March
in 1932. In North China, under Chang Hsüeh-liang's
dominance, the boycott brought about a decline
in Japanese sales of 43 percent between September 1931
and February 1932. Sales reached a low point in
November 1931, when the drop was 73 percent.[77]

Of what significance, then, was the anti-Japanese
boycott in the struggle of Chinese nationalism
against foreign imperialism? In the short term, it
gave the Chinese the means to express their bitterness
with what they regarded as Japanese aggrandizement.
From the Japanese point of view, however, it was
they who had been wronged by the Chinese. Publicized
as a hostile act of economic warfare, the boycott
tended to inflame not only the Japanese military, but
also the more world-trade oriented business circles.

The Wanpaoshan Incident, the anti-Chinese disorders in Korea, and the murder of Captain Nakamura were cited by many Japanese as arguments in favor of a military solution to Sino-Japanese problems. The seizures of Japanese goods by the AJNSA were seen in Japan as similar to the destruction of the Japanese railroad on September 18, 1931, which was falsely blamed on Manchurian soldiers. The Japanese public saw the boycott as a manifestation of Chinese anarchy and lawlessness and did not perceive the message as intended by the Chinese boycotters.

The attempt by Chinese industrialists to expand their domestic manufacturing by means of the anti-Japanese boycott reinforced the view of the critics that aggressive Chinese capitalists had merely used the anti-Chinese "massacres" as a pretext to conspire against Japan's producers and traders. Yet, the boycott notwithstanding, Chinese industrial output actually declined in its share of total production in China after the Japanese manufacturers had resumed their operations in 1932. Only in cotton yarn production did the Chinese make gains over the Japanese in China.[78] Rather than the intended dramatic increase in their production for the home market, the Chinese saw much of that market slip during the boycott into the hands of American and British traders.[79]

Quietly encouraging the anti-Japanese movement were American and British diplomats who hailed the boycott as China's most effective defense. With American exports to China surging despite the depression, Secretary of State Henry Stimson reminded London in January 1932 that it was for "the benefit of the world" that China in its weakness not be deprived of its only weapon against an enemy. He warned that "it would tend to destroy the balance of power" if China should lose its capacity to resist Japan with the boycott.[80] In a more realistic appraisal, the French ambassador to Tokyo cautioned Stimson that the anti-Japanese boycott had, by November 1931, caused Japanese business circles to lose their confidence in world trade and internationalism and turn to the military for security reasons.[81] When the imperial Japanese navy began its armed intervention in Shanghai in early 1932, Western diplomats concluded that the boycott more than any other cause had provoked the Japanese military to action.[82]

Although there may have been no better alternative available to Nanking in 1931, the boycott did not effectively resist Japanese aggression in Manchuria and China; nor did it break the economic hold

that the Japanese had on the Chinese market. Apparently the boycott did push the Japanese civilian
population to support the military leaders who offered
their "fundamental solution" to the matter of Japan's
place in the Chinese economy. Despite the fervor
of some patriotic elements among the Chinese citizenry
against Japan's military and economic imperialism,
the boycott revealed how vulnerable a decentralized,
disunited China remained in 1931. At various
stages of the boycott, the motivations of the in-
fighting Kuomintang factions in Nanking and Canton
seemed self-serving. Prior to the Manchurian Incident of September 18, many Chinese vacillated in
their support of the boycott. The ambiguous support
that the Nanking government provided to the commercial
nationalism expressed in the anti-Japanese movement
was not on a par with the positive influence that
a more centralized political system could wield over
an integrated nation-state. What was better than
nothing was not good enough for China.

NOTES

1. *Foreign Relations of the United States, 1931:
China* (Washington, D.C.: Government Printing Office,
1946), p. 151 and p. 377; and *Foreign Relations of the
United States, 1932: China* (Washington, D.C.: Government Printing Office, 1948), pp. 61-62.
2. C. F. Remer, *A Study of Chinese Boycott, With
Special Reference to Their Economic Effectiveness*
(Baltimore: Johns Hopkins Press, 1933); and Akashi
Yoji, "The Boycott and Anti-Japanese National
Salvation Movement of the Nanyang Chinese, 1908-1941"
(Ph.D. dissertation, Georgetown University, 1963),
p. 20.
3. *Mainichi and Tokyo nichi nichi* (hereafter
cited as *Mainichi*), November 18, 1931, p. 7.
4. *North China Herald*, July 14, 1931, p. 39.
5. *Japan Advertiser* (Tokyo), July 15, 1931, from
Shanghai; *Asahi shimbun*, July 21, 1931, p. 2. See
also Japanese Naval Attaché Kitaoka at Shanghai,
telegram No. 70 (July 14, 1931) to Tokyo, in Reel 27
of the Library of Congress collection of Japanese
Navy and Army Archives.
6. *Mainichi*, July 14, 1931, p. 7; *China Weekly
Review*, August 15, 1931, p. 436.
7. *Japan Advertiser*, July 15, 1931, p. 1, Nippon
Dempo news service at Nanchang, Kiangsi.
8. Remer, *Chinese Boycott*, cites a "National
Salvation Fund Movement" of 1915 (p. 48). See also
Mainichi, November 20, 1931, for the origins of

the 1931 boycott (p. 5).

9. *Mainichi*, September 30, 1931, supplement on the Japanese cotton textile industry.

10. *North China Herald*, July 21, 1931, p. 75; *Japan Advertiser*, July 21, 1931, p. 1, from Shanghai; and *Mainichi*, July 16, 1931, p. 1.

11. *Asahi*, July 20, 1931, p. 2, from its Shanghai correspondent.

12. Wang Hsien-hsiang, "China's Responsibility in Connection with the Anti-Japanese Boycott," *China Weekly Review*, November 21, 1931, pp. 448-49.

13. *Japan Advertiser*, July 18, 1931, p. 1.

14. *Ibid.*, July 19, 1931, p. 1; *Asahi*, July 23, 1931, p. 1, datelined Shanghai, July 22; *Monthly Return of the Foreign Trade of Japan* (Tokyo, August 1931), cited in Remer, *Chinese Boycott*, Appendix I, p. 265.

15. *Japan Advertiser*, July 21, 1931, p. 1; and *Asahi*, July 23, 1931, p. 1. See also United States Navy Office of Naval Intelligence (hereafter ONI), "Report on the Sino-Japanese Situation," July 24, 1931, p. 2.

16. *North China Herald*, August 18, 1931, and October 20, 1931; and ONI report of July 24, 1931, p. 5.

17. *Japan Advertiser*, July 19, 1931, p. 1; *China Weekly Review*, August 29, 1931, p. 501.

18. *China Weekly Review*, July 18, 1931, p. 278; and *North China Herald*, July 14, 1931, featuring historical sketches commemorating Yü's fiftieth anniversary in Shanghai (p. 50).

19. *China Weekly Review*, August 1, 1931, p. 334; and *Japan Advertiser*, July 19, 1931, p. 1.

20. *China Weekly Review*, August 1, 1931, p. 334; and *North China Herald*, August 4, 1931, p. 156.

21. *China Weekly Review*, August 8 and 22, 1931, pp. 394, 474.

22. ONI Naval Attaché report from China, August 7, 1931, p. 7.

23. *Mainichi*, August 12, September 4, September 19, 1931. On these days, the financial page followed closely the sales abroad of Osaka's leading industry.

24. *Ibid.*, August 3, 1931; and *Asahi*, August 12, 14, 15, 1931, from the *Asahi* correspondent in Shanghai and the Rengo news agency there.

25. *Asahi*, August 13, 1931, p. 2.

26. *Ibid.*, August 16, 1931, p. 2, via the Dentsu agency in Shanghai.

27. *Japan Advertiser*, August 13 and 22, 1931; and *North China Herald*, August 25, 1931, p. 257.

28. *Japan Advertiser*, August 16, 1931, p. 1; *China Weekly Review*, June 11, 1932, p. 45.

29. *North China Herald*, August 25, 1931, p. 257; *China Weekly Review*, August 8, 1931, p. 384.

30. *Asahi*, August 29, 1931, p. 2.

31. *Mainichi*, August 18, 1931, p. 1, via the Dentsu service in Shanghai.

32. Meng Chang-yung, "The Boycott Against the Japanese," *China Weekly Review*, August 29, 1931, p. 501.

33. *Ibid.*, p. 501; *Japan Advertiser*, August 13, 1931, p. 3; *Asahi*, August 15, 1931, p. 2; and *Mainichi*, August 18, 1931, p. 3.

34. *Japan Advertiser*, August 26, 1931, p. 4; September 1, 1931, p. 1.

35. *Asahi*, September 2 and 4, 1931, included reports by Dentsu, Rengo, and *Asahi* correspondents on the boycott in Tientsin and Manchuria.

36. *Mainichi*, September 9 and 10, 1931, front page headlines.

37. *North China Herald*, September 29, 1931, p. 444.

38. "Ko-chi tang-pu chih-tao fan-Jih chiu-kao hsing-tung kung-tsu yao-kang" ∠ Outline Directive to All Levels of Party Headquarters for Guidance in Conducting the Work of the Anti-Japanese National Salvation Movement_/ (Nanking, September 25, 1931), an appendix to *The Report of the Commission of Enquiry into the Sino-Japanese Dispute* (Tokyo: League of Nations Association of Japan, 1932).

39. *Kuo-wen chou-pao* ∠ National News Weekly_/, October 5, 1931.

40. *Asahi*, September 25, 1931, p. 3, from Dentsu in Shanghai; and "How Japanese Business Suffers from the Boycott," *China Weekly Review*, October 17, 1931, citing an October 12 report of the Shanghai Japanese Consul General. See also ONI Naval Attaché's China report, November 27, 1931, p. 10.

41. *Japan Advertiser*, September 27, 1931, p. 5.

42. *Mainichi*, September 23, 1931, p. 2, from Nanking; *North China Herald*, September 29, 1931, p. 444; and *Asahi*, September 30, 1931, p. 2, from Shanghai correspondent.

43. *Japan Advertiser*, October 6, 1931, p. 1, via the Nippon Dempo service in Shanghai; and *Mainichi*, October 7, 1931, p. 1, Dentsu agency in Shanghai.

44. *North China Herald*, October 13, 1931, p. 41, from the official Kuo Min news agency.

45. John Israel, *Student Nationalism in China, 1927-1937* (Stanford: Stanford University Press, 1966), and reported by contemporary press.

46. *Foreign Relations, 1931*, p. 126.

47. *Mainichi*, October 22 and November 19, 1931. The financial pages summarized the official investigation of the effects of the Chinese boycott. See also *China Weekly Review*, November 21, 1931, p. 461.

48. *Asahi*, September 27, 1931, with reports on both meetings (p. 2). See also *Japan Advertiser*, September 30, 1931, p. 7.

49. *North China Herald*, October 6, 1931, p. 12; *Asahi*, October 6, 1931, p. 4.

50. *Foreign Relations, 1931*, p. 128.

51. *Mainichi*, October 8, 1931, p. 1.

52. *Asahi*, October 9, 1931, p. 2, from Shanghai; *North China Herald*, October 27, 1931, p. 127.

53. *Japan Advertiser*, October 14, 1931, p. 2.

54. *Ibid.*, January 29, 1932, p. 1; *New York Times*, January 29, 1932, quotes Shiozawa's proclamation (p. 2). For details, see *Wai-chiao yüeh-pao* ∠ Foreign Affairs Monthly_/, Vol. I, No. 1 (July 1932).

55. "Customs Report," Nankai Statistical Service, published in *China Weekly Review*, June 20, 1931, p. 122. See also *Japan Advertiser Annual Review, 1930-31* (Tokyo, 1931), p. 9.

56. *Mainichi*, July 16, 1931, p. 7.

57. *Ibid.*, September 30, 1931. The details in the supplement on cotton textiles (p. 12) are corroborated by the figures on spindles in *China Weekly Review*, February 20, 1932, p. 372. See also Albert Feuerwerker, *The Chinese Economy, 1912-1949* (Ann Arbor: Center for Chinese Studies, University of Michigan, 1968), table 5.

58. Jennings Wong, "New Factory Law and China's Industries," *China Weekly Review*, August 22, 1931, pp. 268-69; *Mainichi*, September 30, 1931, p. 12, cotton supplement; and December 9, 1931, p. 7.

59. *China Weekly Review*, April 11, 1931, p. 241; *Mainichi*, September 30, 1931, p. 12.

60. ONI Naval Attaché report of November 13, 1931, matches the special report from Shanghai, filed for *Mainichi*, November 20, 1931, datelined November 18. See also *Shih-pao* ∠ The Times_/, December 12, 17, 18, 1931.

61. *Mainichi*, December 1, 1931, p. 7, datelined Shanghai, November 23; and December 9, 1931, p. 7.

62. *Chinese Economic Bulletin* (Nanking), September 1931.

63. *Asahi*, September 11, 1931, p. 3; *Japan Advertiser*, September 12, 1931, p. 9; and *Mainichi*, September 12, 1931, p. 7.

64. *Mainichi*, November 3, 1931, p. 7; *Japan Ad-*

vertiser, July 1933 supplement, "Textiles and Tar-
riffs: An International Problem," p. 22.

65. M. Gandhi, *Young India* (Bombay, July 17,
1931); and *Mainichi*, November 1, 1931, p. 7.

66. *Mainichi*, September 26, 1931, p. 7, survey by
the Association of Japanese Spinners in China; and
October 17, 1931, p. 5. See also *Japan Advertiser*, July 1933 textile supplement, pp. 22, 24;
and Feuerwerker, *The Chinese Economy*, tables 5, 8, and
9.

67. *North China Herald*, December 1, 1931, p. 303;
and *Mainichi*, September 30, 1931, p. 12.

68. *Asahi*, September 11, 1931, p. 3; *Mainichi*,
September 19, 1931, p. 7.

69. *Mainichi*, September 16, 1931, p. 7.

70. *Ibid.*, August 14, 1931, p. 1, special feature
on the "South Seas" trade.

71. *Ibid.*, October 10 and 19, 1931, trade page.
See also ONI Naval Attaché report on China, October
30, 1931, p. 10; *North China Herald*, March 15,
1931, p. 403; *Asahi*, October 14, 1931, p. 4, estimates that it would cost the AJNSA 36,000 yüan daily
to pay the 60,000 plus workers while they were on
strike.

72. *Mainichi*, November 18, 1931, p. 7; *Japan Advertiser*, November 24, 1931, p. 7; *China Weekly
Review*, February 20, 1932, p. 372, reprint of Alfred
L. Meyer's investigation of the losses to Japanese
mill owners in *Shanghai Evening Post*.

73. *Japan Advertiser*, January 30, 1932, pp. 5 and
7; February 2, 1932, p. 7.

74. Feuerwerker, *The Chinese Economy*, tables 8
and 9.

75. Report by the Bank of China Research Department, in *China Weekly Review*, February 20, 1931,
p. 370; and February 20, 1932, p. 372.

76. Report of the Japanese Ministry of Finance,
December 15, 1931, in *ibid.*, December 19, 1931, p. 38,
of the Reconstruction Edition. See also Chih Meng,
China Speaks: On the Conflict Between China and Japan
(New York: Macmillan Co., 1932), p. 93.

77. *Japan Advertiser*, March 29, 1932, p. 7.

78. Feuerwerker, *The Chinese Economy*, tables 5,
9, and 23.

79. *Shih-pao*, December 18, 1931; *Mainichi*, December 9, 1931, p. 7; and *China Weekly Review*, July
16, 1932, p. 234.

80. *Foreign Relations, 1931*, pp. 343, 471; *Foreign
Relations, 1932*, p. 62.

81. *Foreign Relations, 1931*, p. 386.

82. *Foreign Relations, 1932*, pp. 61, 202, 211-12,
220-22.

Part 2
Sinkiang and Szechwan in the Era of Japanese Aggression

5

Regionalism and Central Power: Sheng Shih-ts'ai in Sinkiang, 1933–1944

F. Gilbert Chan

Sheng Shih-ts'ai was a regional militarist, yet his rule in Sinkiang was nationally significant. In the pre-1937 years, the province was an arena of international intrigues, with Russia, Japan, and British India competing for influence. It later became the principal avenue through which the Chinese government in Chungking received assistance from Soviet Russia. Throughout Sheng's governorship in 1933–1944, the Nationalist leaders expressed an unusually strong interest in this borderland. Nonetheless, until 1942, they were unable to exert central authority over the province. To a considerable extent, this failure reflected the political weaknesses of the Kuomintang government in China.

Sheng had nurtured important connections in Nanking prior to his departure for Sinkiang. After his ascension to power in Urumchi, however, he moved deliberately away from the central government. He adopted an independent foreign policy, which eventually turned his province into "a voluntary, disguised satellite of the Soviet Union."[1] He claimed to be "a devoted disciple of Marxism-Leninism," and he invited Chinese Communists to serve in his gov-

Acknowledgments are due to General Sheng Shih-ts'ai, Mr. Lin Chi-yung, Mr. Kuang Lu, and Mr. and Mrs. Lin Pai-ya for granting the author interviews, during which they recounted their experiences in Sinkiang. General Sheng died in Taipei in July 1970. As a graduate student at Columbia University in the late 1960s, the author benefited from the guidance of Professor O. Edmund Clubb, who headed the American consulate in Urumchi in 1943.

ernment. While "granting only token allegiance" to
Chiang Kai-shek, he professed that the Nationalists "lacked the power" to deprive him of his
governorship.[2] His twelve years of rule represented
a regression of Chinese sovereignty in Sinkiang.

With Sheng as a case study, this chapter analyzes
the conflict between regional separatism and political integration in the Kuomintang era of Chinese
history. It centers on Sinkiang's intricate relations
with both the Nationalists and the Russians. It
examines Sheng's pro-Soviet leanings in the context
of the central government's ineffectual endeavors
to extend its influence to the northwestern frontier.
Because of active Russian intervention, regionalism in Sinkiang was more than a manifestation of the
failure of national integration; it was also in-
dicative of China's weakness in the face of imperialist aggression.

SHENG SHIH-TS'AI'S EARLY LIFE

Sheng was born in the province of Liaoning in
southern Manchuria on December 3, 1895. During
his childhood, his home region was a "cradle of conflict" between Russia and Japan.[3] He was keenly aware
of the rivalries of these two nations. When he was
seventeen years old, he went to Shanghai to study.
He became friendly with teachers and students
of "radical inclination."[4]

In 1915, Sheng traveled to Tokyo and was enrolled
at Waseda University. He stayed for only one year.
His nationalistic outbursts against Japanese exploitation of China impressed many fellow-students. They
sent him home to take part in anti-Japanese movements
as one of their representatives.[5] This experience
had a profound influence on him and partially
accounted for his hostile attitude toward Japan during
his rule in Sinkiang.

Shortly after his return to China, Sheng entered
a military college in Shaochou, Kwangtung. He won
the support of its principal, Li Ken-yüan, who
was politically influential. Upon Sheng's graduation,
Li recommended him for a post under Kuo Sung-ling,
a subordinate of the Manchurian warlord, Chang Tso-
lin. Meanwhile, Sheng's interest in radicalism
continued. In 1919, he became a Marxist.[6]

Thanks to Kuo's support, Sheng was admitted to
Shikan Gakkō in Japan in 1924. His study was
again interrupted by political upheaval at home, and
he returned to China in the following year. Kuo
was directing a military campaign against Chang Tso-

lin, and Sheng rallied under Kuo's banner. The campaign was doomed to fail, however, because of
Kuo's inadequate strength. Chang protested to the
Japanese government when Sheng tried to resume
his work at Shikan Gakkō. At this critical juncture,
Chiang Kai-shek intervened and offered Sheng financial
assistance to complete his training.

In 1927, when the Northern Expedition was already
in progress, Sheng went back to China and served
under Ho Ying-ch'in at the headquarters of the
National Revolutionary Army. After the reunification
of the country, he expected to receive an assignment
in the new government commensurate with his ability. He was bitterly disappointed.[7] He thereupon turned his attention to the Chinese frontiers,
hoping to advance his career there. At the same time,
he made many friends in Nanking, including P'eng
Chao-hsien, a "powerful political operator."[8]

In 1929, Lu Hsiao-tsu, general secretary of the
Sinkiang government, came to Nanking to seek financial
aid. He was also looking for a capable young man
to take charge of military training in the province.
P'eng spoke favorably of Sheng, and Lu immediately
offered Sheng an appointment.[9] After a delay of eight
months in Peiping, Lu and his new protégé traveled
via the Trans-Siberian Railway to Urumchi, the
provincial capital of Sinkiang.

SHENG SHIH-TS'AI'S RISE TO POWER

Sheng's career in Sinkiang did not begin promisingly. Governor Chin Shu-jen had never dreamed of
enlisting a subordinate with Sheng's qualifications.
Chin's brother, Shu-hsin, was then in charge of
army administration, and he, too, was not pleased to
have an assistant whose training was superior to
his own. With much reluctance, they appointed Sheng
chief of the general staff of the frontier army, a
commission that did not give him a chance to show his
best. Sheng did not betray any sign of discontent,
for his had no intention of returning to Nanking.
Gradually, the governor became impressed, and he approved of Sheng's request for an appointment to
the provincial military college as its principal instructor.

As a military instructor, Sheng had, at least
in Sinkiang, no equally qualified rival. His training
in Japan was an attraction to many young officers.
As his popularity grew, the provincial government, which was incompetent, venal, and backward,
rapidly lost the support of the people. Chin Shu-

jen's ill-advised racial policy toward the Uighurs
proved to be the last straw, and it led to the
outbreak of the Hami Rebellion.[10]

At the beginning of the revolt, Chin resorted to
high-handed suppression. The Uighurs sought assistance from Ma Chung-ying, a chieftain of the powerful
and warlike Tungan clan in Kansu. In May 1931, Ma
marched toward Hami with ambitious plans for a
Muslim empire in Central Asia, based on his expecta-
tion of conquering Sinkiang.[11] With an army of
400 calvarymen, he won a succession of victories.
Hami was besieged and Urumchi threatened.

In order to turn the tables on his adversaries,
Chin called upon his ally in Ili, Chang P'ei-yüan,
to raise the siege of Hami. The governor also commis-
sioned Sheng to be chief of staff. Chang had recently recruited the veteran White Russian mercenary
troops. Known in Sinkiang as the *kuei-hua* army, these
were tsarist soldiers who had escaped to the province
after the Russian Revolution of 1917. In August
1931, they forced Ma to withdraw to Kansu. The Uighurs begged for the termination of hostilities in the
following month.

Personal rivalries developed between Chin and
Chang shortly after the restoration of peace, and
Chang left Urumchi for Ili. Meanwhile, five representatives from Outer Mongolia approached the Uighurs
with promises of material aid if the Uighurs would
renew their struggle against the Sinkiang government.
Chin was conscious of the seriousness of the situation, but Nanking was too far away to render him
any assistance. He turned to the Russians for help.
In return, he concluded with them a trade agreement without prior approval from the central government. This rapprochement with Soviet Russia was
a clear mark of regional independence, and it demonstrated the political weakness of the Nationalists in
the northwestern borderland.

Hostilities with the Uighurs resumed. With Chang
in Ili, Sheng was the only person in Urumchi worthy
of appointment to the post of commander-in-chief
of the army. He was the most experienced, competent,
and, above all, popular militarist in the province.
Since the outbreak of the Hami Rebellion, he had
loyally served one commander after another and he had
favorably impressed the people. Now at the mature
age of thirty-nine, he finally earned a long awaited
opportunity to show his talents.

Meanwhile, the revolt dragged on. The Uighurs
sought to spread the insurrection as widely as
possible. Chaos broke out at Shanshan, Turfan, Kara-

shahr, Kucha, Aksu, and Khotan. In May 1932, Ma
Chung-ying sent his subordinate, Ma Shih-ming, to Sinkiang to help the rebels. Early in 1933, Ma Shih-
ming attacked Urumchi. While the city was in turmoil,
the Northeast National Salvation Army of Manchuria
arrived from Russia on March 27. They were underfed,
insufficiently clothed, and unarmed. Nevertheless,
their arrival at the most critical moment must
have produced a great psychological impact on the
people.[12] The optimism at the capital convinced
the Uighurs to seek additional assistance from
Ma Chung-ying.

Before Ma reentered Sinkiang from Kansu, a
coup d'état broke out in Urumchi on April 12. It
started as a mutiny of the White Russian troops
against Chin Shu-jen. These Russian emigrés had been
largely responsible for the defense of Urumchi against
Ma Shih-ming's attack. Yet, Chin was suspicious of
them and had treated them badly.[13] Prior to the coup,
Papingut, a White Russian, had consulted the leaders
of the Northeast National Salvation Army and been
assured of their sympathy. He had also received support from some of Chin's subordinates, principally
T'ao Ming-yüeh, Ch'en Chung, and Chang Hsin. The
governor escaped and, after attempting in vain
to regain his power, returned to China through Russia.

Sheng was in Uraba on the day of the coup, and
he had apparently not been involved in the plot to
overthrow Chin's government. He contended that the
first news of the coup came to him on the following morning, when Li Hsiao-t'ien flew from Urumchi to
urge him to return to the capital.[14] He was an ambitious man, and he had been dissatisfied with Chin's
policies. He regarded the coup as an opportunity
for personal advancement. Upon his arrival in
Urumchi, he skillfully used the disturbances to promote his own interests.

On April 14, Sheng attended a meeting of different anti-Chin factions. Representatives of
the ethnic groups were also present.[15] In an earlier
meeting held in Sheng's absence on April 12, the
rebellious leaders had already decided to reduce the
power of the governor, who would henceforth be in
charge only of civil administration. Without confer-
ring with the Nationalists in Nanking, they had
named Liu Wen-lung, a provincial bureaucrat, to fill
that position. In the second meeting of April 14,
they elected Sheng to head the Border Defense Commission. As commander (*tu-pan*), he would be responsible for the military affairs of the province.[16]

Sheng's election was a compromise. He was prob-

ably the only militarist acceptable to all factions
in the meeting. He had served Chin loyally and
was therefore a more agreeable choice for the
governor's former subordinates than, say, Chang P'ei-
yüan. His status as an outsider who was relatively
new in the province was one of his important
assets; as such, he was comparatively free of the
bitter rivalries that had characterized Sinkiang
politics. Moreover, he was popular among soldiers;
both the White Russians and the Northeast National Salvation Army had fought under him and respected
him for his abilities. Unlike many of his colleagues,
he had also avoided offending the non-Chinese races.
Above all, his military strength gave him a decisive bargaining power. The anti-Chin factions were
eager to win him to their side.[17] Thus, his selection
as military leader of the province was not surprising.

THE WEAKNESS OF CENTRAL POWER

Sheng's position in Sinkiang was far from secure.
Chin's fall did not create a power vacuum, and Sheng
was by no means his logical successor. The coup
d'état simply removed a leader who had been ineffectual since the outbreak of the Hami Rebellion.
Liu Wen-lung's ascension to the governorship showed
that the old provincial bureaucrats still held a
pivotal position in Urumchi. They had no intention of
yielding any real power to Sheng, who found it necessary to state after his election that he would not
interfere with the civil affairs of the government.
Even as a military leader, Sheng had to face the
challenge of Ma Chung-ying and Chang P'ei-yüan. Ma
was still the greatest menace in the province, and
Chang, now in Ili, was uncooperative. Most im-
portantly, the reaction of Nanking to the coup was
uncertain. In spite of his earlier connections with
the Nationalists, Sheng had risen to prominence in
Sinkiang without Chiang Kai-shek's assistance.
Indeed, the Kuomintang government favored the abolition of the Border Defense Commission, of which Sheng
was chairman, and it had appointed Ma to command the
36th Division of the national army. The fear that
Nanking might support Ma must have haunted the minds
of many provincial leaders. As *tu-pan,* Sheng
needed the recognition of the central government
to legitimatize his authority, so that he could retain
the loyalty of his soldiers and the fruit of years
of struggle.

In May 1933, Ma and his Tungan forces threatened
Kuch'eng. The provincial authorities protested to
Nanking against the conduct of its divisional commander, but they conceded that there could be "no hope
of help from that quarter." The protest was
merely "a matter of correct procedure."[18] In addition to his official commission, Ma claimed to
have "learned the arts of war" from Chiang Kai-shek.
The Tungan's relations with Nanking were embarrassing
to Sheng, who had reason to consider Chiang as his
own patron.[19]

Nonetheless, the apparent support of the central
government could not fully account for the strength
of Ma's military forces. He had received further
assistance from at least one of the foreign powers
having an interest in the province. The weapons used
by his soldiers were British rifles imported from
India.[20] Sheng insisted that Ma had accepted aid from
Japan. The provincial troops captured a Japanese,
Onishi Tadashi, who was attached to Ma's headquarters.[21]

Early in June, Ma telegraphed Sheng to signify
his readiness to negotiate with Urumchi. The
White Russians were against compromise. Sheng, however, believed that it was possible for two rivals to
work out some terms of accommodation in a huge
region like Sinkiang. He was willing to yield the
southern half of the province to Ma in return for
peace in the north. He persuaded the provincial government to send a mission to Kuch'eng to negotiate
with the Tungans. The peace effort failed despite some promise of success.[22] Both Sheng and Ma
were pressed by their war parties to renew hostilities. At this juncture, Nanking intervened by dis-
patching Huang Mu-sung to Sinkiang as its pacification
commissioner.

Since 1928, the central government had been interested in Sinkiang, a province known for its
regional independence. Indeed, Chiang Kai-shek may
have endorsed Sheng's decision to leave for the northwestern frontier in the following year.[23] In 1931,
when Chin Shu-jen negotiated with Russia for assistance, China did not have diplomatic relations with
the Soviet government. Nanking was concerned, and
this probably explained its half-hearted support of
Ma in 1932-1933. Meanwhile, the Nationalists were too
preoccupied with Japanese aggression and anti-
Communist campaigns to be able to help Sinkiang solve
its problems. They were further weakened by
Chiang's rivalries with Wang Ching-wei and other
factional leaders within the Kuomintang. As a result,

Nanking's policy toward the province was fitfully opportunistic, and Huang's mission in June 1933 was a typical example.[24]

Huang's arrival in Urumchi was poorly timed. The province had failed in its search for peace and had been convinced of Ma's insincerity. A new attempt by the central government could not arouse much optimism among provincial officials. Moreover, Huang was ignorant of frontier problems and his arrogant behavior offended some local leaders.[25] Among the many rumors in Urumchi, one alleged that Nanking intended to divide Sinkiang into several smaller provinces. Sheng suspected that Huang's primary duty was to investigate the April 12 coup, instead of trying to bring peace to Sinkiang, and that Huang's report would influence the central government's decision to confirm Liu Wen-lung and Sheng as governor and *tu-pan* respectively.

In this atmosphere of suspicion, Sheng charged that Huang was plotting with T'ao Ming-yüeh, Ch'en Chung, and Li Hsiao-t'ien against the provincial government. According to Japanese sources, Huang was an agent of Wang Ching-wei, who would have regarded the overthrow of Sheng as a setback for his political rival, Chiang Kai-shek. Sheng likewise implied that Wang was involved. In any case, the *tu-pan* took advantage of the factional struggles in Nanking to consolidate his own shaky position at Urumchi. As he maintained, the plot was for Huang to negotiate an alliance with Liu Wen-lung, Chang P'ei-yüan, and Ma Chung-ying. T'ao Ming-yüeh, Ch'en Chung, and Li Hsiao-t'ien would be responsible for Sheng's assassination.[26] Sheng learned of the conspiracy from his subordinates, and he ordered the arrest of T'ao, Ch'en, and Li. They were executed almost in Huang's presence.

In a meeting with provincial leaders, Sheng criticized Nanking for planning to abolish the Border Defense Commission. He tendered his resignation. His colleagues, foreseeing utter chaos, begged Huang to petition the central government to abandon all efforts to change the system. Strongly affected by the executions, Huang telegraphed Nanking to recommend the confirmation of Liu and Sheng. A few days later, he hurriedly left the province. In September, the official endorsement reached Sinkiang and the two leaders were installed in office by Lo Wen-kan, who was concurrently minister of foreign affairs and minister of justice. No matter how elaborate the ceremony was, it was obvious even to such travelers as Peter Fleming that their appointments were the price

Nanking had paid for the life of its pacification commissioner.[27]

Lo's arrival in the provincial capital on
September 2 ushered in a new period of political tension.[28] After Huang's fiasco, Nanking had sent a
number of representatives, including P'eng Chao-hsien,
to the province. Their presence failed to impress
upon Urumchi the importance of loyalty to the central
government. Indeed, the dispatch to Sinkiang of so
prominent a figure as Lo revealed Nanking's desperate
desire to gain control over this northwestern borderland. Lo's mission was another failure. Like
Huang, he was victimized by the skillful political
manipulation of Sheng, who again turned his opponents
into a useful instrument to further his personal
power.

Sheng accused Lo of conspiring to revive an alliance with Liu Wen-lung, Chang P'ei-yüan, and Ma
Chung-ying. Liu's responsibility was to arrange for
Sheng's assassination.[29] Sheng extracted a confession
from Liu and forced him to resign. With Liu's
removal from the provincial government, the bureaucratic hierarchy established by Chin Shu-jen and
his predecessor, Yang Tseng-hsin, ceased to be an important factor in Sinkiang. Sheng created a new
hierarchy by placing his brothers, father-in-
law, brothers-in-law, and other men of his choice in
high government positions. Since Sheng insisted that
Nanking's envoys had instigated plots against him,
Liu's fall was generally interpreted in the province
as a failure of the central government. Lo's
departure from Urumchi marked the beginning of an
era of alienation between Nanking and its northwestern
province.

SHENG SHIH-TS'AI AND SOVIET RUSSIA

Having established himself in power, Sheng concentrated his attention on Ma Chung-ying, who had
allied with Chang P'ei-yüan. He was not so much
threatened by the combined forces of two opposing militarists as by the possibility that Japan might have
assisted them. He had seen Japanese imperialists
in action in other parts of China, and he could not
tolerate the penetration of their influence in
Sinkiang. He was determined to end his struggle with
Ma and Chang once and for all, but the provincial
government did not have the military capability to
press the campaign to a successful conclusion.
Nanking was politically too weak to be helpful. Sheng
was therefore obliged to follow Chin Shu-jen's prece-

dent and turn to Russia for aid.

In October 1933, Ch'en Teh-li and Yao Hsiung departed for Moscow. Sheng claimed that the purpose of their trip was to urge the Russians to supply the province with the weapons they had promised to give to Governor Chin in 1931.[30] Some new arrangements were evidently made, however, for when Ch'en and Yao returned in December, they were accompanied by Garegin Apresoff, the new Soviet consul general in Urumchi. Russian advisers were soon appointed to key positions in the government, and a secret police force was instituted under the command of a Soviet named Pogodin.[31]

In comparing his policy toward Russia with his predecessor's, Sheng argued that while Chin had merely exchanged Sinkiang trading rights for Soviet military assistance, he strove instead to gain Russian friendship.[32] Since his youth, Sheng had been devoted to radical ideals, which doubtless inspired his pro-Sovietism. It is irrelevant whether his actions conformed with Chinese national policy toward Russia; his "was not the first regime to seek Soviet assistance."[33] In the warlord era, it had been a common phenomenon for regional leaders to exercise an independent foreign policy. Before Sheng came to Sinkiang, he had participated in the struggle among warlords by helping Kuo Sung-ling against Chang Tso-lin. It was natural that he should behave like one, particularly when the political authority in Nanking was weak.

Charges of territorial aggression notwithstanding, the Soviet government responded favorably to Sheng's request for help partly for defensive reasons. Japanese and, to a lesser extent, British imperialistic designs on Sinkiang threatened Russia as much as they did the provincial leaders, and Moscow was pessimistic about Nanking's ability to protect its northwestern frontier.[34] Fearing that Ma Chungying's victory might result in the enhancement of Japanese influence in Sinkiang, the Soviets were anxious for his defeat. Hence, when Ma besieged Urumchi in January 1934, Russian troops and airplanes came to Sheng's aid and routed the Tungan forces.[35] Chang P'ei-yüan committed suicide. Ma fled to southern Sinkiang. In July, he yielded to the persuasions of a Soviet consular officer in Kashgar and withdrew to Russian territory with a small retinue of loyal followers.

After the restoration of peace, Sheng turned his attention to the task of provincial reconstruction. He envisioned a "new Sinkiang" with a "revolutionary

administration" to replace "the decadent old regime."[36] Yet, in spite of his rise to prominence, he
lacked firm support from any strong faction in the
government. He had found it expedient to eliminate
one opposing group after another. In December
1933, upon Pogodin's insistence, he purged the White
Russians, whose presence in Sinkiang had proved
irritating to the Soviets. Moreover, as a militarist,
Sheng did not have adequate forces under his command.
In this precarious political and military position,
he had to win the favor of the non-Chinese races.
A liberal government with popular support would be his
best guarantee of political security.

An enlightened racial policy would also gratify
Russia. In order to carry out his ambitious reform
programs, Sheng needed Soviet technical and financial
assistance, since Nanking was not helpful. Before
Ma Chung-ying's flight, Sheng had already been
negotiating with the Russian government for a loan of
4 million gold rubles "for the development of industry and the relief of the poor."[37] The Soviets
were interested in the province for their own reasons,
and Sheng had cause to question their motives. Even
casual observers were puzzled when Ma was offered
sanctuary by the country that had helped to defeat
him. Sheng acknowledged that "Stalin was keeping Ma
as a check upon my own power."[38]

Soviet Russia was clearly trying to play a double
role: an obliging friend as well as a treacherous
enemy. Sheng had to prove his faithfulness to the
Russians in order to win their friendship and to
enlist their help. Any sign of disloyalty would turn
them into dangerous foes and culminate in his replacement, a phenomenon not uncommon in Sinkiang. He
had not gained his position of military leadership
easily, and he did not want his future destroyed
by Soviet interference. Thus, in a discussion with
Apresoff in 1934, he offered to put Communism into
practice in the province.[39]

Henceforth, Sheng's main concern was to remain on
friendly terms with both the ethnic groups and the
Soviet neighbor. His reform programs were geared toward this end. In August 1934, he promulgated an
Eight Point Declaration, aimed at creating a "progressive, united, prosperous province of 4 million
souls."[40] In doing so, he exceeded his authority
as commander of the Border Defense Commission. When
he promised in 1933 that he would leave the civil
administration of the province to the governor, it
was evident that his ambition could not be satisfied
by his appointment as *tu-pan*. His influence increased

when Liu Wen-lung resigned later in the year. Chu
Jui-ch'ih, the succeeding governor, died of illness in
February 1934. Sheng recommended Li Jung as the new
leader of the civil government. Li was an old man
whose long service in Sinkiang had taught him to mind
his own business.[41] With such a figurehead as
governor, Sheng seized complete control of the provincial administration.

In 1935-1936, Sheng proclaimed his Six Great
Policies, in which he emphasized his dual program of
antiimperialism and pro-Russianism.[42] They furnished
an ideological justification for his leanings toward
the Soviet government. He attacked Japan and Britain
for their imperialistic exploitation of Sinkiang.
On the other hand, he regarded Russia as nonaggres-
sive, seeing the Soviet leaders as "determined to put
Leninism into practice" and "ready to aid the weak
races of the world." Without their assistance,
he contended, Sinkiang could not "tread on the path of
antiimperialism."[43]

In late 1936, a Muslim rebellion broke out in
the southern portion of the province. Its leaders were reportedly anti-Russian. Upon Sheng's request, Soviet troops intervened in May 1937.
They remained in Hami after the suppression of
the revolt. Meanwhile, Sheng claimed that Apresoff
was the "mastermind" behind a "Trotskyite plot," which
attempted to "create discord" between Sinkiang and
the Russian government.[44] With Soviet agents participating in the investigation, Russian interference
in the Urumchi administration intensified. More
than 400 people, including Chang Hsin, Ch'en Teh-li,
and Kuang Lu, were convicted of conspiracy. Apresoff
was recalled to Moscow and executed.

By late 1937, Soviet influence had come to
dominate the province. Sheng had gained control of
the Sinkiang government without any aid from Nanking.
His relations with the Nationalists were, at best,
"tenuous."[45] Chiang Kai-shek, politically weakened by
his rivalries with Wang Ching-wei and other dissi-
dents, admitted in 1935 that he was unable to "separate Sinkiang" from Russian domination because he was
"too preoccupied" with Japanese aggression in other
parts of China.[46] With the outbreak of war
against Japan in July 1937, his ability to protect
Chinese interests in the province was open to serious
question.

PRO-RUSSIANISM AND CHINESE SOVEREIGNTY

In comparison with the previous governments, Nan-

king's desire to extend its influence to Sinkiang was
exceptionally strong, and it did not abate after the
unsuccessful missions of Huang Mu-sung and Lo Wen-
kan in 1933. Shortly after Lo's return to the Chinese
capital, the central government established a "commission on Sinkiang affairs ... to devise ways
and means to consolidate Nanking's political power"
in the province.[47] A confrontation with Urumchi soon
developed over Sheng's negotiation of a loan with
Soviet Russia.

In July 1934, Sheng informed Nanking that he had
been negotiating with Russia for a loan of 4 million
gold rubles. He insisted that this was a strictly
"commercial" arrangement with no political impli-
cation.[48] The foreign ministry withheld its approval
of the loan and asked for the submission of a copy
of the agreement. At the same time, Nanking notified
Moscow that it was illegal for a foreign government
to negotiate loans with the provincial authorities.
In May 1935, Sheng succeeded in persuading the
Russians to raise the amount to 5 million gold rubles,
and the agreement was concluded without Nanking's
approval.[49]

Japan was concerned about the increasing Russian
influence in the Chinese northwestern borderland.
In January 1935, Foreign Minister Hirota Kōki warned
the Diet of the "Sovietization of Sinkiang." Wang
Ching-wei likewise charged that Russia "was con-
templating an attempt to establish a Communist government" in the province. V. W. Molotov dismissed
these accusations as "slanderous rumors" and maintained that his government had consistently been an
"absolute adherent of the independence, integrity, and
sovereignty of China ... over Sinkiang."[50]

Despite Molotov's assurances, the Urumchi government continued to keep Nanking at a distance. In
July 1935, when W. W. Yen (Yen Hui-ch'ing), Chinese
ambassador in Moscow, proposed to travel to Sinkiang,
he was discouraged from doing so by the Soviets.
Sheng's independence from the central government was
heightened two years later by the outbreak of the
Sino-Japanese War. China's wartime alliance with Russia lent official sanction to his leaning toward the
Soviet neighbor.[51]

After the formation of the "united front" with
the Nationalists, the Chinese Communists became
interested in Urumchi as a midway station between
Yenan and Moscow. In 1937, Ch'en Shao-yü and K'ang
Sheng arrived in Sinkiang from Russia. Sheng offered
to join the Chinese Communist Party as a full member. Although the application was rejected because of

Stalin's intervention, Sheng enlisted the service
of such prominent Communist leaders as Ch'en
T'an-ch'iu, Teng Fa, and Yang Chih-hua (wife of Ch'ü
Ch'iu-pai) in his provincial government. Mao Tse-
tung sent his brother, Tse-min, to Urumchi to act as
Sheng's "personal adviser and assistant."[52]
     In August 1938, Sheng strengthened his ties with
the Soviet government by traveling to Moscow to pay
homage to Stalin. During his visit, he became a member of the Russian Communist Party. While contending that he acted "in the genuine interests of
new China," he took every precaution to prevent the
Nationalists from learning about his trip. He
gave Stalin "an instrument of blackmail" by subjecting
himself to Soviet party discipline.[53] Henceforth,
Sinkiang appeared to be more a Russian satellite than
a Chinese province.
     In 1940, political tension developed in Urumchi
between Sheng and his intimate friend, Tu Chung-
yüan. They were fellow northeasterners, and they had
both studied in Japan in 1915-1916. After a brief
stay in Sinkiang in 1937, Tu published a favorable account of Sheng's government. When he returned to
Urumchi in 1938, Sheng asked him to head the provincial college. Tu was "a follower of Communist
ideology," and he later confessed to having been
ordered by Chou En-lai to strive for the replacement
of Sheng's government with "a Soviet regime" independent of the Nationalists in Chungking.[54] In September 1940, Tu plotted with Yao Hsiung and Ouyanjak,
Russian consul general in Urumchi, to assassinate
Sheng and other provincial leaders. The conspiracy
ended with a purge of more than 480 people. Tu
was arrested and died mysteriously in prison.
     As the plot evolved, the Soviet government
tightened its control over Urumchi. In November,
Bukulin arrived from Moscow. Without prior consulta-
tion with Sheng, he demanded a fifty-year lease on
Sinkiang's tin mines for Russian exploitation. When
Sheng protested, the Soviet emissary invoked Stalin's
authority and insisted that Sheng, as a Communist
Party member, "should obey the orders of the party."[55]
Sheng yielded and placed his signature on the
proposed agreement without notifying the central government.
     With a "meager defense force" of 10,000 troops,
Sheng was militarily unable to resist Russian aggression.[56] Since late 1937, the Nationalists had
abandoned Nanking and taken refuge in Chungking. They
were even less capable of aiding Sinkiang than
before. They watched helplessly as Sheng sacrificed

China's sovereign rights in the province to protect
his selfish political interests. In 1941, after
the conclusion of the "Sin-tin" agreement, he offered
to establish a "full-fledged Soviet regime" in
Sinkiang. He had previously argued that his pro-
Russian policy was necessary for his combat against
Japanese imperialism. Yet, with the creation of
a nonaggression pact between Moscow and Tokyo
in April 1941, his pro-Soviet leanings could not be
justified in similar terms. When the German
forces threatened Russia in June, he became skeptical
about Stalin's ability to help him in the future.
He began to turn his eyes to Chungking.

SHENG SHIH-TS'AI AND THE CHUNGKING GOVERNMENT

The assassination of Sheng's brother, Shih-ch'i,
in March 1942 triggered his shift of loyalty to
Chungking. There were then about 300 Chinese Communists in the province, and he blamed them for
Shih-ch'i's murder.[57] He had earlier sent another
brother, Shih-yi, to Chungking to negotiate with the
Nationalists. In March, General Chu Shao-liang
visited Urumchi as Chiang Kai-shek's personal envoy.
In the following month, Sheng instigated a purge
of approximately 660 people. Ch'en T'an-ch'iu and Mao
Tse-min were among the victims; they were executed
in September 1943.

In May 1942, General Chu and Weng Wen-hao,
minister of economic affairs, arrived in Urumchi for
additional negotiations with Sheng. They brought
with them a message from Chiang, promising that the
tu-pan would not be prosecuted for his "errors."[58]
They returned to the province two months later with an
official delegation. Russia tried to intervene, but
Sheng had cast his die. In late August, Madame
Chiang Kai-shek traveled to Urumchi to formalize Sinkiang's return to the Chinese fold. In October, Sheng
asked the Russians to withdraw their troops from the
province.

Sheng rationalized his new alliance with Chungking on ideological grounds. He accused Stalin of
betraying the Leninist principle of antiimperialism by
signing the nonaggression pact with Japan. He argued
that the April coup of 1933 had been an integral
part of the nationalist revolution. Until 1942, Sinkiang had been "too backward" to embrace the Three
Principles of the People. He justified the introduction of his Six Great Policies as an important
transition, preparing his people for the eventual
acceptance of Kuomintang ideology.[59] In 1943,

a branch office of the Nationalist Party was instituted, with Sheng as the provincial chief. The
officials in Sinkiang were henceforth required to
study Chiang Kai-shek's writings.

Sheng's political reorientation was also motivated by pragmatic considerations. Japan's attack on
Pearl Harbor in December 1941 had turned the United
States into a powerful ally of the Chungking government. Sheng expected the Nationalists to
gain strength with American support at a time when
the Russians were suffering military defeats. He
was surprised by the rapid improvement of the Soviet
situation. In 1942, he made overtures to Stalin,
offering to place Sinkiang again under Russian
"protection."[60] Stalin was still incensed by Sheng's
earlier betrayal, and he forwarded records of their
communications to the Chungking government.

In June 1943, the Nationalists began to move
their troops into the province. They also attempted
to improve their relations with Russia in order to
buttress their war efforts against Japan. Stalin
demanded Sheng's removal from power. The *tu-pan* was
aware of his unenviable position, and he flew to
Chungking in the fall to discuss his political future
with Chiang Kai-shek.[61] He volunteered to leave
Sinkiang in return for a significant appointment elsewhere in China. To increase his bargaining
strength with Chiang, he charged the Nationalist
officials in Urumchi with conspiring against the provincial government. In April 1944, he placed a number
of them in prison. In the following month, Chiang
proposed to transfer him to Kansu, but Sheng refused
to compromise.[62]

In June, Henry A. Wallace, vice president of
the United States, arrived in Urumchi via Moscow. After staying for two days, he traveled to Chungking
to meet with Chiang. He told the Nationalist leader
that Sheng was an obstacle to the betterment of
Sino-Soviet relations.[63] In August, Sheng arrested
additional Kuomintang officials, including Lin Chi-
yung and Lin Pai-ya. He wanted desperately to remain
in power.[64] Chiang sent Chu Shao-liang back to
Urumchi with the offer to appoint Sheng minister of
agriculture and forestry. In September, Sheng
left for Chungking, thus ending his turbulent rule in
Sinkiang.

Sheng's departure did not herald an epoch of
strong central control in the province. A Kazakh rebellion had broken out along the Outer Mongolian
border in the winter of 1943-1944. In November 1944,
anti-Chinese hostilities exploded into a major

revolt of the ethnic groups against the new provincial administration. Racial problems in Sinkiang gave the Russians a fresh opportunity "to fish in troubled waters."[65] Political integration as a government objective remained as elusive in the post-1944 years as it had been during Sheng's regime.

CONCLUSION

Separated by geographical barriers, Sinkiang has always been isolated from the rest of China. It is inhabited by a variety of races, with the Chinese constituting to only 6 percent of the population. Racial antagonism against the ruling minority was common during the republican era, and the Chinese officials aggravated the problem by assuming an arrogant attitude of superiority. While united by their hatred of the Chinese, the ethnic groups were divided by jealousies and rivalries. Political integration became almost impossible as a result.

Yang Tseng-hsin, Chin Shu-jen, and Sheng Shih-ts'ai served as provincial governors in 1911-1944. None was a native of Sinkiang; they were only interested in their own political aggrandizement. They adopted the policy of "divide and rule," aimed at encouraging racial animosity among the non-Chinese peoples. Sheng's professed concern for the ethnic groups was too much motivated by self-interest to generate any amicable relations among the races. Meanwhile, the governors took advantage of the weakness of the central government in China and they maintained their regional independence at the sacrifice of national integration.

Sheng was a "typical warlord."[66] Despite his progressive beliefs, his rule in Sinkiang was guided primarily by political opportunism. He entertained a contemptuously low estimate of the central government's ability to interfere in provincial affairs. When he was confronted by the threats of internal rebellions and imperialist exploitation, he sought assistance from the Russians instead of from the Nationalists. He flirted with Soviet and Chinese Communists, and he endeavored to attract the support of the subject peoples by initiating a superficially enlightened racial policy. He played the part of a juggler, trying to keep several balls in the air at the same time. With regional separatism dominating the politics of Sinkiang, he impeded the process of national integration in China. He further violated Chinese sovereignty by yielding to Soviet pressures.

The weaknesses of Sheng's leadership could not, however, fully account for the failure of national integration. Because of their political ineptitude, Chiang Kai-shek and his Kuomintang comrades were at least partially responsible for the development of regional independence in Sinkiang during 1933-1944.

Fortified by their nominal success in national reunification, the Kuomintang leaders were eager to consolidate their political gains in the north-western province. Yet, they underestimated the limitations of their authority, and they failed to propose a positive program of provincial reconstruction after Chin Shu-jen's fall from power. More-over, they alienated the new Sinkiang officials by playing one faction against another, thus hurting their chance to bring the province under central con-trol. The estrangement also furnished the Russians with an opportunity to expand their influence over this border region.

Sheng's pledge of allegiance to Chungking in 1942 could have resulted in the resurrection of central authority in Sinkiang. Nevertheless, the Nationalists were too preoccupied with appeasing the Soviets to try to understand the complexities of provincial problems. They permitted Sheng to use their appointees in Urumchi as pawns for political bar-gaining. When Sheng extracted a cabinet appointment from Chungking, his removal seemed to demonstrate more the weakness of central power than its strength. In spite of the Chinese policy of appeasement, the Russians were waiting to reassert their influence in the midst of racial hostilities. In the end, the Kuomintang takeover of Sinkiang did not enhance the prestige of the central government in the province; nor did it halt the erosion of Chinese sovereignty in an era of Soviet penetration.

NOTES

1. Allen S. Whiting and Sheng Shih-ts'ai, *Sin-kiang: Pawn or Pivot?* (East Lansing: Michigan State University Press, 1958), Pt. I, p. 22. Part I of this book, "Soviet Strategy in Sinkiang: 1933-49," is an analysis of the topic by Whiting, while Part II, "Red Failure in Sinkiang," is a translation of Sheng's autobiography; hereafter cited respectively as SSIS and RFIS.

2. RFIS, pp. 201, 207.

3. Owen Lattimore, *Manchuria: Cradle of Conflict* (New York: Macmillan Co., 1932). The first half of this chapter is based partly on my article, "The Road

to Power: Sheng Shih-ts'ai's Early Years in Sinkiang,
1933-1934," *Journal of Oriental Studies*, Vol. VII,
No. 2 (July 1969), pp. 224-60. Acknowledgments are
due to Hong Kong University Press, which publishes the
journal, for permission to reproduce some sections
of the article in this chapter.
    4. SSIS, p. 13.
    5. Tu Chung-yüan, *Sheng Shih-ts'ai yü hsin Hsin-
chiang* ∠ Sheng Shih-ts'ai and the New Sinkiang ∠
(Hankow, 1938), p. 32.
    6. SSIS, p. 15. See also Sheng's letter to
Chiang Kai-shek, July 7, 1942, in *Su-lien tui Hsin-
chiang te ching-chi ch'in-lüeh* ∠ Soviet Economic
Aggression Against Sinkiang ∠ (Taipei, 1950), p. 55.
    7. For reasons for Sheng's failure to earn an
important appointment in Nanking, see SSIS, p. 14; and
Owen Lattimore, *Pivot of Asia: Sinkiang and the Inner
Asian Frontiers of China and Russia* (Boston: Little,
Brown & Co., 1950), p. 70.
    8. O. Edmund Clubb, *China and Russia: The "Great
Game"* (New York: Columbia University Press, 1971),
p. 281.
    9. Kuang Lu, *Kuang Lu hui-i-lu* ∠ The Memoirs of
Kuang Lu ∠ (Taipei, 1964), pp. 126-30. At the same
time, Sheng received offers of appointment from Yünnan
and Szechwan. He chose to go to Sinkiang. See Chan,
"The Road to Power," p. 232.
    10. Chang Ta-chün, *Szu-shih-nien tung-luan Hsin-
chiang* ∠ Forty Years of Turmoil in Sinkiang ∠
(Hong Kong, 1956), pp. 28-29; and Chan, "The Road
to Power," pp. 234-35.
    11. Sven Hedin, *The Flight of the Big Horse: The
Trail of War in Central Asia* (New York: E. P. Dutton &
Co., Inc., 1936), pp. 223-24.
    12. When Japan invaded Manchuria, these soldiers
were driven out of their homeland. They finally
reached Sinkiang after being interned in Russia. Eric
Teichman describes them as "a strong body," and Owen
Lattimore suggests that the Soviet government had
sent them to Sinkiang to strengthen the provincial
military capability. See Teichman, *Journey to Turkistan* (London: Hodder & Stoughton, Ltd., 1937), pp.
20, 187; and Lattimore, *Pivot*, p. 69. Cf. SSIS, p.
16.
    13. Hedin, *Flight*, p. 8. Sheng later accused
Soviet Russia of instigating the coup. See
Sheng, "Hsin-chiang shih-nien hui-i-lu" ∠ Recollec-
tions of Ten Years in Sinkiang ∠, *Tzu-li wan-pao*
∠ Independent Evening Press ∠ (Taipei), October 6,
1952.
    14. RFIS, pp. 159-60. Sun Fu-k'un, a detractor,

146

charges that Sheng had offered great profit to the
White Russians in return for their overthrow of
Chin's government. See Sun, *Su-lien lüeh-to Hsin-
chiang chi-shih* / A Record of Soviet Plundering
of Sinkiang/ (Hong Kong, 1952), Vol. I, p. 8.
   15.   Sheng described Sinkiang, with a population of
fourteen different nationalities, as "a living eth-
nological museum." See RFIS, p. 156.
   16.   Sheng had allegedly surrounded the assembly
hall with soldiers brought back from Uraba and
engineered the election in order to produce the
desired result. See Chang, *Sze-shih-nien*, p. 40.
   17.   Wu Ai-ch'en, *Hsin-chiang chi-yu* / An Account
of Travel in Sinkiang/ (Shanghai, 1936), p. 78;
and Aitchen K. Wu, *Turkistan Tumult* (London: Methuen
& Co., Ltd., 1939), pp. 106-107, 110.
   18.   Wu, *Turkistan*, p. 138.
   19.   *Ibid.*, p. 156. According to David J. Dallin,
Nanking was dissatisfied with the pro-Soviet in-
clinations of the Sinkiang government and was prepared
to recognize Ma's control of the province. See
Dallin, *Soviet Russia and the Far East* (New Haven:
Yale University Press, 1948), p. 97.
   20.   T'ang Chi-ts'ung, "Lieh-ch'iang tsai Hsin-
chiang te yin-mou" / Conspiracies of Foreign Powers in
Sinkiang/, *Pien-shih yen-chiu* / Studies of Frontier
Affairs_/, Vol. III, No. 2 (January 1936), p. 28;
and *China Weekly Review*, February 2, 1935, p. 327.
   21.   RFIS, pp. 160, 192-93; and Lattimore, *Pivot*,
p. 72. Max Beloff, however, suggests that Ma was "not
a likely Japanese puppet." See Beloff, *The Foreign
Policy of Soviet Russia, 1929-1941* (London: Oxford
University Press, 1947), Vol. I, p. 237.
   22.   For details of the mission, see Wu, *Turkistan*,
pp. 148-69. The author was a member of the mission.
   23.   Teichman, *Journey*, pp. 104-105; Owen Lattimore, *Inner Asian Frontiers of China* (New York:
American Geographical Society, 1940), p. 201, *n.* 82;
and Edgar Snow, *The Battle for Asia* (New York: Random
House, Inc., 1941), p. 306.
   24.   Lattimore, *Pivot*, p. 52.
   25.   Wu, *Turkistan*, p. 171.
   26.   RFIS, p. 161. Sheng was "a man possessed of
a spy mania." His "capacity for suspicion was
boundless." According to Wendell L. Willkie, who
visited Sinkiang in 1942, the stories Sheng told him
"of murder, intrigue, espionage, and counterespionage
sounded like a dime thriller." See SSIS, p. xi;
Clubb, *China*, p. 285; and Wendell L. Willkie, *One
World* (New York: Simon & Schuster, 1943), p. 114.
   27.   Peter Fleming, *News from Tartary: A Journey*

from Peking to Kashmir (London: Jonathan Cape, 1936),
p. 250. Cf. Gaimushō (Japan), *Shinkyō chōshō*
/ Records on Sinkiang / (Tokyo, 1935), p. 32. This is
a report on the province written by the Japanese
foreign ministry in 1934.

28. Lo was accompanied by a secretary, Feng Yu-
chen, who recorded the visit in a book, *Hsin-chiang
shih-chia chi* / An Account of the Sinkiang Investigation / (Shanghai, 1934). See particularly pp. 119-
202.

29. Sheng Shih-ts'ai, "Mu-pien so-i: Chien-t'ao
P'eng Chao-hsien hsien-sheng shih-ta tso-wu" / Random
Notes on My Service in the Frontier: An Examination
of Mr. P'eng Chao-hsien's Ten Great Mistakes /, in
P'eng Chao-hsien, Sheng Shih-ts'ai, and Chang Ta-chün,
Wu-shih-nien cheng-hai feng-yün: T'ien-shan nan-pei
/ Fifty Years of Political Turmoil: South and North of
T'ien-shan / (Taipei, 1967), pp. 78-79.

30. RFIS, p. 163.

31. Sven Hedin reports that Apresoff was the only
man "who was more powerful than Sheng" in Urumchi.
See Hedin, *The Silk Road* (New York: E. P. Dutton &
Co., Inc., 1938), p. 166. See also Clubb, *China*, pp.
289-90, on Pogodin's organization of secret police.

32. RFIS, p. 163.

33. *Ibid.*

34. In August 1933, *Pravda* complained about the
"imperialistic infiltration into Sinkiang." A Soviet
diplomat also warned China of the danger of permitting
the province "to become a second Manchuria." See
SSIS, pp. 22, 24; and Theodore White, "Report from
Turkestan," *Time* (October 25, 1943), p. 27.

35. Alexander Barmine, *One Who Survived: The Life
of a Russian under the Soviets* (New York: G. P.
Putnam's Sons, 1945), p. 231.

36. RFIS, p. 164.

37. Quoted from Sheng's telegram to Nanking, July
16, 1934, in *Su-lien tui Hsin-chiang*, p. 32.

38. RFIS, p. 164.

39. See Sheng's letter to Chiang, July 7, 1942, in
Su-lien tui Hsin-chiang, p. 58.

40. RFIS, p. 161.

41. Nelson Johnson described Li as "a figurehead."
See United States Minister in China to Secretary of
State, June 17, 1935, in *Foreign Relations of the
United States: Diplomatic Papers, 1935* (Washington,
D.C.: Government Printing Office, 1953), Vol. III
(Far East), p. 258.

42. F. Gilbert Chan, "Sinkiang under Sheng Shih-
ts'ai, 1933-1944" (M.A. thesis, University of Hong
Kong, 1965), pp. 153-54.

148

43. Sheng Shih-ts'ai, *Cheng-fu mu-ch'ien chu-yao jen-wu* / The Present Major Task of the Government / (Urumchi, 1941), Vol. I, pp. 30-31.

44. RFIS, p. 177.

45. Johnson to Secretary of State, June 17, 1935, in *Foreign Relations, 1935*, p. 259.

46. SSIS, p. 35.

47. Report by Military Attaché in China, January 30, 1935, in *Foreign Relations, 1935*, p. 31.

48. *Su-lien tui Hsin-chiang*, p. 33.

49. For details of the negotiations, see *ibid.*, pp. 32-38.

50. *Contemporary Japan*, Vol. III, No. 4 (March 1935), p. 704; United States Ambassador to Secretary of State, January 8, 1935, in *Foreign Relations, 1935*, p. 7; *China Weekly Review*, February 2, 1935, p. 326; and SSIS, p. 39.

51. SSIS, p. 50.

52. Mao's letter to Sheng, February 4, 1942, in RFIS, p. 232.

53. *Ibid.*, pp. 191, 207.

54. *Ibid.*, pp. 210-18. Tu's confession, dated June 20, 1942, is included in pp. 291-92.

55. *Ibid.*, p. 222.

56. *Ibid.*, p. 226.

57. For a confession of Shih-ch'i's wife, Ch'en Hsiu-ying, see *ibid.*, pp. 293-301. The assassination had "frightened" Shih-ts'ai, who was "afraid for his own life." See Counselor of Embassy in China to United States Ambassador in Chungking, September 9, 1942, in *Foreign Relations of the United States: Diplomatic Papers, 1942 -- China* (Washington, D.C.: Government Printing Office, 1956), p. 237.

58. Sheng's letter to Chiang Kai-shek, November 24, 1946, in *Su-lien tui Hsin-chiang*, p. 70.

59. *Hsin-chiang jih-pao* / Sinkiang Daily / (Urumchi), April 15, 1943; June 18, 1943; and April 14, 1944.

60. John Davies to Administrative Assistant to President Roosevelt, August 6, 1942, in *Foreign Relations, 1942*, p. 227.

61. Sheng to Chiang, November 24, 1946, in *Su-lien tui Hsin-chiang*, p. 71.

62. Kuang Lu *et al.*, *Sheng Shih-ts'ai tsen-yang t'ung-chih Hsin-chiang* / How Sheng Shih-ts'ai Governed Sinkiang / (Taipei, 1954), p. 49; United States Consul at Urumchi to Secretary of State, October 10, 1944, in *Foreign Relations of the United States: Diplomatic Papers, 1944* (Washington, D.C.: Government Printing Office, 1967), Vol. VI (China), p. 816.

63. *New York Times*, August 30, 1944.

64. Kuang *et al.*, *Sheng Shih-ts'ai*, pp. 66-71.
65. SSIS, p. 98.
66. Vice President Wallace to President Roosevelt,
July 10, 1944, in *Foreign Relations, 1944*, p. 240.

6

The Kuomintang and Rural China in the War of Resistance, 1937–1945

Robert A. Kapp

The eight-year War of Resistance, 1937–1945, witnessed the catastrophic decline of the Kuomintang's fortunes and the striking improvement of the Chinese Communist Party's prospects. Yet the causal role of the war in the collapse of the KMT regime and the Communist victory is problematical. With regard to the CCP's success, powerful arguments hold that the Japanese invasion, with its accompanying social abuses, gave rise to new forces of "peasant nationalism," which the Chinese Communist Party was able to harness to its own ends.[1] As for the KMT, it is widely assumed that the wartime dislocations forced upon the Nanking regime -- the loss of prewar revenue bases, the economic and psychological distress caused by long exile in the underdeveloped interior, the rampant inflation caused by material shortages and the hopeless inadequacy of government revenues -- produced pressures with which the Nationalists could not cope and thus dealt a fatal blow to a regime which otherwise might have been able to regain its balance after the war.[2]

On the other hand, scholars have also argued that the Japanese invasion and the long War of Resistance did not in and of themselves kill the KMT or enthrone

The author gratefully acknowledges the support of a research grant from the Joint Committee on Contemporary China of the American Council of Learned Societies and the Social Science Research Council, and the support of the University of Washington Graduate School. In this chapter, KMT and CCP are often used respectively as abbreviations for Kuomintang and Chinese Communist Party.

the CCP. Now-familiar assertions by Mark Selden, Donald Gillin, and others hold that the primary cause of CCP successes in North China was the party's adoption of social programs and organizational methods which permitted it to mobilize the rural populace and carry out its war effort with the aid of the active commitment of the peasantry.[3] And in considering the fate of the Kuomintang regime, whose collapse between 1945 and 1949 took practically everyone -- including the Chinese Communists -- by surprise, Lloyd Eastman and others have argued that the wartime trauma only exacerbated cultural and structural traits that had by 1937 long stifled the revolutionary impulse on which the KMT had ridden to a semblance of national power in 1927.[4] That is, while admitting the disastrous effects of wartime inflation, for example, these writers argue that the KMT already carried within itself the elements of its own destruction, which the war merely brought into sharper relief.

Just as the question of whether the KMT "failed" or the CCP "triumphed" is an oversimplification, there is no single answer to the question of the war's impact on the Chinese political order. Yet the historical outcome is striking: the CCP entered the war period with a remnant of its pre-1935 strength and with its political leaders isolated in a desolate and impoverished outpost of the far Northwest. The Kuomintang regime, even when forced from the Yangtze Valley where it had enjoyed most of its prewar power, retired to a wealthy province, Szechwan, and possessed an enormous army even after suffering brutal losses early in the war. At war's end, the CCP emerged generally united and vigorous, with powerful popular support in wide areas of North China and enhanced organizational strength in the border regions and base areas where it had operated during the conflict. The Kuomintang returned to its old haunts along the China coast and the lower Yangtze disorganized and corrupted, psychologically exhausted, and (it soon turned out) incapable of mastering the tasks of postwar recovery. The CCP's survival in conditions even more stringent than those of the KMT prompts the question: what was the vital difference between the two parties that enabled one to adapt and grow in desperate wartime conditions while the other stagnated and declined?

Such a question, in the case of the KMT, leads toward the arguments that the war itself did not bring about the Nationalist regime's collapse, and that the KMT's fate might have been sealed even before the war began. Yet these arguments would sound unconvincing to many of the people who made the difficult trek to the interior and lived in and around Chungking for eight years amid Japanese bombs, economic collapse, and the phantasm of wartime Nationalist politics, only to return to the chaos of postwar disintegration. Is it only political cant and self-delusion that sometimes seem to make of the prewar "Nanking decade" a period of golden age, spoiled not by its own internal maladies but by events over which the KMT had no control? What does the eight-year war period, during which the Nationalist regime held out in the "great rear area," tell us about the reasons for the catastrophic fate of the Kuomintang?

One answer suggests that the wartime emergency placed the Kuomintang and its national government in touch with Chinese society in ways that it had never been in the Nanking decade. Specifically, the flight to the Southwest left the KMT unprecedentedly dependent on the resources of China's preindustrial economy and society. The peculiarities of the encounter between the Nationalist regime and its main host province, Szechwan, were of course partially conditioned by wartime circumstances. But they were primarily determined by the enduring qualities of the KMT party-state on the one hand and of Szechwanese society on the other; the military exigencies that brought the two sides face-to-face were dire, but tangential. What we learn from the KMT in exile relates to the regime's longer-term interaction with rural China, where the great masses of the population lived and died. An examination of the long KMT sojourn in Szechwan may not prove why the KMT "lost" in 1949, or why the Communists "won," but it should clarify the perspectives from which the transfer of national power in mid-twentieth century China can be viewed. Such an analysis may also be suggestive of the difficulties that the KMT would have faced even if, somehow, it had been able to govern China unchallenged by the Chinese Communists.

The KMT's sudden immersion in the life of the rural interior, far from the great treaty ports and industrial-financial concentrations of the lower Yangtze, blocked the mainstream of prewar Kuomintang spatial and economic strategy. After the establishment of the national government in 1928, the KMT in effect turned its back on the Chinese rural economy; the decision to abstain from any national claim on the land tax and to leave it instead to the provincial governments was realistic, since

warlord governors could do what they liked with the
revenue anyway, but it was also symbolic of the
Nationalist orientation to the big cities and the
modern economic sector, where revenues could
more easily be collected and economic activities could
more easily be dominated. The renewed interest of
the KMT in rural affairs, a response to the Chinese
Communists' rural progress during the early 1930s,
represented not a KMT commitment to the economic and
social development of the countryside -- or even
a KMT policy of reliance on the resources of the rural
sector -- but merely an attempt at tighter rural
administration and control in the interests of anti-
Communism.[5]

It was true, of course, that economic changes in
the late nineteenth and early twentieth centuries
lay behind the Kuomintang's prewar economic approach.
Long before the KMT established its regime, the
land tax had ceased to constitute the largest single
item in central government tax revenues, overshadowed
by salt and customs taxes upon which the Kuomintang
was later to rely. The diminishing significance
of land tax revenues was clear even before the fall of
the Ch'ing dynasty; new forms of economic activity
and sources of revenue signaled the onset of modern
economic changes in China even while established
political institutions remained formally intact.[6]

But the precedent of shifts in the late-Ch'ing
tax mixture is as misleading as it is explanatory.
For there seems to have existed in late Ch'ing an assumption about the interrelatedness of the state
and the rural social economy that was lost by the time
of the Nanking regime's birth. Until virtually the
end of its days, the Ch'ing state assumed the
inseparability of rural social control and rural
revenue extraction and never willingly gave up on
either. The KMT party-state, in many ways a
self-consciously modern and modernizing regime, began
after 1927 without the assumption that the rural
sector was central to its existence. When in the
early 1930s the KMT refocused its attention on rural
control, in the "Bandit-Suppression Zones," it
implicitly accepted the separateness of rural administration from the acquisition of rurally generated
revenues. It was as though, in the onrushing tide
of modernity that swept over China in the early
twentieth century, the significance of China's agrarian society was obscured because modernity could not
be imagined to originate or reside there. By the time
the CCP began to experiment with opposing assumptions -- and it did so slowly and painfully, with many

failures and false starts -- the KMT was locked into
a set of priorities and methods of operation that
precluded any systematic, intensive effort to weld
rural China into its economic and social, as well as
political, domain.

That is precisely what the wartime flight to
the interior and the establishment of the national
government in Chungking demanded that the Nationalists
do. If the KMT had responded effectively to the
challenges of governing the rural interior under difficult circumstances, not only would it have
emerged from the war in better condition inter-
nally and *vis à vis* the CCP; it also would have gained,
as the CCP did elsewhere, invaluable experience in
legitimatizing its power and governing China.

THE KUOMINTANG EXPERIENCE IN SZECHWAN

Once the battle lines in the War of Resistance
stabilized after the fall of Canton and Wuhan in 1938,
the national government found itself in partial or
complete control (in the sense that neither Chinese
Communist nor Japanese governments rivaled the
Nationalist claim to authority) of a crescent of
provinces from Kwangtung and Hunan through Kweichow,
Yünnan, Szechwan and into the Northwest. "Free
China" contained approximately 250 million people.[7]
Chungking had been proclaimed the national capital in
1937, and the final withdrawal of vital government
agencies and personnel from Wuhan in October 1938
completed the transfer of the political power center
to the deep interior. On the eve of Wuhan's fall,
the remaining industrial plants that had been
transported from the lower Yangtze, plus additional
equipment originally based in Wuhan, were laboriously
transported upriver to Chungking and its environs,
effectively completing the heroic movement of
mechanized production facilities into a region of
China that had known practically none before.[8]

Of the provinces left to the Kuomintang after the
great retreat, Szechwan was unquestionably the most
important. As long as the regime sought to retain
substantially the same form and style as it had before
the war -- with complex bureaucratic structures and
urban lifestyles -- Szechwan was indispensable.
It was, for one thing, impregnable. Although Chungking grew panicky when Ichang fell in 1940 and
again when Japanese armies advanced into Kweichow
in late 1944, Szechwan was never lost. Throughout the
war, the national government and Kuomintang depended
much more heavily on that province than on any oth-

er. Greater government attention was paid to political and economic organization in Szechwan, as well as to the extraction of the province's indispensable revenues, than anywhere else in the unoccupied interior. Indeed, Szechwan's potential wartime importance had been discerned in advance; Chiang Kaishek had begun preparations for an emergency withdrawal to Szechwan several years before the war. The retreat was foreseen if not fully planned.

What was less clear in advance was what the KMT and government would find there. The characteristics of the Szechwan environment that greeted the Nationalists must be treated lightly for want of space. The province was then, as it is today, the most populous in China; in the late 1930s, around 50 million people lived in Szechwan. This great population bespoke the richness of Szechwan's agriculture, long renowned for its productivity and for the endless variety of its crops.[9] Such wealth in turn contributed to a tradition of independence and to an economic self-sufficiency qualified in the twentieth century only by shortages of indigenous cotton and of modern manufactured goods from the coast and overseas. Szechwanese independence, sometimes shading off into separatism, also expressed the physiographical facts of life; access to the province from other parts of China proper was difficult, whether via the turbulent and easily defended Yangtze Gorges or by way of mountain paths unsuited to auto traffic. Only in the year preceding the outbreak of full-scale war with Japan did the first interprovincial auto roads begin to link Szechwan with the outside world.[10] Within the province, the modern economic sector -- transportation, raw materials extraction, manufacturing -- remained primitive, though Szechwan compared favorably with neighboring unoccupied provinces like Kweichow and Yünnan.[11] Even with the addition of more than 100,000 tons of industrial equipment hauled into Szechwan during the first eighteen months of the war, a Japanese observer noted, the entire capitalization of the industrial facilities around Chungking (where nearly all of Szechwan's industry was concentrated) barely equaled that of a single large Japanese plant in Manchuria.[12]

The Nationalists entering Szechwan also encountered a world of topographical and socioeconomic variety. Much of the population and agricultural production of Szechwan was concentrated in a core area, roughly coterminous with the Red Basin, which embraced the immensely fertile Chengtu Plain and the navigable sections of Szechwan's major Yangtze

tributaries, the Min, T'o, Fou, Chialing, and Chü
rivers. But large areas of the province were more
mountainous, less productive of staple crops,
less densely populated, and less culturally developed.[13] In the far southeast and along the border with Yünnan and Sikang, non-Chinese populations
predominated, often beyond the reach of Chinese
administrators. Along the province's northeastern
border with Hupei and Shensi lay remote and impoverished counties, where the White Lotus Rebellion
had flourished a century and a half before, and where
the Chinese Communists had made inroads for several
years in the early 1930s. In short, the lion's
share of Szechwan's wealth was to be found in only a
portion of the province's territory; in the large
peripheral zone, the balance between the immediate
costs and benefits of government control was problematical.

Most important, the refugee regime found when it
reached Szechwan an intricately ramified network of
indigenous elites and economic activities to which
it was at the outset utterly external. After the
Ch'ing collapse and the removal of Szechwan from the
routinized intervention of bureaucratic outsiders,
these structures of power had developed with little
interference from beyond Szechwan's borders. The KMT
thus entered a discrete universe of associations,
leagues, and magnates within which the economic and
social life of the province had been defined for
many years. In 1938, two organizations conspicuously
absent from this universe were the CCP and the
Kuomintang.

Szechwan after the collapse of Ch'ing authority
had passed through twenty-five years of political
disintegration, militarization, warlordism, and social
insecurity.[14] The certainties once represented by
the twin pillars of imperial social control --
formal government institutions and the orthodox local
elites who supported those institutions -- had faded
as the traditional examination system receded into
history and the restraining influence of imperial
moralism waned. Instead, amid the generalized insecurity, other less readily defined groups gained
and held de facto power in city and countryside alike.
In particular, the Ko-lao-hui (Elder Brother Society), a semisecret organization of broad social
inclusiveness, emerged as a kind of surrogate government with both protective and entrepreneurial functions throughout much of Szechwan. Already in
1911, the Ko-lao-hui had organized the armed,
guerrilla-like units of the "Railway Protection Army,"

which had put Szechwan beyond the control of the
faltering imperial government.[15]   A quarter of a century later, when the Nationalists arrived in
Szechwan, they confronted in the Ko-lao-hui a loose
but powerful and ubiquitous network whose activities
permeated the everyday economic life of much of
the province and whose millions of members owed no
higher allegiance.[16]

The Nationalists also encountered a militarized
province, whose armies in the 1930s were by far
the largest of any province in China and whose local
militia forces were estimated at an additional half
million men.[17]   Thus the Nationalists had to deal with
both the well-known provincial warlords, one or two
of whom commanded as many as a hundred thousand
soldiers, and with the local powerholders who could
raise armed units in defense either of principle
or of vested interests. Beyond the provincial warlord units and the ubiquitous militia, local bandits
-- armed predators sometimes operating in small
bands of ten or twenty, and sometimes in great forces
of several thousand which could attack and capture
county capitals or put whole counties off limits to
government authority -- were active in most of
Szechwan. The lines between these entrenched groups
-- militarists, local militia chieftains, bandit
leaders, and of course the Ko-lao-hui -- are not clear
now and were not clear then. What matters is that
when the national government and the Kuomintang made
Szechwan their wartime base, the province lay in
the hands of elaborate and interpenetrating networks
of what, in an earlier era when black was black and
white was white, would have been called "hetero-
dox" organizations: secret societies, quasi-independent
militarist establishments great and small, and bandit
gangs. The pervasiveness and complexity of these
groupings, and the fullness of their penetration of
the economic and social life of the province, may well
be attributed to the very factor which made Szechwan
so attractive to the Nationalists in the first
place: the province's wealth.

The slogan employed by the Nationalists in unoccupied China -- *K'ang-chan chien-kuo* (War of
Resistance and National Reconstruction) -- was both
noble and unexceptionable: the government would fight
Japanese aggression while building and developing
that part of the nation which it still retained. The
goal was not merely rhetorical, at least in the early days of the war, before the lifelines to the
outside world were cut off and before Pearl Harbor
left the outcome of the Asian conflict in others'

hands. But from the start the flight to the interior posed urgent new problems. The Chinese armies, decimated by the battles of the lower Yangtze, required endless manpower replenishment and supplies. The refugee government, with its tens of thousands of uprooted officials and their dependents, as well as immigrant universities and other refugee groups, congregated in Chungking and Chengtu, where shortages of housing and manufactured goods[18] arose at once; the threat of food shortages in the refugee centers lay just over the horizon. Thus from the first instant the KMT regime had to deal with pressing problems of supply. With the passage of time, "National Reconstruction" became an ever more hollow rhetorical device. But whatever the reality of military stalemate and torpor along the front lines may have been, "War of Resistance" in Szechwan never lost its currency, for the war was the justification for the government's efforts to dominate Szechwan and extract the province's wealth for its own uses.

The interaction of Kuomintang authorities and Szechwanese society was complex and multifaceted. I will examine three problems central to the regime's encounter with Szechwanese rural society; the restructuring of local government, the acquisition of grain, and the securing of military and labor manpower. These three endeavors, and particularly the last two, were the real points of contact at which the Nationalists came face to face with indigenous customs and indigenous structures of power in rural Szechwan.

In Szechwan, one of the national authority's first tasks was to dominate the provincial government, long controlled by Szechwan's powerful native militarists. This was a delicate matter. The regime had managed to avoid a military showdown with Szechwan's most powerful general, Liu Hsiang, in June 1937, and Liu died in Wuhan in January of the following year. But Liu's former leading subordinates remained jealous of their prerogatives and uneasy about the sudden presence of the downriver authorities, as did other provincial militarists who had once been Liu's major rivals. The central government managed to dispatch some of the Szechwanese armies to the East China front early in the war, where they suffered staggering casualties, but the situation in the province remained awkward. After Liu Hsiang's death, Chiang Kai-shek named a long-time Kuomintang official, Chang Ch'ün, to the provincial governorship. Though Chang was born in Szechwan, he was nonetheless an outsider, whose career had been made in Japan and in

downriver KMT politics. The remaining major militarists protested; Chang's appointment was delayed,
then rescinded. Instead, in April 1938, Wang
Tsan-hsü, one of the Liu Hsiang coterie, was made
governor. A year and one-half later, native
militarist opposition to Wang led to his dismissal,
and Chiang Kai-shek himself assumed the title, leaving
the daily duties of the job to Ho Kuo-kuang, a faith-
ful supporter who had old ties to the Liu Hsiang
clique. Only in November 1940 did Chiang succeed in
placing Chang Ch'ün, his original appointee, in the
position. Chang remained governor of Szechwan for the
rest of the war, but three of Szechwan's most powerful prewar generals, Liu Wen-hui (Liu Hsiang's
uncle and former antagonist), Teng Hsi-hou (another
of Liu Hsiang's major rivals) and P'an Wen-hua (one of
Liu Hsiang's ranking subordinates) maintained both
military forces and active political interests inside
Szechwan. Liu Wen-hui remained untouched in Sikang
west of the Chengtu Plain, which became a separate
province in 1939, and which he ruled until 1949
in feudal isolation.[19]

Despite numerous war scares and rumors of provincial army uprisings against the outsiders, the
national government managed to avoid out-and-out
conflict with disgruntled Szechwanese militarists during the war. By 1940, the provincial government at
Chengtu was firmly in central government hands,
the presence in its upper ranks of numerous influential Szechwanese bureaucrats notwithstanding. Perhaps more in Szechwan than anywhere else in unoccupied
China, and certainly more than in neighboring Yünnan,
where the warlord Lung Yün jealously guarded his
prerogatives until very late in the war, provincial
government in Szechwan became an instrument of central
government power after 1940.[20]

But provincial-level government was inherently
a stepchild, a middle-rank agency whose powers
were many layers removed from the populace of Szechwan.
No amount of central government domination of the
bureaus and offices in Chengtu could provide the local
stability and responsiveness that was so plainly
lacking in Szechwan when the national government came
up the Yangtze. Furthermore, the regime found itself under pressure from quasi-democratic organizations, notably the People's Political Council, to
broaden the bases of popular participation in government and thus enhance its own legitimacy and strengthen
the war effort. Even before the personal problems
of the provincial government in Chengtu were ironed
out, therefore, the regime promulgated its plan

for the restructuring of local politics, the "Outline of County Government Organization," in September 1939. The system described in this document came quickly to be known as the "New Hsien System."[21]

The New Hsien System was neither a specifically wartime program nor unique to Szechwan. Implicit in the decline of centrally directed imperial administration and of the imperial institution itself during the late nineteenth and very early twentieth centuries was the gaping uncertainty as to how local social control was to be structured and political authority defined and exercised. The currency of new-fangled ideas about popular sovereignty and participatory government, and the growing familiarity with the nature of foreign political systems, gave birth around the turn of the twentieth century to the idea of "local self-government." Never precisely defined, the term nonetheless stood as a kind of amulet with which early twentieth century prognosticators could begin to construct a new, national political-administrative ideal to supplant that of the vanishing empire. Sun Yat-sen was one of those who envisioned the articulation of a national, constitutional government from the bottom up, building on the initial achievements of local self-government.[22] After 1927, the Kuomintang government adopted a series of plans prescribing the forms of county and subcounty government and laying out the channels along which various governmental powers were supposed to flow. Thus the New Hsien System of 1939 was not the first Kuomintang plan for county and subcounty administration, even though it differed in superficially important ways from its predecessors.[23]

Intellectual uncertainty over the structure of local power in the aftermath of imperial decline was accompanied by more tangible confusions. Though some lower-level administrative entities, such as provinces and counties, survived the fall of the Ch'ing dynasty, the Chinese administrative system lapsed after 1916 into disorganization and anarchy. This was only to be expected: how could orthodox and predictable definitions of governmental function and systems of power persist, when their historic ideological consensus had been undermined and the imperial institution that had certified the legitimacy of power had ceased to exist? The administrative anarchy of the republican period was one reflection of a much more thoroughgoing disorientation, a loss of common assumptions, which left the very definitions of local power unclear and the determinants of power unspec-

ified. The Nationalists thus faced similar problems
of administrative confusion in all the provinces
they sought to govern: unclear lines of authority
between levels of government whose officeholders themselves were uncertain as to what their duties were;
duplications of function at every administrative
level; independent vertical connections between functionally related agencies at different levels at
the expense of horizontal coordination. The litany
of complaints about local government has a familiar sameness to it: the district magistrate at once
chaired dozens of shadowy "committees" within the
county government and was subject to the orders of
dozens of higher agencies which were not in touch with
one another; subcounty government was burdened with
useless, do-nothing offices at unneeded levels of
administration; real power was not only fragmented
among uncoordinated agencies with formal titles but in
fact lay in the hands of powerful local figures
who were outside the grasp of the formal administrative process altogether; uncorrupted, effective
administrative personnel could not be found.

        This familiar list of woes, which can be found
in any number of sources produced in the 1920s,
1930s and 1940s,[24] rested on three venerable but sometimes incompatible assumptions. First, it was commonly assumed that a strong, modern China required a
new articulation of power between central government and society, so that the centralizing influences
of the government at the top could reach with
unprecedented directness and thoroughness to the
masses at the bottom. In other words, the necessity
for much greater local responsiveness to central
initiative was widely recognized. Second, there was
a widespread belief in the need for "local self-
government," that is, for local residents' participation in formal government and in the selection
of local officials. One expression of this impulse,
the concern for "the people's opinion," or "the
people's will" (*min-i*), informed the late Ch'ing plan
for county and provincial assemblies; it survived
in the up-and-down history of the assemblies during
the early republic and, at least rhetorically, in the
short-lived Provincial Federalist Movement of the
early 1920s. With the forces of local and provincial
self-determination vigorous and unfettered in the
early twentieth century, the impulse to participatory
local government at times ran counter to the concern for responsive, vertically controlled and
centrally directed administration.

        The third assumption underlying the pervasive

dissatisfaction with local government was that too
much centralization of power, even if it were somehow
possible, would result in governmental ineffectiveness, because local conditions varied so greatly.
All-embracing ukases from the center, in other words,
might not offend localistic sensibilities around
the country; they would also probably be useless, since they could not take adequate account of
the locally specific conditions in which they had
to be carried out.

The Kuomintang approach to local administration
before the war was at first lackadaisical. Early
Nanking policies on the reorganization of county and
subcounty government had little effect. The regime
left existing structures pretty much alone, particularly outside of the three or four lower Yangtze
provinces where it had some pretensions to real local
influence. Beginning in 1932, however, as the Kuomintang pursued its campaigns against the Chinese
Communists, new attention was paid to the problems of
local social control. As the regime turned more
seriously to the question, it moved in the direction
of a profoundly bureaucratic, managerial reorganization of local administration. Though the rhetoric
of moral improvement ran through the regime's
pronouncements on the subject in the mid-1930s, the
overwhelming emphasis in Kuomintang policy was on
prevention of local dissidence and on building clear,
vertical channels of administrative power. Thus
the cornerstone of KMT local policy in the "Bandit-
Suppression" period was the resurrected *pao-chia*
system, in which local inhabitants were grouped in
decimal units of mutual responsibility and sur-
veillance and, in principle, linked to county and
higher level authority.[25]

The retreat to the interior in 1937 and 1938,
however, raised several new considerations. With the
war against the Communists suspended, rural pacification and anti-Communist social controls lost their
salience, especially in the Southwest. The administrative anarchy of the southwestern heartland
demanded attention not so much because the Chungking
regime faced organized and ideologically potent social
rebellion but because the Kuomintang was so utterly
without established bases of power in the region
and so bereft of access to local society. Furthermore, the war made access to the wealth of local
society imperative, in ways that the Communist problem
had not. In short, the New Hsien System of 1939 was
heir to an evolving tradition of Chinese local administrative practice and to a decade of Kuomintang

policy in that arena, but it also reflected the peculiar wartime circumstance of the Nationalists' new
dependence on local and rural social resources.

The New Hsien System laid out the proposed structure of local administration and detailed the powers
of various agencies. It provided for *chia* and *pao*
at the lowest levels, for *hsiang* and *chen* (rural areas
defined in relation to their marketing centers) above
the *pao* and *chia*; for *ch'ü* or districts above the
hsiang and *chen* in populous counties, and for county
government itself. Among the features of the 1939
"Outline," whose prescriptions were very detailed,
were the provisions for elected assemblies at the *pao*
and *hsiang* levels, the proposed concentration of
power in the hands of the individuals who headed the
administrative units at each level, including county magistrates, and the emphasis on education and
local self-defense as major responsibilities of the
lowest levels of administration in the system.[26]

Proponents of the New Hsien System argued that it
would bring clarity and systematic regularity to the
chaos of local administration, simultaneously sim-
plifying the impenetrable maze of local structures and
providing formal administration with a flexibility
to meet local exigencies which had hitherto been
lacking. Establishment of low-level organs of popular
opinion (*min-i chi-kuan*) would liberate and develop
the people's commitment to self-government, while
training them in the necessary self-governmental arts.
Rationalization of the welter of local armed units,
and their incorporation into a responsive system
of governmental power reaching up to the national capital, would better provide for local security and
order.[27]

Critics of the system made telling points. The
New Hsien System was overwhelmingly bureaucratic; its
requirements of legions of trained personnel were
hopelessly unrealistic. One critic took as an example
a hypothetical Grade 2 county, i.e., a county of less
than maximum size and complexity. Assuming five
districts, 14 *hsiang* or *chen*, 138 *pao*, and 13,800
chia, the total number of administrators called for
according to the system was 11,000.[28] Another
observer went so far as to calculate the number of
personnel needed to staff the agencies of the New
Hsien System throughout Kuomintang territory and
reached a figure of 11,187,000. Needless to say,
there was no way to staff the new structure effectively, and no way to train the necessary personnel. As
long as the heads of the *pao* and *chia* remained il-
literate in great numbers, to take a single example,

the system could not function as planned.

Other observers pointed out the hollowness of the New Hsien System's democratic provisions. In particular, eligibility to vote or to serve in elective office within the system was confined to the small slice of the population who met the system's requirements of education or prior administrative service. Moreover, the process of creating organs of popular opinion at the several subcounty levels could not take place overnight; in the interim, the Outline of the New Hsien System provided that heads of local units at each level would continue to be appointed by the heads of the units one level above.[29]

The Kuomintang regime's administrative response to the wartime necessity of dealing more closely with local, rural society was thus predictably bureaucratic, inordinately complicated, and impracticable. Although Szechwan proceeded farther in the direction of formal compliance than most other provinces during the war, the erection of the complete edifice of subcounty administration proceeded haltingly. More important, even where the edifice was assembled, the results envisaged by the system -- tighter high-level control of local affairs, politicization of the populace in support of the regime and the war effort -- failed to materialize. Although the documentary evidence is limited, perhaps as a result of wartime censorship, there is good reason to believe that the ornate structure of administrative agencies concocted by the New Hsien System made very little difference in the exercise of local control and authority in Kuomintang China, including Szechwan.[30]

In fact, in Szechwan more powerful considerations compromised the New Hsien System from the start. For one thing, the government's need for the material and human resources of Szechwan was supremely urgent and could not wait until the New Hsien System was operating at full steam. For another, the indigenous structures of power and the people who dominated them were too firmly established to wither in the face of administrative pronouncements from Chungking.

Perhaps if the Nationalists had attempted to articulate a less bureaucratic relationship between themselves and the social communities they sought to govern, they might have managed to alter some of the structures of local power while securing vital wartime necessities from the countryside. Operating instead from the unquestioned assumption that better government depended on better bureaucracy, the Kuomintang proclaimed the bureaucratization of local control, and then looked to the cumbersome administrative

system to serve its immediate needs for material
sustenance and manpower. With effective administrative renovation beyond its grasp and the requirements of the wartime emergency unremitting, the regime
settled for compromise. The fiction of administrative regularity was maintained; *chia*, *pao*, and *hsiang*
units were formed. But the vital functions of local
control remained in the hands of those whom regular
administration was designed originally to circum-
vent, the elites who already exercised social power in
their communities.

The Kuomintang's compromises in the area of local
administration occurred in three ways. First, the
newly named local-level administrative agencies
of the New Hsien System -- *chia*, *pao*, and *hsiang*
organizations -- remained under the influence of those
who had commanded wealth and coercive power at comparable levels before the new system was announced.
Second, the national regime permitted, by neglect at
any rate, those local chiefs whom it relied on to
provide the vital rural resources to enrich themselves
with impunity in the process. Third, at higher
levels of administration, the government sought the
cooperation of powerful provincial leaders --
militarists, financiers, leaders of the Szechwan
gentry -- in mediating its relations with the provincial elites whose support was essential to the
regime's survival.[31]

The two most prominent instances of this process
of interaction and compromise were the Chungking
authorities' programs of grain acquisition and manpower conscription. These lay at the heart of
the Kuomintang's brush with Chinese rural society
during the War of Resistance.

The central government intervened in the
Szechwanese rural economy in numerous ways during the
war, for example by establishing government controls
on the transport and marketing of key export commodities like t'ung oil.[32] But its most extensive
venture into the agricultural economy was the program,
initiated in 1941, to nationalize the land tax and
collect it in kind instead of in money. This tax-in-
kind system, which was accompanied by a program of
compulsory grain sales (later, loans) to the government, aimed at providing the central authorities
with supplies of food with which to feed dependent
urban populations, provision the armies, and if possible retard the advance of the inflation which
already by 1941 was threatening to undo the regime.

Tax-in-kind and compulsory sales were Chungking's
response to a complex of deepening difficulties. By

1940, a food crisis loomed in the major cities, especially Chungking, Chengtu and Kunming, where the wartime refugees had concentrated. In 1938 and 1939, harvests in Southwest China had been good and food prices had increased relatively slowly, at least when compared with the prices of such largely imported commodities as industrial products and such nonfood necessities as fuel. But in the late summer of 1940, just as the harvest began to come in, grain prices shot upward in urban markets, causing panic buying and murmurs of social unrest. Bad war news, including the fall of Ichang just below the Yangtze Gorges in the spring of 1940, contributed to the pervasive sense of insecurity in Chungking and other cities, on which the Japanese continued to rain bombs.[33] But the most disturbing thing about the sudden explosion of foodgrain prices in late 1940 was the abundant evidence that the panic was man-made. Most observers were certain that the oddly timed price leaps were caused by the hoarding of Szechwanese landlords, who recognized the opportunities for self-enrichment offered by artificial scarcities.[34] Among the greatest hoarders was said to be the widow of Liu Hsiang. Another powerful hoarder was said to be P'an Wen-hua, one of Liu's former ranking subordinates, who, as vice commissioner of pacification for Szechwan and Sikang, remained with his armed forces in Szechwan through the war.[35]

The central government, its prewar revenues reduced by 80 percent, had already begun to look at the rural economy of the interior with an eye toward greater revenue. Many observers had noted that, as the value of the regime's currency declined, rural taxpayers whose obligations were calculated in monetary terms were enjoying lighter and lighter tax burdens.[36] Furthermore, the land tax itself did not belong to the central government but to the provincial governments, to whom it had been relegated by the Nationalists in 1928. Thus, to gain access to rural tax revenues, the regime had both to nationalize the land tax and collect it in grain instead of money. When Chungking announced both these policies in the fall of 1941, the government committed itself to the collection of indispensable revenues, not from a few relatively accessible economic nuclei, as had been the case before the war, but from millions of taxpaying rural households. Moreover, the uses to which the government intended to put tax grain -- supplying urban consumers and mitigating inflation -- injected the government into long-established and enormously intricate patterns of grain transport and marketing throughout Szechwan.

Although Chungking agreed to reimburse provincial governments for revenues lost in the nationalization of the land tax, the new program unquestionably strengthened the central government's growing domination of the Szechwan provincial government in Chengtu. Nevertheless, the key to implementation of the tax-in-kind and compulsory sales programs lay in the first instance in delicate compromises with unofficial provincial leadership as well as with Szechwanese representatives of the provincial administration. For example, cooperation had to be established in the first months of the program on the matter of the money-to-grain tax rate, which would determine the real amount of revenue extracted from the grain-holders. With the tax registers in Szechwan utterly out of date and disorganized, formally correct assessments of tax obligations were impossible.[37] The voluntary "land reporting" program and the cadastral surveys about which the regime periodically made pronouncements were barely underway and could not be completed as a prerequisite for the tax-in-kind. As late as 1941, the medium of payment in land taxation varied from locality to locality, and a variety of currencies persisted; what, for example, was to be the conversion rate between silver taels and silver yüan?[38] Even the annual provincial tax grain quota, which the central government initially proclaimed in unequivocal terms, turned out to be negotiable. The head of the newly created Food Ministry, Hsü K'an, was a Szechwanese with long-established connections to H. H. Kung. Hsü in turn relied on Lu Tso-fu, a provincial industrialist and a leading figure among the Szechwan gentry, in quiet negotiations with representatives of Szechwanese landlord interests. As a result, even before the tax-in-kind and compulsory sales programs began to function in Szechwan, the government's original quotas for Szechwan were lowered sharply.[39] The Food Ministry under Hsü and Lu embodied the Nationalists' approach to the immensely difficult problem of taxing the rural sector for nonlocal and nonrural needs. Combining regulation and fiat with the exercise of familiar informal influences on the grain-holding elites of the province, the regime sought the smoothest means possible to acquire a modest portion of Szechwan's agricultural bounty.

The new tax arrangements called for the establishment of provincial and county agencies to manage the collection, storage and handling, and shipment of the vast amounts of foodgrain (mostly rice) that came

into government hands.[40] In the cities, regulations
for the distribution of fixed-price government
grain to specified urban groups imposed an array
of government bureaus on the regular urban marketing
system.[41] In other words, the regime's leap into
the grain economy necessitated development of an
efficient grain management bureaucracy. Yet the new
program left local grain acquisition and storage
in familiar hands. Having taken possession of
hundreds of thousands of tons of rice in the program's
first year, for example, the government found that
it lacked adequate granary facilities. Grain hastily
stored in vacant temples quickly rotted, and rural
riots broke out. The government therefore had to rely
willy-nilly on existing granaries, which of course
belonged to the very landlords and grain-holders
whose produce was being taxed.[42]

Between 1942 and the end of the war, tax-in-kind
and compulsory grain sales gave the Kuomintang
regime enough food to keep the inflation-ridden urban centers from starvation and thus enabled it
to forestall the social disturbances that the 1940
food panic showed to be so near the surface.[43] But if
we examine the program for what it reveals about the
Kuomintang's approach to rural society, the findings are less consoling. The new taxation program
was grafted onto unaltered social and economic structures. As a result, the holders of local power --
the *pao* and *chia* chiefs and the so-called "rotten
gentry" (*t'u-hao lieh-shen*) -- were able to take unto
themselves most of the collection, storage, and
transport functions essential to the operation of
the government's new tax system.[44] Basic-level tax
functions were already dominated by the local elites
when tax-in-kind came along. Theoretically, the
New Hsien System and the Food Ministry's apparatus
were supposed to produce the trained, politically committed, incorruptible functionaries who could effectively carry out the new program, but they never
approached that goal. What was left was a mantle
of central government authority on the shoulders of
the old extortionate collectors and the inclusion
of the central government in a structure of exploitation and corruption hitherto monopolized by provincial and local elites.[45]

Furthermore, and presumably far more important
from the view of small landowners and tenant farmers,
tax-in-kind failed to eliminate the forest of mis-
cellaneous, ad hoc levies known generically as
t'an-p'ai, which were exacted by county or even lower-
level authorities without any higher authorization.

The proliferation of surcharges and one-time-only exactions had begun late in the Ch'ing dynasty, during the financial crises of the late nineteenth and early twentieth centuries. Amid burgeoning war-lordism in Szechwan after 1916, these locally raised fees had spread rapidly. In the Nanking decade, the profusion of *t'an-p'ai* in Szechwan had been no-torious. Indeed one of the professed aims of the tax-in-kind program was to rid rural society of these random exactions, which often added up to a far heavier burden than the basic land tax itself. But, relying as it did on the cooperation of local power holders, the Nationalists' wartime arrange-ments for securing a share of rural revenues left the *t'an-p'ai* problem untouched.[46]

Chungking's attempt to intervene in the grain economy by collecting the land tax in grain raised the hackles of powerful provincial landlords, including Liu Hsiang's widow and other militarists with large holdings in the fertile Chengtu Plain. Its impact was felt even by tenant farmers not officially liable to taxation, who found their rents or rent deposits raised (despite the government's prohibition of such retaliatory practices) after the program went into effect.[47] Nevertheless, the significance of tax-in-kind for the present analysis does not lie in its disrupting social impact, which at any rate would be nearly impossible to measure. In fact, the land tax in Szechwan had claimed a peculiarly small percentage of overall foodgrain production ever since the early Ch'ing dynasty, when low rates were established as an inducement to immigrants to repopulate the province. The staggering wartime urban inflation left the rural sector, which was more self-sufficient, in a comparatively healthy con-dition.[48] The tax-in-kind problem remained primarily a struggle for power between native landed elites and immigrant urban administrative and financial powers, but it struck only marginally at the taproots of the masses' welfare in wartime Szechwan. The other Nationalist campaign which connected the Chungking regime directly to rural society -- the manpower conscription program -- cut more sternly at those roots.

With the Nationalists' retreat into the interior, Szechwan's vital role as supplier of soldiers and laborers quickly emerged. In eight years of war, ac-cording to War Minister Ho Ying-ch'in, more than 2.5 million Szechwanese were drafted for mili-tary service alone.[49] Though the numbers cannot be known, labor requisition affected a great many

more. If the population of Szechwan at that time
was around 50 million, of whom about half were male;
and if half of the male population of Szechwan was
of able-bodied age; and if army conscripts were
drafted for the duration and generally did not return
home once they were conscripted (even if they de-
serted), then the military draft alone took one-fifth
of Szechwan's able-bodied males. Labor conscription
for such projects as interprovincial roadbuilding,
airfield construction and the transport of both
military and civilian supplies including foodgrain,
may have allowed a greater share of the conscripts to
return to their homes, but the effects of manpower
requisition during busy agricultural seasons, for
example, were still disruptive.[50] The social effects
of the conscription were skewed, moreover, by the
exemption of a great many young men of privi-
leged background, who were able to evade conscription
by bribing local officials, hiring impoverished substitutes, or assuming functionary positions that
preserved them from the clutches of the press gang.[51]

As it did with the land tax, the central government issued detailed regulations concerning
manpower conscription. Conscripts' families were supposed to receive financial aid and labor assistance
in periods of peak agricultural activity. Limits
were placed on the number of male children who could
be taken from a single family. The handling and
provisioning of conscripts and trainees were laid out
with great precision. Once again, however, the formal
arrangements were bureaucratic, expensive, and ineffective. Pending the development of procedures that
in effect never materialized, the government left the
conscription system in the hands of provincial and
local authorities; after a brief and unsuccessful
experiment with an ostensibly impartial lottery system
in 1938, the functions of taking and transporting
military manpower in rural Szechwan were left to the
chiefs of the *chia*, *pao*, and *hsiang*. The *hsiang*
organization in particular emerged as the agency with
greatest power in the conscription process. Almost
from its inception, therefore, the conscription
program, like the tax program a few years later, was
able to fulfill its responsibilities to the central
government precisely because it offered to the
local agents with the power to carry it out a whole
array of legitimatized opportunities for aggrandizement of their power and wealth.[52] Essential to
the massive acquisition of soldiers and laborers
was a tacit compromise between central and local authorities, by which the local agents enjoyed Chung-

king's acquiescence in their unrestrained pursuit
of conscripts. In a province the size of Szechwan,
the Nationalists had neither the coercive power
nor the administrative personnel nor the financial
resources to erect and operate a conscription system
independent of local influence. Though these weaknesses were conspicuous in the case of wartime
manpower programs, they were not caused by the war itself, and the conscription situation was not unique.
That the KMT regime managed to acquire so many men
was testimony, not to its own prowess, but rather to
the enormous wealth and population of Szechwan and
to the depth of the regime's compromises with local
elites.[53]

The cases of wartime land taxation and manpower
recruitment in Szechwan may in fact suggest, para-
doxically, that the very wealth of the province, which
was so crucial to the Nationalists' survival, in
some ways did them more harm than good. When all is
said and done, outside of the cities and commercial
centers where "downriver people" concentrated and
where the rampant inflation was most horrifying, the
war seems to have wrought few profound social changes
in Szechwan. The rhetoric changed, of course; *t'an-
p'ai* took on patriotic names, and KMT propaganda
exhortations reached into remote market towns.[54] But
the sporadic tax riots, the persistent sect uprisings, the repeated rumblings of warlord dissatisfaction, and the endemic banditry that thrived on
draft evasion and the opium trade never ignited a
social conflagration or transformed the distribution
of wealth and power in provincial society.[55] Szechwan,
it seems, was rich enough to provide the immigrant
regime with the basic necessities for maintaining its
bloated armies and its bureaucratic governmental
style, while making cooperation with the KMT regime
worth the while of local established elites. One
wonders, idly, how the Nationalists would have fared
if they had retreated into a part of China that
was not only underdeveloped but also poor -- an area
that could not afford the combined costs of central
government bureaucratism and central-local profit
sharing. Would the result have been a more dynamic,
less encrusted approach to the host society, or a
quicker and more total collapse? Conversely, what if
the Chinese Communists had somehow managed to settle in Szechwan after the Long March instead of
in northern Shensi? Was the mass line compatible with
the relative wealth and the enormously complex structures of economic and social power that thrived in
Szechwan? There is no way of knowing. What is clear

is that the KMT regime managed to survive eight years
in Szechwan, but that the local social elites which
effective central government needed either to cir-
cumvent or uproot remained in place, as strong at the
end of the war as they had been at the start.

CONCLUSION

The contrast between the plight of the Kuomintang in Southwest China, degenerating into corruption
and impotence, and the expanding power of the
Chinese Communist Party in Shen-Kan-Ning and the
guerrilla zones, was conspicuous in the 1940s and
remains so today. Amid material conditions far more
forbidding than those confronting the Kuomintang
in Szechwan, the Chinese Communists spent the war
perfecting the programs and work styles that enabled
them to mobilize rural popular support, first for
the anti-Japanese struggle and then for the final push
against the collapsing KMT regime. Given this stark
contrast between the wartime rural experiences of
the KMT and the CCP, an easy assumption would be that
the Nationalists failed because they were too weak,
or myopic, or both, to take the steps necessary
to prevent the Communist rural revolution from taking
hold. Explanations of Kuomintang failure often
stress the urban bases of the KMT regime, the
divorce of the KMT from the realities of peasant life,
and the Nationalists' failure to recognize the overwhelming saliency of the rural crisis -- whose
critical importance was ultimately proven when the
Communists mobilized the peasantry. According to this
line of reasoning, the record of the KMT experience
in wartime Szechwan provides added evidence of the
Kuomintang's utter failure to deal with rural China's
woes; in effect it confirms the rural-centered
explanation of the Nationalist collapse.

Without for a moment arguing that the Kuomintang
really was successful at, or even particularly interested in, a frontal assault on the plight of the
Chinese peasantry either before or during the war, I
think the significance of the Chungking regime's
brush with rural China lies elsewhere. For one thing,
it goes without saying that the degeneration of the
KMT during the war, and the catastrophic denoue-
ment after the conflict with Japan, stemmed from many
sources; the demoralization of KMT officials struggling to survive in the refugee centers of the Southwest, for example, took its toll on the postwar
Nationalist regime, independently of the party's
dealings with rural elites. In other words, the KMT

collapse cannot be solely attributed to its rural
failings.

But beyond that, the fact that the CCP built its
power base among the peasantry and finally seized
national power in 1949 does not prove that only
rural mobilization could keep a regime in power in the
1930s and 1940s. Weak as it was, the KMT regime in
Nanking and Chungking had the primary claim to
legitimate national government status; it is fallacious to argue that as the national government it
should have adopted the same priorities and employed
the same methods used by the Communist movement
that sought to destroy it. The Kuomintang unquestionably did fail, and the CCP certainly succeeded, in
the late 1940s -- but at different tasks. An
examination of how the KMT tried to deal with wartime
rural China has, I believe, less to tell us about
why the Kuomintang found itself out of power on the
Chinese mainland in 1949 than it does about the
daunting challenges of applying central government
control to the rural sector of Chinese society, before
or after 1949. The interesting comparison is between
the KMT in power after 1927, particularly its wartime phase, and the CCP in power since 1949, when it,
too, has had to face the problems of installing its
control over (and obtaining the resources of) rural
China. The parallels are not, of course, precise: the
CCP after 1949 approached rural China with different
visions, a history of vastly different rural social
techniques, and relatively greater domestic power.
And indeed, the CCP since 1949 has been able to
achieve results in rural society that can hardly be
compared with the Nationalists' lack of achievement. Nevertheless, the challenges rural society
placed before the wartime KMT and the post-liberation
CCP were surprisingly similar, and the approaches
of the two parties coincided more than one might
expect.

The KMT's wartime grain control program, for
example, addressed the same issue that any modern Chinese government -- and thus the Communist authorities after 1949 -- had to address: the extraction of
rural economic surpluses by the central government
for national purposes. As riddled with corruption, inefficiency, and abuse as the tax-in-kind and
compulsory grain sales programs in wartime Szechwan
were, they represented a government intrusion into the
rural economy which was to be built upon and refined
a decade later by the Communists. Urban grain
rationing and price controls and fixed government
prices to rural producers for compulsorily-sold grain

were not only the pillars of a KMT policy adopted
out of desperation but of a CCP food program adopted
from a position of vastly greater strength. The
greatest of all the differences between the KMT and
CCP approaches to this basic problem of modern Chinese
government was the CCP's elimination, during land
reform, of the bulk of the local power-holding elite
with which the KMT had neither the wish nor the
strength to struggle. What puts the KMT's wartime
rural acquisition program in the same arena with the
post-1949 CCP program, however, instead of in the
realm of imperial Chinese practices (the Ch'ing
dynasty, after all, collected a land tax, too, and the
KMT's rates were not that much higher than the old
imperial levies), was the Kuomintang's attempt
at feeding the cities on a regular basis. Hoarding
and peculation aside, the aim of wartime rural
taxation was governmental transfer of rural resources
to urban consumers, intervening in established marketing procedures along the way. Of course, refugee
officials, students, and other urban residents with no
local connections were singled out for special attention, but the wartime program was, beyond that, a
forerunner of subsequent CCP food control policies
essential to the development of the Chinese economy.

At the risk of heresy, it might also be pointed
out that the KMT's approach to rural China, both
before and during the war, has often shared with CCP
economic policies a tendency to place greater material
emphasis on nonagricultural development. Despite
the rural surroundings of the successful Chinese Communist social mobilization of the late 1940s, and
the Maoist notion of the moral superiority of
the rural masses, once in power the Chinese Communist
Party looked to the rapid growth of the urban industrial sector for the keys to China's modernization,
relying mostly on social and political reorganiza-
tions for economic growth in the rural world. By co-
incidence, both the Nationalist regime and the
Communist government encountered a severe crisis
after a decade in power, which forcefully brought home
the indispensability of rural resources to the survival of urban China. The Kuomintang, suddenly
deprived of its industrial and commercial centers,
turned to the programs of control and extraction-by-
compromise examined above; the People's Republic
of China, after the economic collapse of the "three
bad years," turned to "walking on two legs" in order
to balance the needs of rural and urban economic
development more successfully. Yet the persistent
fact is that agricultural production in China has

grown more slowly than industrial production, and
that the Peking authorities, like the Nationalists,
have discovered that urban economic growth is -- with
all its technological and financial problems -- more
amenable to sudden stimulation than is the growth
of the immense and diffuse rural economy. As
the Chinese Communist Party declared at the end of
1978, agriculture is "the foundation of the national
economy," but it "remains very weak."[56] The simple
lesson of 1949 -- that the Chinese Communists were
successful in rural China and the Nationalists were
unsuccessful there -- might be true as far as it
goes. But from a longer perspective it is apparent
that the problem of moving the rural economy forward
as fast as the urban sector is a persistent one.
The point is not that KMT and CCP rural policies are
indistinguishable; they have been worlds apart ever
since the days of the first Communist experiments
with land reform in the 1920s, and above all in terms
of the CCP's elimination of landlordism and subsequent
collectivization of agriculture. The point is,
rather, that the task of laying hands on Chinese
rural social structures and economic surplus for the
sake of transcendent national goals presented challenges to the KMT which the CCP still faces, despite
the many transformations of rural life since 1949.
Looking at the Kuomintang's wartime rendezvous with
rural reality, one can hardly conclude that a bright
future awaited the KMT in agrarian China, but neither
can one conclude that the Nationalists' rural activities and policies -- at least in the wartime
Southwest -- lost them the Chinese mainland. And
indeed, as evidence emerges from contemporary China
showing the persistence of familiar rural social
patterns, including "seizure and use of production
teams' labor, funds, and goods without compensa-
tion,"[57] a sense of *déjà vue* is unavoidable. As the
tremendous agrarian social upheaval that brought
the CCP to power recedes into history and the persistence of certain long-standing rural social and
political problems even after the land revolution
becomes more evident, the image of stark and unalloyed
contrasts between KMT and CCP approaches to rural
China may weaken. With hindsight it may well turn
out that the wartime KMT and the CCP in power after
1949 occupied places on a continuum of Chinese rural
social history, rather than holding diametrically
opposed positions on either side of the great revolutionary divide.

NOTES

1.   Chalmers Johnson, *Peasant Nationalism and Communist Power: The Emergence of Revolutionary China, 1937-1945* (Stanford: Stanford University Press, 1962).

2.   Standard textbooks, such as John K. Fairbank, Edwin O. Reischauer, and Albert M. Craig, *East Asia: Tradition and Transformation* (Boston: Houghton Mifflin Co., 1973), pp. 799-807, discuss these matters.   Nationalist degeneration is detailed in Theodore H. White and Annalee Jacoby, *Thunder Out of China* (New York: William Sloane Associates, 1946).

3.   Mark Selden, *The Yenan Way in Revolutionary China* (Cambridge, Mass.: Harvard University Press, 1971); and Donald Gillin, "'Peasant Nationalism' in the History of Chinese Communism," *Journal of Asian Studies*, Vol. XXIII, No. 2 (February 1964), pp. 269-89.

4.   Lloyd E. Eastman, *The Abortive Revolution: China under Nationalist Rule, 1927-1937* (Cambridge, Mass.: Harvard University Press, 1974).

5.   Hung-mao Tien, *Government and Politics in Kuomintang China, 1927-1937* (Stanford: Stanford University Press, 1972).   See also Philip A. Kuhn, "Local Self-Government under the Republic," in Frederick Wakeman, Jr. and Carolyn Grant (eds.), *Conflict and Control in Late Imperial China* (Berkeley: University of California Press, 1975), pp. 256-98.

6.   Yeh-chien Wang, *Land Taxation in Imperial China, 1750-1911* (Cambridge, Mass.: Harvard University Press, 1973), pp. 79-83.

7.   _Daitōashō sōmukyoku somuka, *Jūkei seiken no_ naijō* / Internal Condition of the Chungking Regime_/ (Tokyo, 1944), p. 1.

8.   Lin Chi-yung, *Min-ying ch'ang-k'uang nei-ch'ien chi-lu: Wo-kuo kung-yeh tsung tung-yüan chih hsü-mu* / The Story of the Movement of Privately-Run Factories and Mines to the Interior: First_Act in Our Country's Industrial General Mobilization_/ (Chungking, 1942) is the most detailed account of this industrial migration.

9.   For wide-ranging discussions of the economic background in Szechwan, see Chiang Chün-chang, *Hsi-nan ching-chi ti-li* / Economic Geography of the Southwest_/ (Shanghai, 1946); Lü P'ing-teng, *Ssu-ch'uan nung-ts'un ching-chi* / Szechwan's Rural Economy_/ (Shanghai, 1936); and Kanda Masao, *Shisen shō sōran* / A General Look at Szechwan_/ (Tokyo, 1937).

10.   _Mantetsu chōsabu, *Shina kōsenryoku chōsa hōkoku* / Report on an Investigation of China's Power to Resist_/ (Tokyo, 1970), pp. 237-47.   See also Ku Yüan-t'ien, "Shisen shō ni okeru kōrō no kensetsu"

178

/¯Road Construction in Szechwan Province¯/, in Fang Hsien-ting (ed.), *Shina keizai kenkyū* /¯Research on the Chinese Economy¯/ (Tokyo, 1939), pp. 671-86.

11. Chiang, *Hsi-nan*, pp. 261-72.

12. Kōain seimubu, *Jūkei seifu no seinan keizai kensetsu jōkyō* /¯The State of Affairs in the Chungking Government's Economic Development of the Southwest¯/ (Tokyo, 1940), p. 100.

13. For a discussion of the notion of regional "core" and "periphery" in China, see G. William Skinner, "Cities and the Hierarchy of Local Systems," in G. William Skinner (ed.), *The City in Late Imperial China* (Stanford: Stanford University Press, 1976), pp. 275-346, esp. pp. 282-90.

14. Robert A. Kapp, *Szechwan and the Chinese Republic: Provincial Militarism and Central Power, 1911-1938* (New Haven: Yale University Press, 1973).

15. See, for example, Chung-kuo jen-min cheng-chih hsieh-shang hui-i ch'üan-kuo wei-yüan-hui wen-shih tzu-liao yen-chiu wei-yüan-hui (comp.), *Hsin-hai ke-ming hui-i-lu* /¯Reminiscences of the 1911 Revolution¯/ (Peking, 1962), pp. 42-67, 105-107, 174-76, and 193.

16. Drumwright (Chengtu) to Vincent (Chungking), March 24, 1943, in Vincent (Chungking) to Department of State (893.00/15003); and Liao T'ai-ch'u, "The Ko Lao Hui in Szechwan," *Pacific Affairs*, Vol. XX, No. 2 (June 1947), pp. 161-73.

17. Feng Ho-fa, *Chung-kuo nung-ts'un ching-chi tzu-liao* /¯Materials on the Chinese Rural Economy¯/ (Shanghai, 1933), p. 827.

18. *China Weekly Review*, January 1, 1938, p. 124.

19. Chou K'ai-ch'ing, *Min-kuo Ch'uan-shih chi-yao* /¯Main Events in Szechwanese Affairs During the Republic¯/ (Taipei, 1972), pp. 38-129. On Liu Wen-hui's power in Sikang, see Gaimushō, seimukyoku daigōka, *Seikō oyo Shisen kinjō: Zai Pekin Beikoku taishikan'in no genchi hōkoku* /¯Recent Conditions in Sikang and Szechwan: An On-the-Scene Report from an Official of the American Embassy in Peking¯/ (Tokyo, 1943), a translation of a report by United States diplomat Everett Drumwright. See also A. Doak Barnett, *China on the Eve of Communist Takeover* (New York: Praeger, 1963), pp. 215-29.

20. "Shō Kaiseki no Unnan chūoka kōsaku" /¯Chiang Kai-shek's Labors at Centralizing Yünnan¯/, *Tōa* /¯East Asia¯/, Vol. XIII, No. 3 (March 1940), pp. 30-41.

21. Mantetsu chōsabu, *Shina kōsenryoku*, p. 140.

22. Ch'en Po-hsin, *Chung-kuo ti-fang tzu-chih yü*

hsin-hsien chih ∠ Chinese Local Self-Government and
the New Hsien System⌿ (n.p., 1942; 3rd printing,
1945), pp. 1-15. See also Kuhn, "Local Self-
Government," pp. 280-87.

23. Ch'en, *Chung-kuo ti-fang tzu-chih*, pp. 28-40.

24. An example is Wu Ting-ch'ang, *Hua-hsi
hsien-pi* ∠ Jottings from Hua-hsi⌿ (Kueiyang, 1943).
Wu was for many years governor of Kweichow.

25. For a survey of KMT administrative policy in
"Bandit Suppression Zones," see Ch'en Mou-hsing,
Chiao-fei ti-fang hsing-cheng chih-tu ∠ The Bandit-
Suppression Local Administrative System⌿ (Shang-
hai, 1936). See also Tien, *Government and Politics*,
pp. 96-114.

26. The full text of the "Outline" appears in
Ta-kung pao ∠ L'impartial⌿, September 22, 1939.

27. Liu Chen-tung, "Hsien-cheng chien-she"
∠ Reconstruction of Hsien Government⌿, *Hsin cheng-
chih* ∠ New Politics⌿, Vol. III, No. 6 (April 10,
1940), pp. 1-7.

28. *K'ang-chan chung te Chung-kuo cheng-chih*
∠ Chinese Politics in the War of Resistance⌿ (Yenan,
1940), p. 115.

29. *Ibid.*, p. 111.

30. Barnett, *China*, pp. 103-54.

31. Hsiao Ju-hsien, "Hsin-hsien chih shih-shih
chung fa-hsien chih wen-t'i chi ch'i kai-chin"
∠ Problems Arising from the Implementation of the New
Hsien System and Their Solutions⌿, *Hsin Chung-hua*,
December 1944, pp. 5-11.

32. Chang Yu-chiang and Li Yen-tung, "K'ang-chan
i-lai Ssu-ch'uan chih tui-wai mao-i" ∠ Szechwan's
External Trade Since the War of Resistance⌿, in *Ssu-
ch'uan ching-chi chi-k'an* ∠ Szechwan Economic
Quarterly⌿, Vol. I, No. 1 (December 1943), p. 62;
and Masuda Yoneji, *Jūkei seifu keizai seisaku
shi* ∠ History of the Chungking Regime's Economic
Policies⌿ (Tokyo, 1943), pp. 277-83.

33. Hsü K'an, "Chung-kuo chan-shih te liang-cheng"
∠ China's Wartime Grain Tax Collection⌿, *Ching-chi
hui-pao* ∠ Economic Report⌿, Vol. VI, Nos. 1 and
2 (July 16, 1942), p. 16.

34. Chiang Chieh-shih, "Chiang wei-yüan-chang
liang-cheng hui-i hsün-tz'u" ∠ Chairman Chiang's Message to the Grain Tax Conference⌿, *Ching-chi hui-
pao*, Vol. VI, Nos. 1 and 2 (July 16, 1942), p. 3; and
Ishihama Chikao, *Jūkei seifu taisei ron* ∠ On the
Framework of the Chungking Government⌿ (Tokyo, 1942),
pp. 359-73.

35. Wu Shih, *Ch'ung-ch'ing chien-wen lu* ∠ Seen
and Heard in Chungking⌿ (n.p., 1941), pp. 22-24.

36. P'eng Yü-hsin, Ch'en Yu-san, and Ch'en Ssu-te, *Ch'uan-sheng t'ien-fu cheng-shih fu-tan yen-chiu* / Researches on the Burden of Tax-in-Kind in Szechwan / (Chungking, 1943), p. 43.

37. *Hsin Shu pao* / New Szechwan Post /, December 5, 1941, p. 2. See also Ssu-ch'uan sheng yin-hang ching-chi yen-chiu shih, *Ssu-ch'uan cheng-kou liang-shih pan-fa kai-lun* / On Methods of Collecting and Purchasing Tax Grain in Szechwan / (Chungking, 1941), p. 18.

38. P'eng, Ch'en, and Ch'en, *Ch'uan-sheng t'ien-fu*, p. 43.

39. Kokura Otōjiro, *Jūkei kōsen no gendankai to chihō seiji* / The Present Stage of Chungking's War of Resistance and Local Government / (Tokyo, 1941), p. 29.

40. Ch'en Yu-san, *T'ien-fu cheng-shih chih-tu* / The Tax-in-Kind System / (Chungking, 1945), pp. 16-24. See also Tōakenkyujo, *Shō seiken shita Shina chihō zaisei ni kansuru chōsa* / Investigation of Local Finance under the Chiang Regime / (Tokyo, 1943), pp. 32-33.

41. For excellent discussions of the prewar rice marketing system in Chungking, see Heikan tetsurō (ed.), *Jūkei keizai chōsa* / Investigation of the Chungking Economy / (Tokyo, 1940), pp. 193-96; and Kuo Jung-sheng and Ch'en Wu-i, "Ch'ung-ch'ing shih mi-liang hung-hsü shih-k'uang yü t'ung-chih fang-ts'e" / Conditions of Grain Supply and Demand in Chungking and Plans for Control /, *Chün-shih yu cheng-chih* / Military Affairs and Politics /, Vol. I, No. 3 (May 26, 1941), pp. 27-42. For a detailed discussion of wartime grain controls in Chungking, see Yü Teng-pin, "Chan-shih liang-shih kuan-li cheng-ts'e yü Ch'ung-ch'ing liang-shih kuan-chih" / Wartime Grain Control Policies and the Chungking Grain Control System /, *Ssu-ch'uan ching-chi chi-k'an*, Vol. I, No. 4 (January 15, 1944), pp. 295-313.

42. Ch'en, *T'ien-fu*, pp. 103-104. See also Shih T'i-yüan, "Ssu-ch'uan sheng t'ien-fu kai-cheng shih-wu chih ching-kuo" / The Szechwan Experience with Converting to Tax-in-Kind /, *Ching-chi hui-pao*, Vol. VI, Nos. 1 and 2 (July 16, 1942), p. 6.

43. Arthur N. Young, *China's Wartime Finance and Inflation, 1937-1945* (Cambridge, Mass.: Harvard University Press, 1965), pp. 23-31.

44. Daitōashō, *Jūkei seiken no naijō*, pp. 51-52; and Gaimushō, *Seikō oyo Shisen kinjō*, p. 39.

45. Of the 136 *hsien*-level land tax control bureaus established under the new system, more than ninety were formed by merely "reorganizing" existing

hsien collection bureaus (*cheng-shou chü*), which had survived repeated attempts to eliminate them or curtail their excessive independence. See Shih, "Ssu-ch'uan sheng t'ien-fu," p. 41. Particularly vivid evidence of this can be found in *Jūkei jōhō* ∠ Chung-king Intelligence Report ∠, May 19, 1941; and *Hsin-hua jih-pao* ∠ New China Daily ∠, December 3, 1939, quoted in Kariya Kyūtaro (ed.), *Shina nōson keizai no shin dōkō* ∠ New Trends in the Chinese Rural Economy ∠ (Tokyo, 1940); and two speeches by Sun Fo, in *Ta hou-fang yü-lun* ∠ Public Opinion in the Great Rear Area ∠ (n.p., 1944), pp. 49-50.

46. Wu Tan-ko, "Ssu-ch'uan te ti-fang t'an-p'ai" ∠ Szechwan's Local Levies ∠, *Ssu-ch'uan ching-chi chi-k'an*, Vol. I, No. 2 (March 15, 1944), pp. 174-98; and *Hsin Shu pao*, February 8, 1942.

47. Hsü Ti-hsin, *Hsien-tai Chung-kuo ching-chi chiao-ch'eng* ∠ Manuel on the Contemporary Chinese Economy ∠ (Shanghai, n.d.), pp. 269-71.

48. Young, *China's Wartime Finance*, p. 317.

49. Chou K'ai-ching, *Ssu-ch'uan yü tui-Jih k'ang-chan* ∠ Szechwan and the Anti-Japanese War of Resistance ∠ (Taipei, 1971), pp. 245-46.

50. *Kuo-min ts'an-cheng hui Ch'uan-K'ang shih-ch'a t'uan pao-kao-shu* ∠ Report of the Investigative Team on Szechwan and Sikang of the People's Political Conference ∠ (Chungking, 1939), p. 290, is one of many references to this.

51. Tai Kao-hsiang, "K'ang-chan shih-ch'i chih Ssu-ch'uan i-cheng" ∠ Wartime Conscription in Szechwan ∠, *Ssu-ch'uan wen-hsien* ∠ Documents on Szechwan ∠ (July 1963), p. 24. See also *Kuo-min ts'an-cheng hui*, p. 287; and Mantetsu chōsabu, *Shina kōsenryoku*, pp. 116-19.

52. A description of the recruitment mechanism appears in Chou, *Ssu-ch'uan yü tui-Jih k'ang-chan*, pp. 238-47.

53. In addition to *ibid.*, useful sources on war-time conscription in Szechwan are: Ch'en Hung-chin, "Ts'ung Ssu-ch'uan ping-i wen-t'i lun nung-ts'un cheng-chih te kai-ke" ∠ On the Conscription Problem in Szechwan and Rural Political Reform ∠, *Chung-kuo nung-ts'un* ∠ Rural China ∠, Vol. VI, No. 5 (n.d.), pp. 7-10; Li Ch'uan-sheng, *Jūkei no higeki* ∠ The Tragedy of Chungking ∠ (Shanghai, 1941); Mantetsu chōsabu, *Shina kōsenryoku*, pp. 112-19; and *Kuo-min ts'an-cheng hui*, pp. 315-19.

54. H. L. Richardson, "Szechwan During the War," *The Geographical Journal*, Vol. CVI, Nos. 1 and 2 (July-August 1945), p. 17. See also Gunther Stein, "A Journey in Szechwan," *China Quarterly*, No. 5

(1939-1940), p. 487.

    55.   Materials on banditry in wartime Szechwan are abundant. See, for example, *Kuo-min ts'an-cheng hui*.

    56.   "Chung-kuo kung-ch'an-tang te shih-i-chiai chung-yang wei-yüan-hui ti-san-tz'u ch'üan-ti hui-i kung-pao" ∕ Report of the Third Plenary Session of the Eleventh Central Committee of the Chinese Communist Party ∕, *Kuang-ming jih-pao*, December 24, 1978, p. 1.

    57.   *Ibid*. For discussions of the revival of other long-standing agricultural practices, including rural fairs, see the same newspapers, August 18, 1978; September 1, 1979; and October 14, 1978.

Part 3
The Communists, 1927–1949:
In Search of Revolutionary Models

7

The Origins of Communist and Soviet Movements in China

Ilpyong J. Kim

The Chinese Communist movement in the 1930s had its roots in the development of the concept of the soviets. The breakdown of the Kuomintang-Communist alliance in 1927 created uncertainty, frustration, and organizational crisis within the Communist movement in China. The party organization was on the verge of total collapse, and its leaders were looking for a conceptual framework within which to redirect the revolution, to reorganize the party structure, and to bridge the gap between the party and the masses. The soviet seemed to be the best answer. The soviet movement of the 1930s, indeed, served as the conceptual and institutional foundation for the Chinese Communist leadership to achieve revolutionary victory in 1949.

It is therefore important to examine the Communist perception of the crisis. The development of the concept of the soviet in the post-1927 period must be understood and analyzed in the light of the methods used by the Chinese Communist leaders to restructure the revolutionary movement. Their adoption of the "Resolution on the Organizational Questions of the Soviet Government" at the Sixth Party Congress in Moscow in June-July 1928 was by no means a sudden occurrence; it was rather a part of their continuing search for organizational techniques for mass political action.[1] A long series of theoretical discussions and deliberations preceded the final adoption of the concept of the soviet as the premise for seizing political power and winning mass support for the party's revolutionary strategy. The concept of the soviet as an organizational technique for mass political action had begun to emerge shortly after the 1927 debacle. When it was transformed into an actual institution in the 1930s,

it succeeded remarkably well in bridging the gap between Chinese Communist policy and the people by
making rapid mass mobilization possible.

This chapter discusses, first of all, the origins
of the concept of the soviet as it was developed by
V. I. Lenin during his struggle for power in Russia and then briefly surveys the Stalin-Trotsky controversy over the establishment of the Chinese
soviets. The final portion of the chapter analyzes
the vacillating attitude of the Chinese Communist
leaders toward the concept at the time when they were
searching for a new structure for their revolutionary strategy. There are also some significant
questions that must be dealt with. For example: why
and under what circumstances did the Chinese Communist leaders decide to establish the soviets? How
did the function of the soviets change between the
enlarged Politburo meeting of November 1927 and the
Sixth Party Congress of July 1928? In order to answer
these and other related questions concerning the
establishment of the soviets in China, this chapter
studies and analyzes two important documents: the
"Resolution of the Enlarged Politburo Meeting
of November 1927"[2] in which the slogan "Establish
Soviets" was first proclaimed, and the "Resolution on
the Organizational Questions of the Soviet Government" which, adopted by the Sixth Party Congress,
incorporated the resolution of the Politburo meeting
of November 1927.

In addition, this chapter analyzes such important
editorials and articles as "Long Live the Soviet
System," "The Soviet System and Socialism in China,"
and "Democracy and the Soviet System of Government." They appeared in the theoretical journal, *Pu-
erh-sai-wei-k'o* (Bolshevik), of the Central Committee of the Chinese Communist Party and were
written by Ch'ü Ch'iu-pai between the November Politburo meeting of 1927 and the Sixth Party Congress
of 1928. These writings provide a vivid picture of
the way the Chinese Communist leaders perceived
and analyzed the revolutionary situation in China and
of the process by which they sought to develop the
soviet system of government in Kiangsi. Before discussing the Chinese soviet system, however, it is
necessary to trace the concept of the soviet as
it was developed by Lenin.

LENIN'S CONCEPT OF THE SOVIET

The soviet organization sprang up spontaneously
in Russia during the 1905 revolution as a body of

deputies elected by their fellow factory workers.
Lenin's attitude toward the soviet was ambivalent at
the time of its emergence. The local leaders of
the Bolshevik movement in St. Petersburg reportedly
boycotted the soviet organization in the beginning
and asked its leaders to join the Bolsheviks in
an effort to overthrow the tsarist government.
Lenin's flexibility in dealing with the non-Bolshevik
groups helped to solve the problems of working with
the newly emerged soviet organizations. As a
close observer of Soviet politics notes:

> Impressed by the mass support which the
> soviet rallied, Lenin saw in it both
> a field of activity for the expansion of
> Bolshevik influence and the germ of a
> provisional revolutionary government to
> replace the autocracy.[3]

Lenin's intention at this time was not to boycott the
soviets, but to intensify the Bolshevik activity
within them in order to establish control. As it
turned out, his opponent Leon Trotsky and the
Mensheviks played a far more active role in the organization of the soviets in 1905 than he and the
Bolsheviks did.

The word "soviet" in Russian means "council,"
yet it acquired a special significance during
the revolution of March 1917. As one of the two centers of power (the other being the Duma), "the
Soviet of Workers' and Soldiers' Deputies" began
its activities on March 12, 1917, "when a miscella-
neous group composed of left-wing Duma deputies,
members of the labor group of the War Industries Committee, and representatives of trade unions and
cooperatives constituted a Temporary Executive Committee and invited delegates from factories and
regiments to assemble that same evening in the Tauride
Palace to organize the soviet."[4] The soviet organization was thus established. Since the Duma, the
other center of power, was extremely weak, the soviet
quickly assumed such governmental functions as the
regulation of food supplies and the organization of
a workers' militia as a temporary substitute for
the police. "From the beginning, the soviet was far
closer to the workers and soldiers than was the
Duma," and "its decrees carried a persuasive power
that no official body could command."[5]

The dual system of power emerged in Russia when
the provisional government was created with formal
authority on the one hand, and the soviet was estab-

lished with most of the actual power of veto and
decision on the other. Hence, the soviet enjoyed the
confidence of the masses. The relationship between
the first provisional government and the soviet
was "a fragile truce rather than a solid agreement."[6]
War Minister A. I. Guchkov of the provisional
government wrote in March 1917:

> The provisional government possesses no
> real power and its orders are executed
> only in so far as this is permitted by the
> Soviet of Workers' and Soldiers' Dep-
> uties, which holds in its hands the most
> important elements of actual power, such as
> troops, railroads, postal and telegraphic
> service. It is possible to say directly
> that the provisional government exists
> only while this is permitted by the Soviet
> of Workers' and Soldiers' Deputies.[7]

During the spring of 1917, the soviet organization was formed throughout Russia as a rallying point
and coordinating mechanism for revolutionary activities. The authority of the soviets was strengthened
when Lenin called on the Bolshevik leaders to "prepare for the seizure of power by the Soviets of
Workers' Deputies."[8] His plan was to seize political
power through the existing mechanism of the soviets,
and he demanded a complete break with the old line of
"revolutionary defensism" and a repudiation of the
provisional government.

In a speech delivered to his followers on April
17, 1917, Lenin called for "a Republic of Soviets
of Workers', Agricultural Laborers' and Peasants' Deputies throughout the land, from top to bottom,
abolition of the police, the army, the bureaucracy,"
as well as an arrangement of a new organization
by which "all officers were to be elected and subject
to recall at any time, their salaries not to exceed
the average wage of a competent worker." In the
same speech, he also proposed the "confiscation of all
private lands, nationalization ... immediate merger
of all the banks in the country into one general
national bank, over which the Soviet of Workers' Deputies should have control ... control of social
production and distribution of goods."[9]

Lenin's proposed program was based on the
assumption that the bourgeois-democratic revolution
had been completed and was being transformed into
a socialist stage of revolution. As he maintained:

> The peculiarity of the present situation
> in Russia is that it represents a *transition*
> from the first stage of revolution, which
> ... led to the assumption of power by
> the bourgeoisie, to its second stage which
> was to place power in the hands of the
> proletariat and the poorest strata of the
> peasantry.[10]

To Lenin, the Soviet of Workers' and Soldiers' Deputies was the realization of "the revolutionary-
democratic dictatorship of the proletariat and peasantry." The emergence of the soviet in Russia was the
reality of political life in which the bourgeois-
democratic revolution had been transformed into the
socialist stage of revolution.

Under the dual system of power, Lenin maintained,
the provisional government had to be overthrown by
winning over the majority of the soviets. For such
purpose, he proclaimed the slogan "All Power to
the Soviets!" It was sufficient by June 1917 for him
to create a national organization, since the soviets
were widely spread throughout the country. As John
Hazard observes, "The Congress of Soviets provided Lenin with a valuable instrument for maintaining the power which had been seized, and he turned
to it immediately."[11] Therefore, Lenin asked the
congress to enact a program that would implement the
two principal aims of the Russian revolution: peace
with Germany and socialization of land.

To Lenin, the soviet was an organization of both
the working masses and the exploited class. It was
to function as the instrument of the working masses in
their seizure of power, as well as in their participation in the management of their own political
life. As Lenin perceived, it was an apparatus to
unify the working masses and the oppressed people and
to bring them into the government's decision-making
processes. Not only did he advance the idea of
the soviet system as a technique of seizing political
power through mass participation in Russia, but he
also laid the groundwork for the development of
a conceptual framework by which workers and peasants
of the colonial countries could build such an
organization.

Lenin stressed the leadership role of the industrial workers, with the peasants playing a supporting part. During the Second Congress of the
Communist International (Comintern) in 1920, he talked
at great length of the formation of "peasant soviets"
and defined the leadership role of the workers as

the essential element in the revolutionary movement
of the underdeveloped and colonial countries. He
asserted:

> Only when the soviets have become the sole
> state apparatus is it really possible to
> ensure the participation, in the work
> of administration, of the entire mass of the
> exploited, who, even under the most en-
> lightened and freest bourgeois democracy,
> have always actually been excluded 99
> percent from participation in the work of
> administration. It is only in the soviets
> that the exploited masses really begin
> to learn -- not in books, but from their
> own practical experience -- the work
> of socialist construction, of creating a new
> social discipline and a free union of free
> workers.[12]

With regard to the role of the soviets in the
rural areas of the colonial countries, Lenin continued
to emphasize the workers when he delivered his speech
on "Preliminary Draft Theses on the Agrarian Question" at the Second Comintern Congress in July
1920:

> The Communist parties must exert every effort
> to begin, as speedily as possible, to set
> up Soviets of Deputies in the country-
> side, and in the first place soviets of
> *hired laborers* and *semi-proletarians*. Only
> if they are linked up with the mass
> strike struggle and with the most op-
> pressed class can the soviets perform their
> functions, and become consolidated enough
> to influence (and later to incorporate)
> *the small peasants*. If, however, the strike
> struggle has not yet developed, and the
> agricultural proletariat is as yet incapable
> of strong organization owing both to the
> severe lack of support from the industrial
> workers and their unions, then the formation
> of Soviets of Deputies in the rural areas
> will require lengthy preparation.[13]

Thus, by 1920 when Lenin was interested in spreading
revolution to the economically backward countries,
he realized that there was almost no industrial
proletariat in those countries. Since a purely proletarian movement was therefore practically im-

possible, the peasant soviets must mobilize the peasant masses in the same way as the workers' soviets
were mobilizing the workers in the urban centers.

While there was structural similarity between
Lenin's ideas about organizing peasant soviets in the
colonial and backward countries and what Mao Tse-
tung was actually creating in Hunan, there was also
a functional difference between Lenin's peasant
soviets and Mao's peasant associations. Lenin believed that the industrial proletariat must assume a
leading role in the peasant soviets, as the peasantry
was incapable of taking the revolutionary leadership in the backward countries. Nonetheless, on
the basis of his direct participation in the peasant
movement, Mao was convinced that such progressive
elements as the farm laborers and poor peasants must
assume the leadership of the peasant associations.

According to Lenin, it was not possible to have
revolutionary peasant movement, whether domestic
or foreign, without the leadership of the proletariat.
The basic ideas in his speech of July 1920 served
as the conceptual framework within which the revolutionary leaders of the colonial countries -- including
the Chinese Communists -- developed their organizational strategy to win the support of the peasant
masses in the rural society. The effort of the
peasants was to be subordinated to the revolutionary
effort of the urban workers.

The observation of the Chinese Communist leaders
of the structure and function of the soviet system
in Russia in the 1920s served as an inspiration for
the subsequent development of their own ideas
about the soviet organization. A fifty-four member delegation representing both the Chinese Communist
Party and the Kuomintang attended the Congress of
the Toilers of the Far East in Moscow in 1922.
While in Russia, the Chinese delegates had the opportunity to tour the countryside and observe the
operation of the soviet system under the leadership
of the industrial proletariat. This experience later
helped the Chinese Communists in their plan to set
up urban soviets in China.[14]

In response to the questions raised by the
Chinese delegates about the way the soviets functioned, Lenin's expert on East Asian affairs,
M. Safarov, stated at the Tenth Session of the Congress of the Toilers of the Far East:

> The representative of the Kuomintang, Com-
> rade Tao, has asserted that the principles of
> the soviet system and the basic demands of

the Soviet revolution are nothing new in
China. He said, if I am not mistaken, that
the Kuomintang has been propagating these
ideas for the last twenty years.[15]

Safarov challenged the misunderstanding of the Chinese
delegation with the following words:

In China, the working class is just learning
to walk, just beginning to develop. The
peasant masses are brow-beaten and ignorant,
and therefore do not put forward their own
demands and views. ... As long as we want
to organize the masses under our banner,
and have the majority of the people on our
side, we must touch upon the vital interests
of the masses, in order that these masses
may follow us to the end, that they be
ready to die for our and their cause.[16]

The underlying concept of the soviet advanced by
Lenin in the early 1920s was the rapid mobilization
and increased participation of the masses. They,
however, had to be subordinated to the leadership of
the industrial workers in the management and administration of state affairs. As Lenin contended,
the revolutionary conquest of power was unattainable
without the mass mobilization and participation of
the proletarian class. In presenting his ideas about
the role of the soviets in a revolutionary situation, Lenin consistently argued that the Soviets of
Workers' and Peasants' Deputies must serve as the
rallying point for the revolutionary working masses.
He envisioned the possibility of having every member
of the society -- including house-wives -- participate
in the administrative processes after the elimination
of the bourgeois type of bureaucracy and management
system. His concept of the soviet was therefore
based upon a committee system of organization rather
than upon a single leader's responsibility, which
was later tried in the Kiangsi soviet base.
    In contemporary Russia, Lenin's concept of the
soviet system continues to serve as the ideological foundation of the Russian attempt to construct a
Communist society. In defining the role of the
soviets in the future, the program of the Communist
Party of the Soviet Union asserts:

The role of the soviets, which are an all-
inclusive organization of the people
embodying their unity, will grow as Com-

munist construction progresses. The
soviets, which combine the features of a
government and a mass organization of
the people, operate more like social
organization with the masses participating
extensively and directly in their
work.[17]

What then will happen to the soviets after a stateless Communist society has been achieved? As the
Russian political thinkers envisioned: "The soviets
may survive as the backbone of a stateless Communist
society where socialist statehood has fully grown
into Communist public self-administration.[18]
According to the program of the Communist Party
of the Soviet Union:

Communist self-administration will embrace
the soviets, trade unions, cooperatives,
and other mass organizations of the people.
The soviets, which represent and unite
all the people, are best suited to become
the basis of Communist public self-
administration.[19]

No matter how lofty and novel it may have been in
the minds of Russian political thinkers, Lenin's
concept of the soviet system failed to have any significant impact on the Chinese Communist movement
in the 1920s and 1930s. Within the general framework
of the united front policy of 1923-1927, the revolutionary effort of the Chinese Communist leaders was
directed at achieving political unity and national
independence by expelling the "foreign imperialist powers." The complexity of the Chinese revolution
during the 1920s was very much affected by the
Stalin-Trotsky controversy over its direction. The
shift in Stalin's policy toward China in the late
1920s, and the activities of different Comintern
agents with different approaches to the revolution,
had an important impact on the course of the Chinese
revolution.[20]

As one historian of the united front policy
observes, the Chinese Communists and Stalin were "unable to create an independent force capable either
of unified action or of withstanding determined
military attempts" by the Kuomintang to break up the
united front and suppress the Communists even when
the Chinese Communist Party had acquired the capacity
to initiate and influence the Chinese revolution.[21]
In 1926, Stalin even countered his own China ex-

pert, Pavel Mif, when Mif suggested that soviets be
established in the countryside of China to assume the
leadership of the revolutionary situation. As
Stalin asserted:

> It would be ridiculous to think that there
> are sufficient revolutionaries in China
> for this task .... Anyone who thinks
> that some tens of thousands of Chinese
> revolutionaries can cover this ocean
> of peasants is making a mistake.[22]

Thus, Stalin insisted that the united front
policy, which maintained the Kuomintang-Communist alliance in an effort to expel "foreign imperialism"
and achieve the goal of national liberation, must
serve the objectives of the Chinese revolution.
As long as these objectives were being carried out,
why should there be any need to establish soviets in
China? Even more gratifying to Stalin was the fact
that the Chinese Communist Party was making apparent
progress within the organizational framework of the
united front policy in the national revolutionary
movement as well as in agrarian reform. A logical
course of action at this juncture was to continue the
facade of the united front policy even after Kuomintang suppression of the Communists in Shanghai in
April 1927, no matter how contradictory the policy
may have appeared to Stalin's opponents. Stalin
therefore continued to direct the Chinese Communists
to ally themselves with the left-wing Kuomintang
leaders in the Wuhan government.

Nevertheless, as Lyman P. Van Slyke states, the
"united front policy of the Comintern could give
no consistent guidelines because it was, in
fact, self-contradictory."[23] The inconsistency of
Stalin's China policy was traceable to his argument
with Trotsky over the formation of Chinese soviets.
Hence, a discussion of their controversy may provide
a new perspective on the problems of institution-
building that the Chinese Communist leadership had to
come to grips with following the 1927 debacle.

THE STALIN-TROTSKY CONTROVERSY OVER THE CHINESE
    SOVIETS

The leadership of Ch'en Tu-hsiu, who served as
general secretary of the Chinese Communist Party, had
been seriously undermined as the result of Stalin's
changing views on revolutionary strategy, as well
as his approaches to revolutionary tactics. Ch'en

was alleged to have sided with Trotsky and was
removed from his position of leadership in the party
even before the August 7 Emergency Conference convened in 1927. Ch'en, however, countercharged that
Stalin, rather than Ch'en himself, should be responsible for the failure of the Chinese revolution,
since it was Stalin who had misjudged the revolutionary situation in China and had, on that basis,
sent erroneous directives to the Chinese Communist
Party.[24] A variety of sometimes conflicting and
contradictory Russian policies in the early 1920s was
similarly reflected in the controversy over the
establishment of soviets in China after the 1927
crisis.[25]

The power struggle between Stalin and Trotsky
was largely couched in terms of the opposing concepts
of revolutionary strategy which these two men held.
Stalin did not believe that a successful world
revolution was likely in the immediate future. He
therefore hoped to build up Soviet Russia as both
a headquarters and a strong base for future world revolutionary movements. Trotsky disagreed. He
demanded an immediate overthrow of capitalism, and
he urged the Chinese Communists to withdraw from their
coalition with the Kuomintang. During his debate
with Stalin in 1926-1927, Trotsky and the so-called
left-wing opposition in Russia advocated the immediate
establishment of soviets in China to overthrow the
existing capitalist system. They criticized the
policy of Stalin and the Comintern, which advocated
continued cooperation with the Kuomintang.

Stalin believed that he could accomplish the
final goal of the Chinese revolution through the Kuomintang which was, to him, the most progressive
organization in China. Consequently, he did not see
the need to set up soviets. Trotsky, on the other
hand, urged the Chinese Communists to organize soviets
as centers of political power, through which to lead
the agrarian revolution in rural China. The soviets in towns and countryside were authentic political
organs of mass mobilization.[26] Trotsky's idea was
closer than Stalin's to the Leninist model of
institution-building, since Trotsky also emphasized
proletarian leadership in the soviet movement,
with the peasantry playing a supporting role.

Stalin disagreed with Trotsky on the strategy for
the Chinese revolution even after the Shanghai coup
of April 12, 1927. He contended:

> To organize the Soviets of Workers' and
> Peasants' Deputies now, let us say on the

territory of the Wuhan government, would
mean to create a diarchy, to launch a
struggle to overthrow the Kuomintang Left
and form a new soviet authority in
China.[27]

What then should the function of the soviets be? According to Stalin, who opposed their establishment
at this stage, "the Soviets of Workers' and Peasants' Deputies are the organs of a struggle to overthrow the existing authority and establish a new
one."[28] Yet he saw no reason to overthrow the
existing authority of the Kuomintang. He maintained
that the soviets should only be formed at the stage of
the socialist revolution. During the bourgeois-
democratic revolution, the Chinese Communist leaders
should use the left-wing Kuomintang in Wuhan to defeat
both the imperialist forces and the northern warlords, who were considered the tools of the imperialist powers in the mid-1920s. Trotsky, however,
stressed the need to promote the "uninterrupted revolution" in towns and countryside through the
establishment of soviets. This would bypass the
bourgeois-democratic stage, with China moving directly
into the socialist revolution.
     In their debate over the problems of the Chinese
revolution during the crucial years of 1926-1927,
both Stalin and Trotsky agreed that the goals of the
revolution in China were to overthrow the "foreign
imperialist powers" and their agents (such as the
landlords and the compradors) and then to establish a
Communist government. Nonetheless, the two leaders
disagreed on their perception of the Kuomintang
as a political force in China. Despite every indication that the Kuomintang would eventually turn against
the Communists, Stalin regarded the Kuomintang as
a progressive organization, helpful in the battle against foreign imperialist powers. Trotsky, on
the other hand, insisted that the Kuomintang had
become a reactionary force after the April coup of
1927. He argued that the revolution led by the
Chinese bourgeoisie had already failed. In his opinion, the Chinese Communist Party should sever its
relationship with the Kuomintang and transform
the revolution into a socialist movement. Soviets
should be established at once to carry out the
"uninterrupted revolution" through the mobilization of
the working masses.
     No matter how perceptive it may have been,
Trotsky's analysis of the Chinese revolution did not
prevail either in the policymaking organs of the

Comintern or in the Russian government. The Chinese
Communist leaders were in need of a new organizational strategy with which to maintain the sustained
growth of their revolutionary activities. Although
Trotsky proposed a policy that would have helped them
accomplish the objectives of the Chinese revolution,
Stalin had the power to control the policymaking
machinery of both the Comintern and the Chinese Communist Party.

During the fateful years of 1924-1927, the Russian leaders could draw on Lenin's teachings, as
well as on the Russian revolutionary experiences of
1905 and 1917. They did not, however, understand
either the realities of the Chinese revolution or the
thinking of its leaders. Moreover, they did not
know when the soviets should be introduced into an
economically backward and politically fragmented
country like China; nor could they determine the extent of the involvement of the peasantry and the
national bourgeoisie in the soviets of China.

Stalin's attitude toward the establishment of
Chinese soviets was consistent with his belief that a
coalition should be maintained between the revolutionary proletariat and the national bourgeoisie at
the stage of bourgeois-democratic revolution. He
could not therefore understand why it was desirable to
organize soviets in China in the 1920s. In late
1926, when Pavel Mif, a Russian expert on China and
one-time president of Sun Yat-sen University in
Moscow, suggested the formation of Chinese soviets,
Stalin responded:

> Comrade Mif believes that we should call
> at once for the formation of soviets,
> or peasant soviets, in the Chinese country-
> side. I believe that this is a mistake.
> Comrade Mif is too much in a hurry.
> It is out of the question to form soviets
> in the countryside and to leave out the
> industrial centers in China. Yet the
> question of forming soviets in the Chinese
> industrial centers has not yet become
> the order of the day. Furthermore, we
> must not forget that soviets cannot
> be considered independently of their con-
> nection with the whole situation. It
> would be possible to organize soviets, i.e.,
> peasant soviets, only if China's peasant
> movement were reaching its zenith, were
> breaking down old power and creating a new
> one -- on the assumption that the indus-

trial centers of China had already broken
down the barrier and entered on the
phase of forming a soviet government. Can
it be said that the Chinese peasantry or
the Chinese revolution as a whole has
already entered on this phase? No, this
cannot be said. Therefore, to speak
of soviets now is to try to outpace the
situation.[29]

THE CHINESE COMMUNIST ATTITUDE TOWARD THE SOVIETS

When the enlarged meeting of the Politburo convened in November 1927, the Chinese Communist
Party was under the leadership of Ch'ü Ch'iu-pai.
This plenum decided to proclaim the formation
of soviets in China. It was characterized by its extreme "left" position under the direction of a new
Comintern policy. The so-called leftist adventurism
reached its peak. The meeting laid down the policy
line of shifting the revolutionary center from the
countryside to the cities, thus reversing the earlier
decision made at the August 7 Conference to carry
out the peasant uprisings in rural China.

The November plenum called for the establishment
of urban-oriented soviets in China. It adopted
Lenin's concept of the soviets as an ideological
foundation on which a new theory of revolution was
to be formulated. At the same time, it used the concept as a part of the reality of the Chinese revolution and as a new model for the development of
organizational strategy. In doing so, the Chinese
Communist leaders encountered serious problems
of theoretical justification. They had to transform
an urban-based revolutionary strategy into one
based on the rural sector of society, while staying within the framework of bourgeois-democratic revolution.

Contrary to what Stalin believed, the reality
of the Chinese revolution was at its lowest ebb after
the 1927 debacle. "What was required of the party
as a whole was to retreat in a proper way instead of
continuing the offensive."[30] Yet, under the assumption that the revolutionary tide was indeed rising,
the new leadership of the Chinese Communist Party
practiced the techniques of urban revolution in the
rural areas. The Autumn Harvest Uprising, staged
by Mao Tse-tung, and the occupation of Swatow by Yeh
T'ing and Ho Lung resulted in tragic failure.
Although there were indications of a down-surge of
the revolutionary wave, the enlarged meeting of the

Politburo in November 1927 reversed the decision of
the August 7 Conference to concentrate on the
revolution in the countryside. As Trotsky had contended in his debate with Stalin, the Politburo
reaffirmed that the existing Chinese political
situation was a part of the "uninterrupted revolution." Since the process would continue for a long
time, the Chinese Communist leaders urged party
members not to harbor any illusion of achieving instant victory.[31]

As both the resolution adopted by the November
Politburo meeting and the theoretical writings
published in *Pu-erh-sai-wei-k'o* seem to indicate,
the Chinese Communist leaders were split into a number
of factions after the August Emergency Conference of
1927. Two major factions, divided along the lines
of opposing concepts of the Chinese revolution,
played a dominant role in theoretical debates and discussions. On the basis of their analysis of the
revolutionary situation in China and their positions
on the policy issues, the members of the Politburo
could be classified as the militant "left" and
the moderate "right" at the time of the November
meeting.

The militant "left" faction, which took over the
leadership of the Politburo, contended that the
bourgeois-democratic revolution in China had been
transformed into the socialist stage. The Chinese
Communist Party should therefore adopt a socialist program. The leaders of this faction demanded not
only changes in party policy in accordance with the
new revolutionary situation, but also transformation
of the peasant associations into a soviet type of
proletarian organizations. "Only the Bolshevik type
of organization can help the proletarian class to
struggle resolutely against the foreign and domestic
bourgeoisie," an editorial of *Pu-erh-sai-wei-k'o*
asserted. It outlined the tasks of the new organization as follows:

> It will also help the peasants and poor
> people to overthrow courageously the rule
> of the gentry and bourgeois class; to
> eliminate feudalistic exploitation by the
> confiscation of the land owned by the
> landlord class; and to establish the
> soviet system for the implementation of
> the dictatorship of the proletarian
> masses.[32]

The principal contention of this faction was that

the proletarian class had to take over the leadership of the revolutionary movement after the 1927 debacle. The social forces with which the Chinese
Communist Party should be allied at the stage
of socialist revolution were the urban proletariat and
the rural laborers. This militant "left" faction
was led by Ch'ü Ch'iu-pai, who succeeded Ch'en Tu-hsiu
as the general secretary of the party. He was supported by such other members of the Politburo as
Li Li-san and Ch'en Tu-hsiu. According to these leaders, only the urban proletariat could lead the
Chinese revolution. Once the proletarian class was
placed in the position of power, it would continue to
hold power and keep the revolution "uninterrupted"
until socialism was achieved in China. In this way,
the two revolutions -- bourgeois-democratic and
proletarian-socialist -- could be combined into one
"permanent revolution" without interruption. On the
basis of this assumption, the Chinese Communist
leaders formulated a policy of military "putschism,"
which assumed the form of military uprisings in urban
centers during the late 1920s.
    On the other hand, the moderate "right" faction
argued that the Chinese Communist Party must continue the bourgeois-democratic revolution and introduce the soviets only as a "transitory form of
revolutionary government." The Chinese revolution was
making a graduate transition from the bourgeois-
democratic stage to the socialist stage. It had not,
however, quite reached the stage of socialist revolution yet. The moderate "right" leaders saw the
achievement of socialism in China as the climax of a
long process of development, not as a sudden transformation brought about by skipping the stage of
bourgeois-democratic revolution. In this transitional
bourgeois-democratic stage, the soviets under proletarian leadership were to play the key role of not
only mobilizing the masses in the revolutionary
processes, but also of bridging the vast gap between
party policy and the realities of the revolutionary
situation, a gap created by the breakdown of the
united front policy. The views of the moderate
"right" leaders were thus based on their assessment
of the revolutionary situation in China. The revolutionary tide had already begun to subside when the
Kuomintang turned against the Communists in April
1927, and it reached its lowest ebb when the Wuhan
government, led by the left-wing Kuomintang,
broke away from its coalition with the Chinese
Communist Party. As the moderate "right" leaders
perceived, the revolutionary upsurge was not likely

to occur in the near future.

What was now required of the Chinese revolution, according to the moderate "right" faction, was to continue the strategy of the bourgeois-democratic revolution, in which the national bourgeoisie ought to play an important role, under the leadership of the working class. The aim was to achieve the unification and independence of China by overthrowing the "foreign imperialist powers," and the eradication of the feudalistic and exploitative system by carrying out the land revolution. This faction was led by Chang Kuo-t'ao and supported by Hsiang Ying, Ts'ai Ho-sen, and Lo Chang-lung.[33]

The question of different stages of the Chinese revolution aroused furious controversies among Chinese Communist leaders during the months between the August 7 Conference of 1927 and the Sixth Party Congress of June-July 1928. The breakdown of the united front inevitably affected the course of revolutionary action. What ought to be the role of the soviets? Should they be introduced at the bourgeois-democratic stage of the revolution or only at the socialist stage? During this period, the views of the Chinese Communists shifted and their attitudes vacillated. This was due partly to the fluid revolutionary situation in China. Nonetheless, there was also the problem of choosing between two opposing concepts of revolutionary strategy. Other related questions had to be answered: Which social force should assume the leading role in the existing stage of the revolution? How should the current stage of the Chinese revolution be determined? Which organization should be responsible for implementing the revolutionary policy of the Chinese Communist Party?

The controversy between the militant "left" and the moderate "right" over the nature and the role of the soviets was reflected by their different approaches to the Chinese revolution in the post-1927 years. Representative of the positions of the militant "left" faction were three articles signed by Ch'ü Ch'iu-pai and three editorials which were probably written by Ch'ü as well. They were all published by the party journal, *Pu-erh-sai-wei-k'o*.[34] According to these writings, the Chinese revolution was already in the socialist stage; the dictatorship of the proletariat and the peasantry ought to be established within the institutional framework of the soviets. As one editorial in the journal stressed, "The soviets are the most suitable political system for China at the present stage of the revo-

lution."[35]   It quoted Lenin's dictum that "once the
soviet system appears, the democratic parliamen-
tary system will disappear" and maintained that "the
soviet system is the form of the dictatorship of
the proletarian class" for China in the late 1920s.[36]
It concluded:

> Between the bourgeois-democratic system,
> i.e., so-called Western democracy, and the
> soviet system, i.e., proletarian democra-
> cy, there is absolutely no other form
> of political system which could be applied
> to the current stage of the Chinese
> revolution.[37]

In sum, the militant "left" leaders insisted that the
Chinese Communist Party ought to define the current
Chinese revolution as being in the socialist stage and
introduce the concept of the soviets as the institutional value of the revolution.

On the other hand, the moderate "right" faction
argued that China in the late 1920s was not yet
ripe for a socialist revolution. A sharp distinction should be made between the successive stages of
bourgeois-democratic revolution and socialist revolution. The first stage had to be completed before
the Chinese revolution could embark on the second.
The Chinese Communist Party must formulate a policy to
promote the first stage of revolution. To win the
support of the masses, it had to organize soviets.
This would enable the masses to participate as fully
as possible in the execution of the agrarian revolution. In a rebuttal to the claims of the militant
"left" faction, the moderate "right" leaders contended
that "it is incorrect to say that the Chinese soviets
have already become the form of the dictatorship of
the proletariat."[38]   Instead, they "ought to be
organized at the time of the uprising to provide leadership for the revolutionary masses."[39]

According to the moderate "right" faction, the
soviets should be organized under the following three
conditions: (1) at the time of the actual revolution
to insure greater participation of the masses, including soldiers and ordinary working people; (2) when
the political and economic crisis became so critical
that the existing regime was losing its power base;
and (3) when the Communist Party planned to seize
power with the support and participation of the majority of the working class. But could the soviets be
established in colonial and semicolonial countries
like China at the stage of precapitalist development?

Could they function as the instrument of the dictatorship of the proletariat?

According to Lenin, a nationalist revolution was
a "bourgeois-democratic revolutionary movement."
During this stage, "the important classes to be allied with in the backward countries are the peasant masses." The moderate "right" faction of
the Chinese Communist Party concurred. Its leaders
contended:

> The peasant masses under feudalistic
> oppression and exploitation should be able
> to understand and accept the meaning and
> significance of the soviets and be willing
> to participate in their organization.[40]

This faction believed that the Chinese revolution had
moved from the stage of coalition with the bourgeois
class to the stage of opposing it. Under such circumstances, the revolution should call for the
establishment of the soviets.[41] Nevertheless, the
"right" leaders emphasized:

> We must make it clear that the soviet is
> not supposed to function as the instrument
> of the dictatorship of the proletariat,
> but to serve as a transitory form of
> government with the support of the workers
> and peasants.[42]

Thus, this moderate faction clearly supported the
argument put forward by Lenin after the March revolution of 1917 in Russia. As the bourgeois-democratic
revolution had not yet been completed, the soviets
should only serve to fulfill the objectives of that
existing stage of the revolution.

The central questions in the controversy between
the militant "left" and the moderate "right" persisted: Who should assume the leadership of the
Chinese revolution? Which group should initiate the
formation of the soviets? How were the soviets to
be organized and operated? While the Politburo of the
Chinese Communist Party adopted the slogan "Establish
Soviets" and turned its revolutionary efforts from
the countryside to the urban centers, the controversy
between the two factions continued into the first
half of 1928. Faced with both the organizational problems of the party and the problems of revolutionary strategy, the Chinese Communist leaders
labored to search, through debates and discussions,
for a new form of organization by which they could not

only appeal urgently to the masses but also involve
them in revolutionary activities. A product of this
search was the development of a new concept of the
soviets meant to satisfy the opposing "left" and
"right" factions.

This new concept of the soviets redefined the
current stage of the revolution and placed the soviets
within it. The soviets now functioned as an organizational technique of fusing the two stages of revolution. The Chinese revolution was still in the
bourgeois-democratic stage, and the most essential
function of the soviets was to mobilize the working
masses in both urban and rural areas and to unleash their revolutionary strength for the final victory. As the resolution of the November Politburo
meeting asserted, "to establish the soviets is
actually to continue the revolutionary struggle."[43]
With such a justification, the Chinese Communist leaders proclaimed the slogan "All Power to the Soviets!"
just as Lenin had done during his struggle to gain
political power in Russia. The ambiguity of the concept, however, created many problems at the local
administrative level, as the Chinese Communists
continued to implement the dual goal of carrying out
the bourgeois-democratic revolution at the national
level and of legislating and implementing socialist programs at the local level in Kiangsi.

Based on the new concept of the soviets, the
party's new policy must incorporate the programs of
"mobilizing the masses to help stage uprisings and of
generating revolutionary consciousness for the sake
of seizing political power."[44] To win mass support, as the Chinese Communists perceived, was a step
on the way to the seizure of political power; the
class struggle was no longer the chief task of the
Chinese revolution. According to the Politburo
resolution, "all class struggles must be converted to
the struggle for the seizure of political power within
the institutional framework of the soviets." Under
this new policy, the Chinese Communist Party depended
on the soviets for the mobilization of the masses,
as well as the creation of the objective conditions
in which they were to participate in the revolutionary
seizure of power. The "mass-line" technique had thus
risen to the level of a revolutionary strategy in
which the soviets were to perform the important function of bridging the gap between the party and the
masses by mobilizing them for the revolutionary
movement. How then were the soviets to be formed?

According to the resolution of the November
Politburo meeting, the soviets were to be organized

only when the *pu-tung* (insurrection) took place in a
given region and when it persisted for a certain
period of time. When the guerrilla-type peasant army that had staged the insurrection moved away
to stage another *pu-tung* in another region, a revolutionary committee was to be organized to provide
leadership for the local area. This committee had the
administrative responsibility of conducting local
elections and supervising the establishment of the
soviet system of government in the region. The
Politburo resolution instructed:

> As soon as the peasant uprising takes place
> in a village, the local organization like
> the peasant association should be immediately
> transformed into the revolutionary commit-
> tee with direct participation of the
> three elements of local power: the party,
> the army, and the mass organization.[45]

The primary function of the revolutionary committee was to mobilize the masses of the region
by including them in the administrative processes of
confiscation and redistribution of land. It was also
to eliminate such oppressive elements as local
gentry and bandits, to exterminate every aspect of
the traditional feudalistic social structure, and to
carry out guerrilla activities at the regional
level. The guerrilla struggle was "to disarm the
enemy forces and organize a revolutionary army unit
with direct participation of the workers and the
peasants."[46] These activities were designed to lay
the groundwork for the establishment of the soviets in
the villages after the peasant uprisings had taken
place.

Although the organizational concept of the
soviets was explicitly outlined in the resolution
adopted by the November meeting of the Politburo in
1927, the soviets were still only an ideal form
of governmental institution which the Chinese Communist leaders hoped to create rather than a revolutionary reality already in existence. In their search
for a new concept of political structure, as well as
in the course of creating a new power base, the
Chinese Communists were able to come up with the
organizational model of the soviets. Not only would
this institution create a new value system, but it
would also designate the roles of various groups
within the Chinese revolution. It would further serve
as a rallying point on which the two contending factions of the party were able to compromise their

conflicting approaches to the Chinese revolution --
the revolutionary strategy of militant "putschism" and
the policy of moderate "gradualism." The concept
of the soviets was so broadly defined that both
factions could use it to justify their course of
action. While the Sixth Party Congress was held in
June-July 1928 under the direct influence of the
Comintern authority in Moscow, that influence was
minimal when the November Politburo meeting developed
its concept of the soviets in 1927.

In the Sixth Congress, the Chinese Communists
concluded that the overall policy of both their party
and the Comintern since the August 7 Emergency Conference was basically correct. Nevertheless, in their
implementation of the policy, some leaders had failed
to mobilize the masses broadly enough to help them
participate in the execution of the urban revolution
of military insurrections. The question in June-
July 1928 was how to restructure the party organization and reorient its revolutionary strategy.
This became the focus of policy disputes and factional struggles within the Chinese Communist leadership. The influential militant "left" faction in
the Politburo had favored the policy of shifting from
rural revolution to armed uprisings in urban centers. Its leaders came under severe criticisms at the
Sixth Congress of the party.

In many respect, the Sixth Party Congress
of 1928 was a particularly interesting and important
event in the history of the Chinese Communist movement. This was so not simply because the meeting
was convened in Moscow, but rather because the
Communist leaders in this congress were able to reach
a compromise solution to the conceptual problems of
the Chinese revolution and to define the concepts
of the soviets as an organizational form of mass
political movement. It was also at this congress that
the dispute over the policy issues became an open,
all-out struggle between the two major factions. The
split within the 176-member delegation was caused
not so much by the differences in their approaches
to the Chinese revolution as by the manner in which
the Politburo, under Ch'ü Ch'iu-pai's leadership,
attempted to resolve the organizational problems of
revolutionary strategy.[47]

As the party's general secretary, Ch'ü gave a
political report to the plenary session of the
congress. This was followed by the eminent Comintern
leader Bukharin's speech on "The Present Situation
of the World Revolution and the Tasks of the Chinese
Communist Party." The political resolution of the

congress was drafted and subsequently adopted by
the participants on the basis of these two reports.
It read in part:

> The crux of the Chinese revolution and the
> fundamental and central tasks of the
> Chinese Communist Party at the moment are
> to drive out the imperialists in order
> to bring about the real unification
> of China, and to carry out a thorough
> agrarian revolution, abolishing the private
> ownership of land by the landlord class.[48]

As the resolution stressed, it was erroneous to think
that the present Chinese revolution was being transformed into the socialist stage. It was also incorrect to suggest that the revolution in China was an
"uninterrupted revolution." Thus, the policy line
of the Chinese Communist Party, as adopted at the
Sixth Congress, was considerably influenced by such
moderate leaders of the Comintern as Bukharin, who was
attacked and ousted by Stalin a year later.
Earlier in the Politburo meeting of November
1927, the Chinese Communist leadership had insisted
that the revolution was being transformed into the
socialist stage, because the bourgeoisie in China had
been incapable of overthrowing the feudal and military class by means of a democratic revolution. Under
such circumstances, the Chinese revolution could not
wait "until the conclusion of the bourgeois-democratic
revolution. *It should move directly into the socialist revolution.*"[49] What the Politburo suggested
was that the party must follow the tactics of the
socialist revolution even though the "main task of the
bourgeois-democratic revolution had not been accomplished." The adoption of such a resolution in
the November meeting was a compromise between the two
opposing concepts of revolutionary strategy that
had split the Communist leaders into two principal
factions. In this sense, the revolutionary strategy
adopted at the Sixth Congress in 1928 was a logical
development of compromise rather than a sudden
and dramatic decision.
Such a compromise came about not because of
changes in the objective conditions in China, but because of changes in the subjective element of power
in the leadership of the Chinese Communist movement. The militant "left" faction had controlled the
policymaking organ of the party since the August 7
Emergency Conference and had implemented the policy of
military "putschism." It was now in retreat because

the moderate "right" faction, having gained enough
support among the delegates, began to criticize
the party leadership and to exert their influence on
the policymaking process. This faction was still
led by Chang Kuo-t'ao, Ts'ai Ho-sen, Hsiang
Ying, and Lo Chang-lung.[50]

As the political views of the delegates to the
Sixth Congress were polarized, so was the political alignment of the factional groups. On the
one hand, the "left" faction, including Ch'ü Ch'iu-
pai and his followers, argued that the revolutionary
strategy of the Chinese Communist Party since the
August 7 Emergency Conference had been basically
correct. Further to the left was a faction that might
be called the "extreme" left. It attacked Ch'ü's
policy on the grounds that it was not really radical
enough to carry out the socialist revolution. This
group was reportedly supported by the followers
of Ch'en Tu-hsiu who did not attend the congress, such
as Wang Lo-fei and Wang Tse-k'ai.

The "right" faction, on the other hand, demanded
that Ch'ü and his supporters publicly confess their
errors and admit their mistakes in the execution
of party policy. Otherwise, they should neither be
allowed to remain in positions of leadership nor
be permitted to carry on the party's work. In between,
however, a moderate center was beginning to emerge
with such leaders as Chou En-lai, Li Li-san, and Teng
Chung-hsia. This group of delegates proposed a policy
that would avoid the "putschist" strategy of Ch'ü
Ch'iu-pai and would help organize the urban proletariat as well as the rural peasantry. They also
proposed the creation of rural soviets and of a Red
Army, similar to what Mao Tse-tung and Chu Teh
were organizing in the Kiangsi soviet base. In
the minds of many delegates, the rural soviets had
become the core of the Chinese revolution. Nevertheless, the moderate center continued to emphasize
the cities as the focus of the revolution in China,
with the countryside being merely an important
auxiliary to the urban-centered movement.

The difference over policy issues and the conflicts of the factional groups were reflected in the
election of the seven-member Politburo, which represented the dichotomy between the "left-right" policy
lines. While Ch'ü Ch'iu-pai was representative of
the "left" faction, Chou En-lai, Li Li-san, and
Hsiang Chung-fa belonged to the moderate "center"
group. Chang Kuo-t'ao, Hsiang Ying, and Ts'ai Ho-sen
represented the "right" faction of the congress
delegates. Hsiang Chung-fa was elected to the post

of general secretary as a compromise candidate. He
also had the support of Pavel Mif, the Comintern
expert on Chinese affairs. Mao Tse-tung did not go to
Moscow to attend the Sixth Congress, and he was not
elected to the Politburo. He was, however,
elected to the Central Committee of the party
in recognition of his work in creating the rural
soviet in the border region of Kiangsi.

The conflicting policy issues of the "left-right"
groups were hence resolved with the election of
leaders representing all main factions and with the
adoption of a revolutionary strategy of the moderate
"center." The congress had reversed the earlier
"putschist" strategy and turned to the cautious and
moderate policy line of the bourgeois-democratic revolution. The party's new policy was to organize
the urban proletariat quickly and, at the same
time, to promote the kind of rural soviets and Red
Army that Mao and Chu Teh were building up in Kiangsi.
The slogan "Establish Soviets," which had been
adopted earlier in the November Politburo meeting
of 1927, was transformed into a concrete and practical
policy when the Sixth Congress passed the "Resolution on the Organizational Questions of the Soviet Government."[51] The concept of the soviets
was meant to be a compromise solution to the problems
of conflicts and of opposing strategy between the
"left" and "right" factions. It had now become the
institutional basis of the bourgeois-democratic revolution, as well as the organizational technique
for implementing the party's new programs.

The concept of the soviets was crystallized even
further in the Sixth Congress as the basic value
underlying the organizational techniques by which
three important policies were to be implemented. They
were, namely, the execution of the agrarian revolution, the expansion of the Red Army, and mass
mobilization. The soviets were perceived by the
Chinese Communist leaders as the most effective form
of political organization to bridge the gap between
the party's policy and the masses of the people.
According to the resolution:

> The soviets should be organized on the
> principle that the working masses provide
> the direction of the organization and
> the industrial workers take the leadership
> in it.[52]

The party's new policy was to direct and promote the
kind of rural soviets that Mao and Chu were creat-

ing in Kiangsi. But, the working class was to assume
the leadership role, and the urban centers were to
be the primary focus of revolutionary strategy,
with the rural areas being only an important auxiliary.

To define the functions of the soviets, the
Sixth Congress adopted a resolution on their organization which served as the guiding principles of
the soviet system of government from 1928 to
1937:

> We must remember Lenin's definition of the
> soviets: the soviets are a new form of
> state organ and their functions are
> as follows: (1) the strength of the workers
> and the peasants lies in the maintenance
> of a close relationship with the
> masses; (2) the soviets ought to keep
> a close contact with the masses; (3) since
> the soviets are organized by the general
> election of the people, they should be
> administered according to the will of the
> people and bureaucracy should not be
> permitted; (4) the soviets can improve
> the various problems of the people, since
> they maintain close contacts with all
> kinds of professional organizations; (6)
> the soviets should perform the dual
> function of legislation and administration,
> since they are directly elected by the
> people.[53]

On the basis of the policy formulated at the
Sixth Party Congress, the Chinese Communist leaders
prepared for the organization of the soviets,
which were designed to lead the mass political movement in both the urban and rural areas. Even the
Comintern leaders were gradually persuaded that the
mission of the Chinese Communist movement was to win
over the broadest possible mass support in order
to create a new revolutionary upsurge in China. The
task of implementing such a policy, however, remained
in the hands of the Chinese Communist leaders.
Therefore, their major activities from the Sixth
Congress to the peak of Li Li-san's insurrectionary
policy were directed toward the full establishment
of the soviets for the purposes of carrying out
the agrarian revolution, the expansion of the Red
Army, and the consolidation of the base area.

The concept of the soviets, originated by Lenin
as an organizational technique of mass political

movement, was borrowed by the Chinese Communist leaders and adapted to meet the demands of realities in
China after the failure of their attempts to carry
out an urban-oriented revolution. They accepted the
soviets as the organizational technique of the
"mass-line" style of leadership in the effort to
win over mass support and bridge the gap between the
party's new policy line and the masses of the
people. The concept of the soviets, however, was
gradually adapted to the peculiar revolutionary
situation of China in the course of shifting the
urban-based revolution to a rural-centered revolution
and of resolving the structural problems of the
party and the government. The soviets were thus
developed by such leaders as Mao Tse-tung and Chu Teh
in their endeavor to resolve the particular problems
of the Chinese revolution. These problems were,
for example, the creation of a new political order by
overthrowing the existing political institutions,
the execution of land reform programs by eliminating
the oppressive landlord class, and the expansion
of the Red Army by recruiting and training the
peasant masses. When this framework of a "mass-line"
style of political movement became more universally
applicable, it served as the foundation for developing governmental institutions based on the Kiangsi
soviet. The political institutions developed since
the founding of the People's Republic of China
in 1949 were inspired by the experiences of institution building during the Kiangsi soviet period.
Mao's experiment in the rural base of Chingkangshan in
the 1930s provided the foundation on which he was
able to extend his political institutions throughout
China after his 1949 victory.

NOTES

1. _"Su-wei-ai cheng-ch'üan tsu-chih wen-t'i chüeh-
i-an" ⁄ Resolution on the_Organizational Questions
of the Soviet Government_⁄, adopted by the Sixth
Congress of the Chinese Communist Party on July 9,
1928, in Moscow. The document is included in
Wang Chien-min, *Chung-kuo kung-ch'an-tang shih-kao*
⁄ A Draft History of the Chinese Communist Party ⁄
(Taipei, 1965), Vol. II, pp. 166-79.
2. For the text of this resolution, see *Pu-erh-
sai-wei-k'o* ⁄ Bolshevik ⁄, No. 6 (November 28,
1927), pp. 140-50. This was an official publication
of the Chinese Communist Party Central Committee.
Its first issue appeared in Shanghai on October 24,
1927. The Library of Congress in Washington,

D.C., has Nos. 1-19 (incomplete). The party's Central Bureau of the Soviet Area also published a journal with the same title. See *Pu-erh-sai-wei-k'o*, No. 1 (July 1934), collected in Shih Sou Collection (21 reels of microfilm made available by the Hoover Institution on War, Revolution and Peace, at Stanford University), Reel 15. Hereafter cited as *Shih Sou Collection in Microfilm*.

3. Merle Fainsod, *How Russia Is Ruled* (Cambridge, Mass.: Harvard University Press, 1965), p. 51.

4. *Ibid.*, p. 61.

5. *Ibid.*

6. *Ibid.*, p. 62.

7. A. Shlyapnikov, *Semnadtsatyi god* / The Year 1917_/ (Moscow-Leningrad, 1925-1927), Vol. II, p. 236. Cited in Fainsod, *How Russia Is Ruled*, p. 635.

8. V. I. Lenin, *Collected Works* (London: M. Lawrence Ltd., 1929), hereafter cited as *CW*, Vol. XX, Book 1, p. 21.

9. Lenin, "Speech Delivered at a Caucus of the Bolshevik Members of the All-Russian Conference of the Soviets of Workers' and Soldiers' Deputies" (April 17, 1917), *CW*, Vol. XX, Book 1, pp. 95-103.

10. Lenin, "On the Tasks of the Proletariat in the Present Revolution," *CW*, Vol. XX, Book 1, p. 107.

11. John N. Hazard, *The Soviet System of Government*, 4th edition, revised (Chicago: University of Chicago Press, 1968), p. 40.

12. V. I. Lenin, *Collected Works* (Moscow: Progress Publishers, 1966), Vol. XXXI, p. 188.

13. *Ibid.*, p. 164; and V. I. Lenin, *Selected Works* (New York: International Publishers, 1935), Vol. III, p. 146. Emphasis added.

14. Chang Kuo-t'ao, Ts'ai Ho-sen, and Pien Shih-ch'i were reportedly among the leaders of the fifty-four member delegation. This was the first participation of the Chinese Communist Party in an international conference. See *Shina nenkan* / China Yearbook_/ (Tokyo, 1935), p. 1599.

15. For the statement by Safarov, see Xenia J. Eudin and Robert North, *Soviet Russia and the East, 1920-1927: A Documentary Study* (Stanford: Stanford University Press, 1957), p. 227.

16. *Ibid.*, p. 228.

17. The Program of the Communist Party of the Soviet Union may be found in Jan F. Triska (ed.), *Soviet Communism: Programs and Rules* (San Francisco: Chandler Publishing Co., 1962), pp. 23-129.

18. Victor Kotok, "How the Soviets Function," *The Soviet Representative System* (Moscow: Progress Pub-

lishers, n.d.), pp. 5-31.

19. Triska (ed.), *Soviet Communism*, pp. 23-129.
The quotation appears in Kotok, "How the Soviets
Function," pp. 5-31.

20. See, for example, Allen S. Whiting, *Soviet
Policies in China, 1917-1924* (New York: Columbia
University Press, 1953); Conrad Brandt, *Stalin's Fail-
ure in China, 1924-1927* (Cambridge, Mass.: Harvard
University Press, 1958); Harold R. Isaacs, *The
Tragedy of the Chinese Revolution* (Stanford: Stanford
University Press, 1961); Robert C. North and Xenia
J. Eudin, *M. N. Roy's Mission to China* (Berkeley:
University of California Press, 1963); Robert C.
North, *Moscow and the Chinese Communists* (Stanford:
Stanford University Press, 1963); C. Martin Wilbur and
Julie Lien-ying How, *Documents on Communism,
Nationalism, and Soviet Advisers in China, 1918-
1927* (New York: Columbia University Press, 1956); and
Richard C. Thornton, *The Comintern and the Chinese
Communists, 1928-1931* (Seattle: University of
Washington Press, 1969).

21. Lyman P. Van Slyke, *Enemies and Friends: The
United Front in Chinese Communist History* (Stanford: Stanford University Press, 1967), p. 23.

22. Joseph Stalin, "The Prospects of the Revolu-
tion in China" (Speech delivered to the Chinese
Commission of the Executive Committee, Communist
International, November 30, 1926), *International Press
Correspondence*, No. 90 (December 23, 1926), pp.
1581-84.

23. Van Slyke, *Enemies and Friends*, p. 29.

24. For Ch'en's stand on the failure of the
Chinese revolution, see Ch'en Tu-hsiu, "Kao ch'üan-
tang t'ung-chih shu" $\angle$ An Open Letter to All Comrades
of the Party $\angle$/, in *Kung-fei huo-kuo shih-liao hui-
pien* $\angle$ Compendium of the Historical Materials on the
Communist Bandits Ruining the Country $\angle$/ (Taipei,
1964), Vol. I, pp. 427-45. This work, classified "top
secret," consists of three volumes compiled by the
Kuomintang in Taiwan. An unabridged text of Ch'en's
statement is also included in Hatano Ken'ichi,
Chūgoku kyōsan-tō shi $\angle$ History of the Chinese Communist Party $\angle$/ (Tokyo, 1962), Vol. I, pp. 405-24.
This work consists of seven volumes.

25. Whiting, *Soviet Policies*, p. 6.

26. For Trotsky's view, see Leon Trotsky, *Problems
of the Chinese Revolution* (New York: Pioneer Publishers, 1932). For Stalin's view, see Stalin, "The
Prospects of the Revolution in China," pp. 1581-84;
and his statement at the tenth session of the
eight plenum of the Executive Committee of the Commu-

nist International on May 24, 1927, "China on the Eve of the Bourgeois-Democratic Revolution," reproduced in Eudin and North, *Soviet Russia*, p. 369.

27. Quoted from Eudin and North, *Soviet Russia*, p. 369.

28. *Ibid.*

29. Stalin's speech to the eight plenum of the Executive Committee, Communist International, May 24, 1927, in *ibid.*, p. 291.

30. Hu Chiao-mu, *Thirty Years of the Communist Party of China* (Peking: Foreign Languages Press, 1959), p. 31.

31. *Pu-erh-sai-wei-k'o*, No. 6 (November 28, 1927). This is a special issue devoted to the enlarged meeting of the Politburo of the Chinese Communist Party in November 1927.

32. *Ibid.*

33. These ideas emerged from my conversation with Chang Kuo-t'ao in Hong Kong in December 1964._ See also his memoirs, "Wo te hui-i" ∠ My Memoirs_/, published serially in *Ming-pao*, a Hong Kong monthly, beginning in March 1966.

34. For the editorials, see "Proclamation of the Publication of *Pu-erh-sai-wei-k'o*," No. 1 (October 24, 1927); "Long Live Bolshevism!" No. 6 (November 28, 1927); "Long Live the Soviet System of Government!" No. 11 (December 26, 1927). For the three important articles signed by Ch'ü Ch'iu-pai, see "What Kind of Revolution Is the Chinese Revolution?" No. 5 (November 21, 1927); "The Question of Armed Insurrections," No. 10 (December 19, 1927); and "Democracy and the Soviet System," No. 15 (January 30, 1928).

35. "Long Live Soviet Power!" in *Pu-erh-sai-wei-k'o*, No. 11 (December 26, 1927), p. 307.

36. *Ibid.*, p. 308.

37. *Ibid.*, p. 309.

38. "The Chinese Soviet System and Socialism," *Pu-erh-sai-wei-k'o*, No. 14 (January 16, 1928), p. 427.

39. *Ibid.*

40. *Ibid.*, p. 429.

41. *Ibid.*

42. *Ibid.*

43. For the text of this resolution, see *Pu-erh-sai-wei-k'o*, No. 6 (November 28, 1927).

44. *Ibid.*

45. *Ibid.* It is interesting to note that during the Great Proletarian Cultural Revolution of 1966-1968 the Chinese Communist leaders once again revived the concept of the revolutionary committee. Under the principle of "the three-way alliance,"

the representatives from the revolutionary mass
organizations, the People's Liberation Army, and the
revolutionary cadres (of the party and the government) were able to participate in the policymaking process.

46. *Ibid.*

47. Chang, "Wo te hui-i," *Ming-pao*, No. 29 (May
1968), p. 96.

48. A full text of the resolution, "Chung-kuo
kung-<u>ch</u>'an-tang ti liu-tz'u tai-piao ta-hui chüeh-i-
an" ∠ Resolution_of the Sixth Congress of the Chinese
Communist Party_/, is available at the Division of
Orientalia, Library of Congress, Washington, D. C.   It
is also included in *Shih Sou Collection in Microfilm*,
Reel 15, Item 34.

49. *Pu-erh-sai-wei-k'o*, No. 6.   Emphasis added.

50. A slate of candidates presented by Ch'ü
Ch'iu-pai to staff the eight other committees was
rejected by the congress because the slate excluded
the people who either had opposed the policy of
the Ch'ü Ch'iu-pai leadership or were suspected of
being critical of the policy at various committee
meetings.   Each of these committees was to draft one
resolution on the peasant movement, the land question,
the trade union movement, the women's movement, the
youth movement, the propaganda work, the organizational questions of the soviet government and
the Chinese Communist Party.   What Ch'ü apparently
wanted to do was to avoid any criticism of his
own policy by placing his followers on various draft
committees.   When Ch'ü failed to get approval of
his slate of candidates, he walked out of the congress.   See Chang, "Wo te hui-i," p. 97.

51. "Su-wei-ai cheng-ch'üan," quoted in *n*. 1.

52. *Ibid.*

53. *Ibid.*

8

Chinese Communist Land Reform and Peasant Mobilization, 1946-1948

Jane L. Price

During the third revolutionary civil war (1946-
1949), the Nationalists and Chinese Communists
waged their final campaigns for leadership over China
and for the allegiance of the Chinese people.
Scholars are still debating the sources of the
Communist victory in 1949, but part of the answer
lies in what happened in the Chinese countryside.

One central issue of the civil war was the land
revolution in the liberated areas. In contrast to the
Nationalists, whose agrarian policies were very
weak and superficial, the Chinese Communists paid
considerable attention to land reform. The fact that
they did so during a life-and-death military struggle suggests the importance of agrarian policy
for the war effort.

This subject has posed problems for scholarly
research. Through wartime dislocations, source
materials for the liberated areas were lost or destroyed. Key Communist periodicals ceased publication
when the Nationalist armies overran the liberated
areas. Still, the civil war was decisive for China.
To the extent available information permits, it needs
assessment.

From V-J Day to 1949 Chinese Communist agrarian
policy passed through several phases. A series of
land reform measures between mid-1946 and 1948
tried to balance policies that were radical or moderate in scope, especially concerning the extent of
equalization of wealth and property and the role of
poor peasant leadership.

Shifts in agrarian policy were in response to the
complex requirements facing the Chinese Communist
movement during the civil-war years: accelerat-
ing grass-roots mobilization, smashing local elites,

restructuring rural political power, and maximizing
agricultural production while grappling with a
nationwide military campaign. As the civil war
progressed, the Chinese Communist Party increasingly
relied on the radicalization of the peasantry in
the liberated areas. It promulgated agrarian legislation that went far beyond earlier land reforms and
promised gains in landholdings to the rural poor
whose needs had not been met through earlier
expropriation campaigns. Poor peasants were singled
out for leadership roles in village affairs. Nevertheless, the radicalization of the poor peasants alienated other segments of village society at a
time when the Chinese Communists could least afford
to lose a broad base of support. Thus, Communist
leaders had to reconcile the narrow class interests
of the poor peasants with the larger goals of agrarian
reform: maximizing production and mobilization for
the war effort. Reflecting these contradications,
Chinese Communist agrarian policy displayed a "pendu-
lum" effect, swinging from right to left and back
toward the right during the civil war period. This
chapter examines these shifts in agrarian legislation,
thereby exploring the intricate relationship between
land reform and military and movement-building
requirements of the Chinese Communist Party before
1949.

CHINESE COMMUNIST PEASANT STRATEGY BEFORE THE CIVIL
   WAR

     Historically, the Chinese Communist Party had
employed agrarian reform to promote mass mobilization,
as well as economic and social change. Despite its
long association with the peasant movement, the
Communist leadership had never considered agrarian
reform an end in itself. While there were many
impoverished peasants throughout China who would benefit from either rent and interest reductions or
equalized landholdings, the Chinese Communist Party
was ideologically committed to creating a nation
in which private property would ultimately be
abolished altogether.
     In working toward this goal, the "fury of hur-
ricane" among peasants -- aroused by the land revolution -- helped promote class conflict and eliminate
the landowning elite of the "feudal" society.
Agrarian reform was also a technique for political
reeducation. From their experience in managing
agrarian campaigns, peasants developed a sense of participation in local political life and a capacity

to run village affairs. Such involvement could,
under party leadership, lead to the restructuring of
political power upward from the grass-roots level.[1]
At the same time, the redistribution of large
landholdings among those with little or no land
was to raise the incentive to increase agricultural
output and to encourage more modern forms of production. As rational economic forces prevailed, individual landownership was to give way to collective
ownership and eventually to complete nationalization
of landholdings.

During their experimentation with the peasant
movement in the 1920s, some Chinese Communists
had relied on agrarian reform for mobilizing military
and political support from the rural population.
The promise of rent and interest reduction, as well
as land redistribution, facilitated the formation
of peasant soviets. After the counterrevolution of
1927, the fate of the Chinese Communist Party hinged
increasingly on the rural areas. Apart from shifts
in party line and factional disputes, the Chinese Communists geared their land policy to mobilization
requirements, with the extent of land redistribution
dependent on the type of popular support the party
needed at one particular time.[2]

The aim of the land policy in the soviet areas
around 1930 was to gain broad peasant support.
Although the party leadership treated the landlords
harshly, it permitted the rich peasants to retain the
land they tilled themselves. When the "exploitative" rich peasants came under attack in 1932, the
situation had changed. The Kuomintang's fourth
encirclement campaign and Japanese military activities
in China had exerted pressure on the soviets. Under
these circumstances, the Chinese Communist leadership
felt that the advantages of heightening mobilization
through intensified class struggle outweighed the
drawbacks of narrowing its base of support.[3]

There were also situations in which the Chinese
Communist Party preferred a "moderate" land policy.
During the anti-Japanese war, the Communists tried
to cultivate the support of the broadest possible segment of the Chinese population. This included the
landlord class that had traditionally come under
Communist attack. As part of the "united front" policy, large landholders were not publicly expropriated. Meanwhile, the party enforced rent and
interest reduction to retain peasant support and di-
minish the local influence of the landlords.[4] It
undermined the power of the wealthy in some areas by
restricting usury, taxing rich landholders, and

confiscating their holdings if they did not meet
these obligations.[5] In Manchuria and North China,
where many large landowners were either Japanese or
their collaborators, extensive expropriation took
place in regions liberated by the Communist forces.[6]

The wartime agrarian policy remained in
effect after the anti-Japanese war. The continuation of "moderate" land reform measures in part
reflected the uncertainty among Chinese Communist leaders about the prospects for their struggle
with the Nationalist government.[7] From 1945 on,
however, their land policy was more "radical"
in reality than in name. The party leadership officially called for rent and interest reduction, yet
it tacitly allowed local cadres to implement whatever
policies best suited the conditions of their area.
These included outright confiscation of the holdings
of large landlords.[8] With the end of the war, it
was again possible to intensify class struggle in the
countryside. In the Shansi-Chahar-Hopei, Shansi-
Suiyüan, Shantung, Shansi-Hopei-Shantung-Honan,
Kiangsi, and Anhwei liberated areas, as well as some
regions in Manchuria, rent and interest reduction
was fused with more radical campaigns. In the
"settling accounts" movement, the peasants confronted
their most hated landlords and demanded restitution
of land and money for all past grievances. The
"antitraitor" movement focused on the expropriation of
Japanese collaborators, extremely exploitative landlords, usurers, and evil gentry.[9]

Winning these concessions from landlords raised
the hopes of the peasants, who began to demand more
land. This pressure from below pushed the Chinese
Communist agrarian policy toward the left. The
peasants were most aroused in Shansi, Shantung, Central China, and Hopei.[10] Without formalizing
these local expropriation movements with a Central
Committee directive, the Chinese Communist Party
examined the experiences of the regional work teams
and extracted features most conducive to mass
mobilization for an impending civil war.[11]

On May 4, 1946, when hostilities appeared im-
minent, the party leaders incorporated these features
into the Central Committee "Directive on the Land
Question" (commonly known as the "May 4 Directive").
It raised the slogan of "land to the tiller" and
instructed party members and cadres to lead peasants
in the "antitraitor" and "settling accounts" movements. Although the cadres were to provide resolute
leadership, the tone of the directive was essentially
cautious, reflecting an awareness of the problems

that had already risen during the local campaigns.

According to the directive, tyrants, traitors, and big landlords were to be expropriated, while small and medium landlords were to be handled via negotiations. All landlords were to be left with a means of livelihood. Those who had actively participated in the anti-Japanese resistance efforts were to be treated leniently and encouraged to join a "united front against feudalism." To prevent serious damage to production, the directive forbade the confiscation of the industrial and commercial property of the landlords, as well as the landed holdings of the middle peasants. It also discouraged the expropriation of the rich peasants.

In addition, in areas that were either weakly consolidated or close to enemy territories, peasants were to refrain from demanding land and to rely instead on rent and interest reduction. The directive stressed the need to activate the masses to develop local democratic government, cadres, and party organizations.[12] The Central Committee, however, did not elaborate on the procedures for implementation; rather, it depended on the agrarian legislation subsequently formulated by individual liberated areas.

Following the "May 4 Directive" as a guideline, these regional laws were sensitive to differing local conditions. They called for the confiscation of all landholdings above a certain size and the compulsory sale of holdings that remained in excess after a landlord had "settled accounts." In northern Shensi and some parts of Manchuria, government bonds were issued to landlords in exchange for their land. Government banks in Shantung and Hopei loaned money to peasant associations, which in turn lent it to their members for purchasing the excess holdings of the landlords. In the firmly consolidated areas of Shensi-Kansu-Ninghsia and Shansi-Chahar-Hopei, village public opinion was often strong enough to pressure landlords to donate their land to needy peasants.[13]

Many large landholdings in the liberated areas were redistributed through legislation on the regional level. As the New China News Service in Yenan reported in February 1947, 60 million poor and hired peasants in the liberated areas had received land. In the Shansi-Chahar-Hopei liberated area, one million peasants were each given an average of three to six *mou*. About 15 million in the Shansi-Hopei-Shantung-Honan liberated area received an average of two *mou* each. Three to five *mou* each were distrib-

uted to 15 million poor peasants in the Shansi-
Suiyüan liberated area, and 15 million peasants in
the Kiangsi-Anhwei liberated area were reported
to have also obtained land. Land reform was completed
in Jehol and Chahar outside the Nationalist-
controlled areas. In the eastern Hopei plain near
Peiping, 3.5 million peasants, constituting 80 percent
of the area's population, received a total of 1.7
million *mou*.[14]

The Chinese Communist leadership was very impressed with the effect of these agrarian reform
measures on popular mobilization for the civil war.
As Mao Tse-tung reported:

> The experience of these three months has
> proved that the peasants stood with our
> party and our army against the attacks of
> Chiang Kai-shek's troops wherever the
> Central Committee's directive of May 4 was
> carried out firmly and speedily and the
> land problem was solved radically and
> thoroughly. The peasants took a wait-and-
> see attitude wherever the "May 4
> Directive" was not carried out firmly
> or the arrangements were made too late,
> or wherever this work was mechani-
> cally divided into stages or land reform
> was neglected on the excuse of preoc-
> cupation with the war. In the coming few
> months all areas, no matter how busy
> they are with the war, must resolutely
> lead the peasant masses to solve the land
> problem, and on the basis of the land
> reform, make arrangements for large-scale
> production work next year.[15]

At the outset of the civil war, the odds apparently weighed heavily against the Chinese Communists. Their forces numbered between 1 million
and 1.2 million men, while those of the Nationalist
government were between 3 million and 4.3 million.[16]
The Chinese Communists occupied only one-fifth
of the territory of China, with about one-third of the
total population. There was neither major city nor
industrial center in the liberated areas. The
party had meager financial resources and less than
six hundred pieces of artillery and no tanks. On the
other hand, the Kuomintang government controlled
the principal industrial and urban areas in China.
It would receive 2 billion dollars of aid from
the United States between V-J Day and 1949, including

large quantities of military equipment.[17]

To overcome these disadvantages, the Chinese Communists counted on their ability to mobilize every village in the liberated areas. They asked the inhabitants to harvest more crops, manufacture more clothing and simple military equipment, and send more men to the militia and the regular forces. The most effective incentive for mobilization was land. Peasants were willing to work harder at producing and fighting when they were given land.[18] The necessity to safeguard newly acquired holdings was a powerful argument for work teams to recruit for the local militia and regular army. Regional legislation that followed the "May 4 Directive" specified that families of the members of the People's Liberation Army were to receive shares of land equal to those of other peasants, and it made provisions for tilling the land in the absence of the soldiers.[19]

In some instances, the results of recruitment were overwhelming. In Chi County in southern Hopei, peasants were "eager to fight." A three-day recruitment campaign netted four thousand volunteers, of whom only the best were selected.[20] Between August 1946 and the beginning of 1947, one hundred thousand peasants from Shantung agreed to join the People's Liberation Army to defend their new property.[21] According to one observer, "troops fought harder at the front when they learned that their families had been distributed land."[22]

The realization that extensive popular mobilization could meet the demands of a prolonged war distinguished the Chinese Communist military effort from that of the Nationalist government. During the first year of the civil war, the Kuomintang forces overextended themselves in their attempt to overrun the liberated areas, reoccupy Manchuria, and control all main lines of communication. On the other hand, the Chinese Communists avoided prolonged positional battles and attacked only the weak spots of the enemy. Through guerrilla tactics and with the cooperation of the local population, they were able to render untenable the areas occupied by the Nationalist forces. Moreover, organized villages and their militia helped the Communists to create a stable rear-area for their own regular forces without tying down troops in garrison and supply duties.[23]

By the summer of 1947, the Kuomintang position had deteriorated. The ambitious surge northward to Manchuria and other liberated areas had weakened the Nationalist government in its own territory. The

Chinese Communists took advantage of this situation
and began to deploy large-scale units in limited
counteroffensives on southern and northern fronts.
　　　Commanded by Liu Po-ch'eng and Teng Hsiao-p'ing,
the Shansi-Hopei-Shantung-Honan Field Army forded
the Yellow River in Shantung on June 30, 1947.
It crossed the Lunghai Railway and thrust into the
Tapieh Mountains.　On August 23, the T'aiyüeh
Army under Ch'en Keng and Hsieh Fu-chih crossed
the Yellow River from southern Shansi and marched into
western Honan.　The Eastern China Field Army under
Ch'en Yi and Su Yü moved from central to southwestern
Shantung, while the Shantung Army, commanded by
Hsü Shih-yu and T'an Chen-lin, initiated a counteroffensive in eastern Shantung.　Led by P'eng Teh-huai
and Chang Chung-sun, the Northwest Field Army
turned to northern Shensi.　Early in September,
the Shansi-Chahar-Hopei Field Army started an offensive along the northern section of the Peiping-
Hankow Railway.　Under Lin Piao and Lo Jung-huan,
the Northeast Field Army launched a large-scale autumn
attack on the Changchun-Kirin-Szepingkai region and
on the Chinhsi-Ihsien section along the Peiping-
Liaoning Railway.
　　　These military operations marked a turning point
in the third revolutionary civil war.　By the summer
of 1948, the Chinese Communist Party had established itself in Central China between the Yellow
River and the Yangtze.　It had destroyed the chief
lines of communication in North China and Manchuria.
With the Nationalist troops limited to the areas
surrounding several large cities, the Chinese Communists routed their enemy in Manchuria, North
and Central China in the autumn of 1948.　In the following spring, they crossed the Yangtze.　The Communist consolidation of the mainland followed
soon after the founding of the People's Republic of
China on October 1, 1949.[24]
　　　Both offensive and defensive operations put
enormous strains on the Communist resources.　Even
more troops, supplies, and support workers were
needed to block Nationalist advances into the liberated areas and to stage counteroffensives on enemy
terrain.[25]　Moreover, invading Nationalist armies
were restoring landlords' property rights in the areas
recovered from the Communists.　The Chinese Communist Party in 1947 may have felt that it had to
step up its struggle against local power-holders in
order to maximize support from other quarters,
even if this meant more social disruption.[26]

THE OUTLINE OF THE LAND LAW

The radicalization of the Communist agrarian
reform program can be seen as a response to the
strategic and political pressures of the civil war.
There remained many dissatisfied peasants in the liberated areas who had not benefited from earlier
land reforms. Furthermore, the results of land redistribution were "uneven" in many areas where
the "May 4 Directive" had been applied.[27] Reports
stated that in some areas middle and small landlords
retained 50 percent more land than the middle peasants. "Progressive" landlords who had been active against the Japanese or had family members in the
party, the People's Liberation Army, or mass organizations were allowed two times as much as an average peasant.[28] These old elites often continued to
dominate village affairs.

During the land campaigns, the "activist" peasants often received land and they were not always
the most deserving ones.[29] As the Chinese Communist
leadership believed, these inequities discouraged
a large portion of the population in the liberated
areas from being mobilized for a large-scale
offensive.[30] By "intensifying" agrarian reform
toward equalizing all landholdings throughout the liberated areas, the party hoped to appeal to those
peasants who still had not received their fair share
of land. Both the receipt of land and participation in the process of redistribution would help activate these peasants to support the Communist war
effort.

Parallel to the shortcomings in land reform were
the deficiencies in local party leadership. Just as
the redistribution of land had been "uneven," the
composition of local party ranks was "impure." With
the rapid territorial expansion between 1937 and
1949, Communist party membership increased from about
40,000 to 2,759,456.[31] The bulk of this spectacular
growth occurred during the latter phase of the
anti-Japanese war, as well as during the civil war.
Given the urgent need to furnish leadership in
the liberated areas, the Chinese Communist Party had
not been able to carry out sufficient investigation
of the class background of its members or to promote inner-party education on the local level.[32]

During this time, many landlords, rich peasants,
and their children joined the Communist Party
because of its stand against the Japanese. They
also hoped to use the prestige of the party to protect
their own interests and to retain their influence

over village affairs.[33] In addition, there were a
considerable number of poor and middle peasants who
had joined the party during previous land reform
campaigns. Many of them had been briefed for only
several weeks by Communist political workers and
quickly moved on to organize other villages.[34] With
little understanding of either Marxism-Leninism
or correct work style, even party members of peasant
background fell back on traditional methods of
leadership. When they were authoritarian, bureaucratic, and distorted Communist policies, they alienated the masses from the party.[35]

The tendency to misconstrue party directives was
accentuated by the intense localism in the liberated areas during the first two years of the civil
war. Many of the revolutionary bases had existed as
scattered autonomous units. Even the higher levels
of the party were separated geographically when
the Nationalist forces tried to overrun Yenan in
early 1947.[36]

The "impure" composition of local party leadership was partially responsible for the inequities
in land distribution, the violent attacks against middle peasants, and the destruction of rural "industrial and commercial" property. It was necessary to
overhaul local party ranks to accomplish agrarian
reform.[37] The Chinese Communist leadership envisioned
that the dynamics of the land revolution itself would
promote party "purification." At the same time, the
campaigns to equalize landholdings would arouse
the peasants to criticize the manner in which local
cadres and party members had handled the agrarian
reform of the past. Through these evaluations
of local party branches, the Communist leaders would
determine which members required reeducation, censure,
or expulsion from the ranks. Party "purification"
was essential to the civil war effort. It would
insure thorough agrarian reform, as well as maintain
reliable leadership in the rear areas of the People's
Liberation Army.

The decision to "purify" local party ranks
throughout the liberated areas coincided with the attempt to intensify agrarian reform. In September
1947, more than one thousand cadres from all liberated
areas assembled in Hsipaip'o Village of P'ingshan
County in Hopei. After extensive discussions, they
adopted the Outline of the Land Law, which was
officially promulgated by the Central Committee on
October 10, 1947.[38]

As with the "May 4 Directive," the National Land
Conference tried to evaluate the experiences in land

reform throughout the liberated areas. It formulated
as guidelines the most effective measures already
in operation in Communist-controlled areas. Although
the law was to be applied to all liberated areas,
each region had the option of working out "concrete
methods appropriate to local conditions."[39]

The Outline of the Land Law called for the
abolition of landownership rights of all landlords,
ancestral shrines, temples, monasteries, schools, and
other institutions. The confiscated land was to
be redistributed among poor and landless peasants,
with holdings of equal size for each member of
the village population. The size of these holdings
would be adjusted to consider the quality and
fertility of the land. There were provisions for such
special types of property as woodlands, water-works,
wasteland, and public land. The houses, agricultural implements, grain, and animals of landlords and
rich peasants were similarly subject to confiscation.

Members of the People's Liberation Army and
their families[40] -- as well as the families of Kuomintang soldiers, officers, and officials -- would receive shares of land equivalent to those of other
peasants. Since landlords were to be eliminated "as
a class" and not as individuals, they were also
entitled to a portion of the land. Although "national
traitors" could not receive land, their families
were eligible. All rural "industrial and commercial"
holdings were to remain intact. Unless demanded
by the peasants, redistribution was unnecessary in
areas where there had been previous movements to
equalize landholdings.[41]

The Outline of the Land Law differed from the
"May 4 Directive" in both tone and content. Although
both documents called for "land to the tiller," the
rhetoric of the 1947 land law was more forceful.
It demanded an end to the entire "agrarian system
of feudal and semifeudal exploitation" and the total
elimination of landlords as a class, with no
preferential treatment for "progressives."

Moreover, the most outspoken peasants and meri-
torious cadres had generally been the first to
receive land under the "May 4 Directive." According
to the Outline of the Land Law, however, land was
to be so redistributed that all holdings were
of equal size, regardless of the qualifications of the
recipients. It also stipulated that the legal executive organs for land reform were specific peasant
organizations, while the "May 4 Directive" had left
this matter to the governments of individual liberated

areas. Under the 1947 land law, such institutions
as temples, schools, and ancestral halls were
subject to expropriation along with the lands of
individuals, although families of Kuomintang soldiers
and officials could receive land. The "May 4
Directive" was silent on these points.

There were six features of the Outline of the
Land Law that affected its implementation. First, it
vested all legal authority for supervising land
reform in meetings of village peasants and their
committees, then in the Leagues of Poor Peasants and
the associated committees. The latter groups were
composed of hired farm laborers, tenant farmers,
and land-poor peasants. Unlike the Associations of
Peasants, they excluded middle and rich peasants.
In contrast to the "May 4 Directive," the 1947 land
law stressed the leadership and interests of the
poor peasants without opposing the encroachment on
middle peasants.

Second, the Outline of the Land Law did not give
any criterion either for demarcating rural classes
or for identifying poor peasants. Third, it was
applicable to all liberated areas, including those
recently occupied by Communist forces. Fourth, the
law upheld the protection of rural "industrial and
commercial" property without providing any definition
for these holdings. Fifth, it did not specify if
landholdings were to be equalized by pooling all
property together, or whether middle and rich peasants
could keep most of the land, with minor adjustments
in cases of excess. Last, it stipulated that land
did not have to be redistributed in areas that
had experienced previous agrarian campaigns. Nonetheless, it furnished no standard for evaluating the
success of past redistribution movements.

Following the National Land Conference, there
were large regional meetings of cadres in the
liberated areas to discuss land reform and party
"purification."[42] The governments of every liberated
area could either accept the land law as promulgated
or amend it to meet local conditions. The Shansi-
Chahar-Hopei liberated area chose the former option,[43]
while the Northeast and Shansi-Hopei-Shantung-
Honan liberated areas preferred the latter. The
supplementary measures compensated for some of
the ambiguities of the 1947 law. For example, those
adopted by the Shansi-Hopei-Shantung-Honan liberated area clarified the differences between the cancellation of commerical and noncommercial debts,
as well as prohibited the confiscation of the houses
and property of rich middle peasants. They also

suggested voluntary migration from overpopulated regions as a means to relieve the hardship of the poor peasants.[44]

Even these "supplementary measures," however, could not insure the smooth execution of the land reform. The legislation was still too general to fit the needs of every village. There were neither adequate guidelines for flexible application of the reform nor instructions to provide different implementation procedures in new and older liberated areas.

As a result, difficulties that had appeared in earlier land campaigns were intensified in the initial stages of executing the 1947 law. During the application of the "May 4 Directive," the Communist leaders had reported many "right" deviations, such as allotting landlords too much land and failing to employ the "mass line." There were also such cases of "left" deviations as attacking middle peasants and rural industrial and commercial holdings. Because of the radical character of the 1947 land law -- particularly the emphasis on the equality of landholdings and on the authority of the Leagues of Poor Peasants -- the "left" deviations became more widespread.[45]

Contributing to the prevalence of deviations in the work of land reform was the dispersion of the Central Committee in 1947-1948. After the Nationalist invasion of Yenan, Mao Tse-tung, Chou En-lai, Jen Pi-shih, and Lu Ting-yi were among those who wandered for almost a year in northern Shensi. Liu Shao-ch'i headed an alternate leadership group (which also included Chu Teh) that was designated the Working Committee of the Central Committee. It made its headquarters in Hsipaip'o Village of P'ing-shan County in Hopei and took charge of the National Land Conference. The Working Committee was dissolved when Mao's group reached Hsipaip'o Village in May 1948 and the Central Committee resumed its normal functions.[46] Physical separation probably delayed the reaction of the ranking leaders to the "ultraleft" line in land reform. Many tasks were heaped on the Working Committee, and Liu was allegedly in charge of the land reform work.[47]

Given the demands of the civil war, the local composition of the Chinese Communist Party, and the complex nature of Chinese agrarian society, it is not surprising that the party leadership encountered difficulties in controlling the social forces unleashed by successive land reform measures. During the Cultural Revolution of the 1960s, however, the issue of "leftist" deviations was personalized.

According to the charges, Liu Shao-ch'i was responsible for the ultraleft excesses in the land campaigns: "kicking aside old cadres," sanctioning too
many killings, and encroaching on middle peasants.[48]
He himself confessed in 1966 that he was to blame for
the mistakes in the agrarian reform of 1947.[49]

As one Cultural Revolution document insists,
Liu and the Working Committee arrived in the spring
of 1947 at Foup'ing, the site of the Chin-Ch'a-Chi
(Shansi-Chahar-Hopei) Central Bureau. Liu reportedly
criticized the agrarian policy of the Chin-Ch'a-Chi
liberated area as "right opportunist." He called
for more "thorough" measures at a bureau meeting.
Pressure from him resulted in a twenty-day "May Reinvestigation" campaign that led to serious "leftist
excesses" -- especially violent beatings of landlords and other people who were considered troublesome. In P'ingshan County alone, more than 130
individuals were allegedly beaten to death during the
"May Reinvestigation" campaign.

According to this document, Liu pressed for
intensifying land campaigns and for making P'ingshan
the model for Communist agrarian reform. He dispatched two work teams -- headed by Feng Wen-pin and
Ch'ien Chün-jui -- to P'ingshan. On the basis of
their findings, Liu convened the National Land
Conference at Hsipaip'o in September 1947. It promulgated the "left" land reform line of "doing everything as the masses want it done." Liu also called
for the dissolution of all party branches and the
disclosure of the names of party members to the
masses. At P'ingshan, the work teams took over the
functions of local party committees, with almost
all cadres below the district level removed from their
posts. Moreover, the Cultural Revolution document
charges the work teams with neglecting "class
analysis," resulting in the infiltration of the
Leagues of Poor Peasants by "bad elements," as well as
in the misclassification of upper-middle, middle,
and even poor peasants as landlords and rich peasants.
More than six thousand of the nine thousand cadres
in P'ingshan were either expelled from the party or
halated in their activities, and 70 percent of
the middle peasant households suffered violations.[50]

While the objectivity of the Cultural Revolution
sources is questionable, there is a passage critical
of Liu Shao-ch'i in Mao Tse-tung's "Speech at a
Conference of Cadres in the Shansi-Suiyüan Liberated
Area" of April 1, 1948. As Mao claimed, Liu had
issued instructions in the spring of 1947 to
convene a conference of secretaries of prefectural

party committees of the Shansi-Suiyüan Subbureau.
This conference, held in June, criticized the "right"
deviations of past programs. It resolved to intensify land reform and party consolidation work.
While Mao granted that "in the main, the conference
was a success," he felt that it had helped promote
"left deviations." It did not issue any instructions
to differentiate land reform in old, semiold, and
new liberated areas. Its resolutions put forward criteria to identify class status that were too
harsh and overemphasized unearthing the hidden wealth
of the landlords. These mistakes were committed
under the slogan of "doing everything as the masses
want it done."[51]

There are very few village-level accounts of
developments in the liberated areas during the
implementation of the Outline of the Land Law; not all
available accounts are rich in detail. While the
problem of sources rules out a definitive analysis of
the agrarian reform in 1947-1948, those accounts
that are available are useful illustrations of both
the complex nature of the land revolution and the
various problems that arose during its course.

The Outline of the Land Law was implemented simultaneously in the old, semiold, and new liberated areas.[52] On the whole, the difficulties
in agrarian reform were related to the length of time
an area had been "liberated." Reports from new
liberated areas stressed the attempts of the "feudal
reactionary" forces to thwart the efforts of the
Communist cadres. In their implementation of the land
law, these cadres frequently pushed for the equalization of all landholdings within several months,
without allowing the land revolution to go through
all stages appropriate to newly consolidated
areas. Profiting from the haste of the cadres,
many landlords continued to remain in power and often
tricked the peasants into attacking each other.[53]

For example, in the Chinghai and Antzu areas of
central Hopei, which bordered on enemy territory,
several villages were reported to have executed the
land law as if they were in an old liberated
areas. Some Chinghai villages neglected to set
up local self-defense corps and openly organized a
League of Poor Peasants. The landlords and rich
peasants who were allowed to stand sentry secretly informed the enemy. The league suffered a surprise
attack, which resulted in the seizure of two men. All
local cadres were subsequently "dismissed." When
the enemy struck again, no cadres could be found.
Several "struggles" against the landlords took place

later, but the peasants did not immediately distrib-
ute the "fruits." The enemy returned and robbed
the village of twelve cattle, five carts, and more
than twenty sacks of grain.

Antzu had only a few cadres, who managed to set
up Leagues of Poor Peasants in two villages. One
village was so unstable that the cadres tried to ex-
propriate the landlords as quickly as possible. They
neglected to go through the "speak bitterness"
phase of agrarian reform that preceded "settling
accounts." Consequently, the majority of the peasants had no opportunity to identify criminal
landlords, some of whom later infiltrated the Leagues
of Poor Peasants. The leagues did not ally with
middle peasants. In confusion, some individuals even
asked their landlords for forgiveness.[54]

Areas that had been under Chinese Communist
influence also experienced serious problems in land
reform. Whereas too much power remained among
the landlords in the new liberated areas, it was
handed to the masses in the old and semiold areas.
The cadres failed to separate the leadership role of
the party from the Leagues of Poor Peasants. Under
the influence of the "poor peasant line," they
gave in to the demands of the peasants and allowed
them to seek the land and property they needed.

In areas where there had been prior expropriation
campaigns, the middle peasants became objects of
attack and were frequently misclassified as rich peasants or landlords. Unshielded from the demands of
the poor peasants, they were increasingly afraid
to continue production for fear that their surplus
would be confiscated. There arose the danger that the
middle peasants as a class would stop supporting the
Chinese Communist Party and its war effort. On the
other hand, the poor peasants wasted their energy in
futile hunts for more land and hidden wealth instead of concentrating on production. Many
industrial and commercial holdings in the countryside
were reported to have been damaged.[55]

For example, representatives from two districts
of Kuo County in Shansi met during the last ten
days of November 1947 to implement the Outline of
the Land Law. It took two months to "struggle"
against landlords and divide their property. The poor
peasants assumed control of village affairs and
organized Leagues of Poor Peasants in all but several "backward" villages. After the work team cadres
had departed, only seven men remained to supervise
the two districts. In thirty-three natural villages
of these two districts, forty-three rich peasants

had been misclassified landlords, 106 middle peasants
were wrongly labeled rich peasants, and five others
were misclassified "bankrupt landlords."[56]

Middle peasants had also suffered misclassification in the administrative village of Tsaichiaai in
Hsing County of the Shansi-Suiyüan liberated area.
Of a total of 552 households, thirty-one middle
peasant families had been identified as "bankrupt and
declining landlords." Among them fifteen had been
classified according to the status of either
their father or their grandfather, five on account of their holdings before the anti-Japanese war,
and seven on the basis of the household possessions.
Three independent cultivators had been misclassified because they had been adopted by or sold to landlords or rich peasants. One wrongly labeled middle
peasant had been an orphan hiring others to work
his lands before he came of age.[57]

ADJUSTMENTS IN AGRARIAN POLICY IN 1948

Once aroused, the radical forces on the grass-
roots level proved difficult to ignore and even more
difficult to control. In the spring of 1948, the
Communist leadership was confronted by demands
from the poor and hired peasants to press further for
equalized landholdings.[58] By the end of 1947, however, some leaders had begun to take steps to
curtail "leftist" excesses in land reform.

The Central Committee group -- led by Mao Tse-
tung and cadres from the Shensi-Kansu-Ninghsia
and Shansi-Suiyüan liberated areas -- met at Yangchia-
k'ou on December 25-28, 1947. They discussed certain tendencies within the party, as well as
policies concerning land reform and mass movements.
In the report of December 25 on "The Present Situation
and Our Tasks," Mao called for "firm unity with the
middle peasants." He cautioned that "rich peasants should generally be treated differently from
landlords" and that "care must be taken to avoid the
mistake of classifying middle peasants as rich
peasants." He continued: "It is necessary to listen
to the opinions of the middle peasants and make
concessions to them if they object." The discussions on the land question at the December meeting
were summarized in Mao's article of January 18,
1948: "On Some Important Problems of the Party's Present Policy." The Communist leaders censured adven-
turist policies toward middle peasants and middle
and small industrialists in the countryside.[59]

Other statements by party leadership advanced the

protection of middle peasants as the overriding issue
in land reform.[60]   The purpose was to apply brakes
to the activities of the poor peasants and to disman-
tle the Leagues of Poor Peasants. Detailed instructions for righting the wrongs against middle
peasants appeared in an address by Jen Pi-shih to a
meeting of the Northwest Front Committee of the
People's Liberation Army on January 12, 1948.
Speaking on "Several Problems Concerning Agrarian Reform," Jen stressed the necessity of "unity with
the middle peasants for victory in the civil war."
He estimated that the middle peasants constituted 50
percent of the population of the old liberated
areas. As he pointed out:

> They have done meritorious work in the
> fight against Japan. Also at the present
> time in fighting Kuomintang reaction-
> aries, they are relied on for a large part
> of the manpower and grain. In our liber-
> ation army at present, 30 to 40 percent
> are middle peasants. If we injure the mid-
> dle peasants, or even go so far as to
> stand in opposition to them, this will
> cause us to be defeated in the war.

To prevent abuses against the middle peasants,
Jen recommended that, first, their holdings should not
be expropriated during land redistribution. Holdings of even the well-to-do middle peasants could not
be touched without their consent. Moreover, lower
middle peasants were entitled to some land "for
the sake of unity." Second, the middle peasants were
to share in managing village affairs in proportion
to their representation in the village population.
Decisions of the Leagues of Poor Peasants were to be
approved by the Associations of Peasants, which
included all classes of peasants. Third, the middle
peasants were not to shoulder by themselves the burden
of supplying grain and manpower to support the front.
Last, restitution was to be made in all cases of
misclassification of middle peasants, and the class
standing of each person was to be determined correctly.
Jen also warned against executing land reform
too quickly. He called for the expropriation of only
the "exploiting feudal classes," which, in the new
liberated areas, were limited to big landlords,
"evil gentry," and members of the armed forces of the
landlords. Only when an area had been militarily
consolidated and sufficiently organized could land

be thoroughly redistributed. According to Jen's
estimate, no more than 8 percent of the rural population should come under attack, with the remainder
supporting the Chinese Communist Party, to insure victory in the civil war.[61]

Jen cited two 1933 documents, which had been
reissued by the Central Committee in December 1947, to
help the cadres delineate rural classes. They were
entitled "How to Analyze Classes" and "Decision on
Some Questions from Agrarian Struggles," and they defined each rural classes by the extent to which it
engaged in exploitation:

1. Landlords owned relatively large plots
of land, did not labor themselves, and
either rented their land or practiced usury.
2. Rich peasants also had sizable landholdings, animals, and agricultural implements. They worked, however, some of the
land themselves and hired the labor of
other peasants.
3. Middle peasants were independent owners
of land, animals, and farm implements, but
they cultivated their own land with little or no "exploitation" of others. The income from "exploitation" for middle peasants could not exceed 25 percent of
their gross income.
4. Poor peasants owned little land,
agricultural implements, or animals. They
cultivated their own land but also sold
a portion of their labor to others.
5. Hired peasants owned no land, animals,
or farm implements, and they sold all of
their labor power.

These definitions did not apply to widows, invalids,
physicians, primary school teachers, and workers
who could not till their own land but were obviously
not landlords or rich peasants.[62]

On February 22, 1948, the Central Committee
issued a directive "On Land Reform and Party Purification Work in the Old and Semiold Areas" that
discussed the different stages in land reform. There
were three classifications of old and semiold liberated areas based on the extent of progress in agrarian
reform work. The first type was usually found in
the old liberated areas where land reform and party
consolidation work had been basically thorough.
The middle peasants -- more than half of whom had
received land in previous campaigns -- constituted 50

to 80 percent of the population. In the eyes of the
Central Committee, there was no need to redistrib-
ute land again. Instead, the party encouraged
those cadres with more land and implements than the
average peasants to help the needy from their own
households. Existing Leagues of Poor Peasants
were to be transformed into "poor peasant groups." To
curtail their authority, they were to be placed within the general Associations of Peasants.

Although the second type had experienced the
same agrarian reform procedures as the first, the Central Committee judged the outcome unsatisfactory.
Only 20 to 40 percent of the population had attained
middle peasant rank, with very few beneficiaries
of past land campaigns. Hence, the instructions for
the second type did not call for redivision of
landholdings, unless it was demanded by the majority
of the peasants. The Leagues of Poor Peasants were
allowed to continue in their leadership role if
they would work with the "new" middle peasants.[63]
The Central Committee anticipated that these leagues
would be converted within one to two months into
"poor peasant groups" within the Associations
of Peasants.

Land reform in the third type was rated poorly,
either because of ineffective implementation of
previous reform legislation or because of proximity to
enemy territory. In these areas, the Central Committee favored the expropriation of rich peasants and
landlords. The operations of the Leagues of Poor
Peasants were to continue for another three to four
months.

Outside of this projection was the timetable for
the new liberated areas, where land reform was to
proceed slowly in distinct stages. In the first
phase which lasted about two years, the landlords were
to be expropriated gradually, with large landlords
being the first to come under attack. The confiscation of the property of the rich peasants and the
equalization of holdings were both withheld until the
second stage. The Associations of Peasants were to
be organized several months after the Leagues of
Poor Peasants. The activists of the leagues were
envisioned as the backbone of leadership in the
Associations of Peasants, with strong participation
from the middle peasants.[64]

The Central Committee defined a number of areas
as "guerrilla zones," where unstable conditions ruled
out either land reform work or mass organizations.
Communist activities there were to be limited
to propaganda, covert organizational work, and the

distribution of some movable property.[65]

Additional evidence of the Central Committee's efforts to mitigate the effects of agrarian legislation on middle peasants can be found in the new edition of the Outline of the Land Law issued in the spring of 1948. Appended to Article Six was a "note" with the following instruction:

> When equally distributing land, you should pay attention to the opinions of the middle peasants. If the middle peasants do not agree, then you should give in to them. Moreover, you should allow the middle peasants to hold comparatively more land than the average amount received by the poor peasants. When equally distributing land in the old and semiold liberated areas, you should proceed according to the Chinese Communist Party Central Committee Resolution of February 22, 1948.[66]

PARTY PURIFICATION AND CONSOLIDATION

The measures adopted at the National Land Conference for party purification were implemented at every level of the Chinese Communist Party from the top down in the months that followed. In most cases, the implementation of the Outline of the Land Law and party purification did not reach the grass-roots level until 1948.

Like agrarian reform, the timing of party purification was tied to developments in the civil war. By January 1948, the military position of the Chinese Communists was substantially stronger than it had been six months earlier. The liberated areas were no longer threatened by Nationalist invasion, and new areas were being consolidated. Consequently, the Communist leadership was not afraid to make local party membership lists available for public inspection.[67]

Moreover, it took time to train the land reform work teams[68] that were to assist in the implementation of the land law and party purification. These teams began their training soon after the land law was promulgated in 1947. Around the New Year holiday of 1948, every college in Pei-ta and Lien-ta had put aside its regular curriculum to study agrarian problems. Students and teachers received training in land reform work and then moved into the countryside. After the completion of their assignments,

scheduled for the early summer of 1948, they would
resume their regular studies on campus.[69]

Liu Shao-ch'i's report on the experience of work
teams in P'ingshan County in western Hopei signaled
the launching of party purification work on a mass
scale.[70] P'ingshan contained both old and semiold areas. In the old areas, the poor peasants made
up 30 to 40 percent of the population, but only 20
percent lacked good land. The poor peasants who
did not have good land constituted 40 percent of the
population in the semiold areas. Almost all the
rich peasants and landlords were family members of
cadres or party members.

According to Liu, the party was dominated by
"landlord elements" in many villages. When the party
branches tried to examine themselves, they made few
changes. Meanwhile, many party members and cadres
under criticism were beaten by peasants. In some
cases, the peasants were incited by rich peasants and
landlords who avenged their losses in past agrarian
campaigns. Some work teams prevented peasants
from participating in land reform and party purification work, while others permitted them to attack
all party members and cadres indiscriminately.
These work teams occasionally "overly aroused" the
masses to struggle against landlords who had already
been expropriated.

These mistakes were corrected when land reform
was combined with procedures for democratizing the
party. Non-party activists were invited to party
branch meetings to help examine the cadres, who under-
went the processes of criticism and "three checkups"
(class origin, ideology, and work style). Punishment
was not harsh and few were expelled from the party.
In most cases, the transgressors were told to
reform themselves through education.

According to Liu, these meetings had a salutary
effect on popular participation in mass organizations. The peasants were more comfortable working
with local party branches where the members could no
longer use the party's authority to mask their
wrongdoings. Although all party branches were subject to public scrutiny, the process of party purification was soon brought under control. Earlier
excesses were avoided by working through party
branches rather than beyond them. Improved purification procedures also facilitated the recruitment of
local activists into the Chinese Communist Party.[71]

Despite the recommendations in Liu's report,
party purification, like agrarian reform, produced
both "right" and "left" deviations. The "right" de-

viations -- bureaucratism, authoritarianism, "impure" work style, and failure to examine class
background -- prevailed during the early stages of the
agrarian reform in the civil war years. They were
criticized at the regional conferences of cadres
that followed the National Land Conference in the
autumn of 1947. By early 1948, however, there had appeared "left" deviations. In the work of party
purification, such manifestations were termed
"tailism," referring to the failure of local leaders
to educate and guide the masses while making concessions to popular demands.

In this atmosphere, many cadres suffered unwar-
ranted criticism and punishment was occasionally
too severe. Some land reform work teams chose
to view the Leagues of Poor Peasants as more reliable
leadership groups than the local party branches.
They were misled by the ties of some party members
with rich peasants and landlords, and they hastily concluded that all party branches were under landlord influence. Some work teams used class origin
as the only basis of evaluating local cadres.[72] The
Chinese Communist programs for cadre training and
intraparty education could not keep abreast of
membership expansion. Most local cadres therefore
lacked the theoretical or practical expertise to
direct a vast and extremely complex social movement.
Even those with desirable class background had
difficulty in comprehending the objectives of Chinese
Communist land policy. Rather than viewing agrarian
reform as a mobilization technique for the war effort, they tended to stress the creation of absolutely
equal landholdings as an end in itself. Expectations
were distorted and the cadres were blamed for their
failure to achieve the impossible.[73]

As the purification movement progressed, under-
estimation of land reform work and excessive criticism
of cadres shook the party at its foundation. To
restore morale, Mao Tse-tung delivered his "Speech
at the Conference of Cadres in the Shansi-Suiyüan
Liberated Area" on April 1, 1948. He assured
the cadres and party members that their work had been
basically successful and that the "left" deviations
in agrarian reform and party purification had been
curtailed. Mao underlined the real goals of the
agrarian reform as "abolition of feudalism" and progress in economic production. He insisted that "we
do not advocate absolute equalitarianism. Who-
ever advocates absolute equalitarianism is wrong."

Mao's speech indicated a tactical shift toward
subordinating the divisive aspects of the land revolu-

tion to the development of production:

> The task before the Shansi-Suiyüan party
> organization is to make the greatest
> effort to complete land reform and party
> consolidation, to continue to support the
> People's War of Liberation, to refrain
> from any further increase of the people's
> burden but to appropriately lighten it,
> and to restore the development of
> production. You are now holding a con-
> ference on production ... The devel-
> opment of agricultural production is an
> immediate aim of the land reform. In
> every area, as soon as feudalism is
> wiped out and land reform is completed,
> the party and the democratic govern-
> ment must put forward the task of restoring
> and developing agricultural production,
> transfer all available forces to the coun-
> tryside for this task, organize cooperation
> and mutual aid, promote seed selection
> and build irrigation work -- all to insure
> increased production.

At the same time, Mao called for the creation of
"people's conferences," based on the Leagues of
Poor Peasants and the Associations of Peasants. They,
as Mao maintained, included "representatives of all
democratic strata -- workers, peasants, independent craftsmen, professionals, intellectuals, national
bourgeois industrialists and merchants, and enlightened gentry." This conference was to "become
the local organ of people's power," with "all due
authority ... vested in it and the government council
it elects." Even if the land reform had not been
completed, these conferences were to supplant
the legal authority of the Leagues of Poor Peasants
and the Associations of Peasants.[74]

In areas authorized to undertake land reform
work, the Chinese Communist leadership issued instructions designed to minimize the damage to production.
Mao had drafted for the Central Committee the
directive of May 25, 1948, on "The Work of Land
Reform and Party Consolidation in 1948," listing steps
for land reform in the areas designated by the bureaus and subbureaus of the Central Committee.

The procedures included: uniting local party
branches with work teams prior to launching land reform; organizing Associations of Peasants and Leagues
of Poor Peasants; correctly determining rural

classes; forming people's representative congresses
to elect government councils on local levels; proper
organizational consolidation of party branches;
insuring that land redistribution was "considered
fair and reasonable by all the main strata;"
and, once these conditions were fulfilled, shifting
work from land reform to promoting agricultural
production. In areas with sizable variations in
landholdings, the Communists were to concentrate on
production, party consolidation, and the formation of
political organs to support the front.

Following up on the February 22 instructions,
this directive discussed the preconditions for
agrarian work in areas that would be designated to
undergo land reform from June to August 1948. In
these areas, distribution of land and property would
be initiated only if (1) the region was militarily
stable; (2) the majority of hired, poor, and middle
peasants demanded land; and (3) party cadres were
adequate in number and quality to exercise firm
leadership. If these conditions had not been met, an
area was to limit its agrarian work to the application of rent and interest reduction. Included
within this category were the newly liberated areas
in northern and eastern China, sections of Northeast
and Northwest bordering on enemy territory, and the
region covered by the Yangtze, Huai, Yellow, and
Han Rivers.

As the Chinese Communist Party extended its
operations further into enemy territory, it became
increasingly concerned with tightening its organizational apparatus. Liberated areas were linked
together and a number of cities were placed under
Chinese Communist administration.[75] With the party
extending its jurisdiction over a wider area, the
fulfillment of its responsibilities necessitated a
higher degree of organizational centralization than
had prevailed under the guerrilla conditions of
the past.

Consequently, the May 25 directive confronted the
organizational problems. It instructed that land
policies and party consolidation measures were to be
explained clearly and thoroughly at the conferences
of cadres. All cadres involved in land reform and
party consolidation were required to study the
contents of all documents issued by the Central Committee, and they were prohibited from making un-
authorized changes. They were instructed to prepare
carefully for their discussion and analysis of
problems in the conferences. All levels of the
party -- from the Central Committee to the local par-

ty branches -- were asked to establish close contacts with the various movements and to report and cor- rect mistakes promptly.[76]

Thus, by the summer of 1948, Chinese Communist land policy had bifurcated into a continuation of land redistribution and party consolidation in the old and semiold areas and the application of rent and interest reduction in the new liberated areas. Directives for the new liberated areas were issued on a regional basis.[77] This return to a cautious land policy for the new liberated areas, placing production objectives above poor peasant interests, did not mean that the party's "radical" programs for social change were unsuccessful. The Chinese Communists did not reverse their entire agrarian policy, and the Outline of the Land Law remained in effect in the old and semiold areas. As an interim measure for areas that could not be rapidly consolidated, rent and interest reduction was useful for meeting some of the needs of the impoverished peasants, while neutralizing potentially hostile landlords and rich peasants.[78]

CONCLUSION

Chinese Communist agrarian policy was closely tied to strategic and mobilization requirements during the civil war period. In late 1947, such priorities, along with mounting pressures from the grass-roots level, were among the factors in the Communist decision to move leftward in agrarian reform legisla- tion. In the course of implementation, the Outline of the Land Law produced side effects that threatened economic output and dedication to the war effort in the liberated areas. While the radicalization of the poor peasants furnished the driving force behind intensified mobilization of the liberated areas, appeals to poor peasant interests overly narrowed the party's rural base of support. Party purification likewise fell prey to the same sets of pressures as land reform, with the authority of local Chinese Communist branches excessively undermined. By early 1948, Chinese Communist agrarian policy had swung toward moderation, both to balance the detrimental effects of "leftist" excesses and in response to changing conditions in the civil war.

As the areas under Chinese Communist control mushroomed in 1948, the problems of insuring orderly administration took precedence over intensified mobilization work. Although "radical" land reform legislation had accelerated mobilization in the liber-

ated areas, successful implementation in recently
conquered regions required painstaking attention to
local conditions and strong local party leadership. Such conditions were increasingly difficult
to meet as the Chinese Communist Party spread throughout a territory three times its original base.

Movement-building needs during the final phase
of the civil war were redefined as a general drive
toward stability, administrative efficiency, and centralization. The mixed land policy for consolidated and unconsolidated areas stressed attention
to stages of agrarian work and concern with developing production. It was to help insure uninterrupted supplies of food to the People's Liberation
Army, as well as to the cities it liberated. Geared
to the party's attempts to assert control over vast
reaches of former enemy territory and urban areas,
the agrarian policy set in mid-1948 did not change until after the end of the civil war. Further land
reform work took place under Chinese Communist
consolidation of the entire mainland, when the People's Republic of China promulgated the Agrarian
Reform Law on June 30, 1950.

Although the Communist agrarian reform policies
brought uneven results, they helped the Communist
movement destroy the old power structure in the
countryside and build a new one in its place. Land
reform was an important technique for mobilizing
manpower and resources to back military efforts. And
Communist attempts to equalize wealth and deliver
social justice helped undermine Nationalist
legitimacy in the eyes of the Chinese people. In all
these ways the Communist agrarian policies fed into
the final confrontation between the Kuomintang and
the Chinese Communist Party.

NOTES

1. Ilpyong J. Kim, "Mass Mobilization Policies
and Techniques Developed in the Period of the Chinese
Soviet Republic," in A. Doak Barnett (ed.), *Chinese
Communist Politics in Action* (Seattle: University
of Washington Press, 1968), p. 81.
2. It is beyond the scope of this study to discuss the evolution of Chinese Communist strategy
and organizational techniques concerning the peasant
movement. See, for example, Carol Corder Andrew,
"The Relationship Between the Chinese Communist Party
and the Peasant Movement, 1921-1927: Ideological
and Organizational Aspects" (M.A. thesis, Columbia
University, 1964); Ilpyong J. Kim, *The Politics*

of Chinese Communism: Kiangsi under the Soviets
(Berkeley: University of California Press, 1973);
Mark Selden, *The Yenan Way in Revolutionary China*
(Cambridge, Mass.: Harvard University Press, 1971);
and Roy Hofheinz, Jr., *The Broken Wave: The Chinese
Communist Peasant Movement, 1922-1928* (Cambridge,
Mass.: Harvard University Press, 1977).

3. Kim, "Mass Mobilization Policies," p. 92.

4. Chao Kuo-chun, *Agrarian Policy of the Chinese
Communist Party, 1921-59* (Bombay: Asia Publishing
House, 1960), p. 39.

5. Donald Gillin, "Peasant Nationalism in the
History of Chinese Communism," *Journal of Asian
Studies*, Vol. XXIII, No. 2 (February 1964),
pp. 282-86.

6. Chang Hsi-chang, "Land Policies in Communist
China" (unpublished manuscript, February 1948), p.
3; Shen Chien-tu, "Red Land Reform Great Stimulant:
140,000,000 Declared Affected," *China Weekly
Review*, November 9, 1946, p. 258.

7. Ozaki Gorō, "Chūkyō tochi seisaku no shinka
to tō-nai junka undō" _/_ Evolution of Chinese Communist Land Policy and the Intraparty Purification
Movement_/_, in *Zen'ei* _/_ Vanguard_/_, No. 33 (December
1948), p. 15.

8. Betty Graham, "Communist China's Land Reform,"
China Weekly Review, February 22, 1947, p. 320; and
David and Isabel Crook, *Revolution in a Chinese
Village: Ten Mill Inn* (London: Routledge & Kegan Paul
Ltd., 1959), p. 110.

9. Li Ming-hua (ed.), *Chung-kung te t'u-ti tou-
cheng* _/_ The Chinese Communist Land Struggle_/_ (Taipei,
1965), p. 203.

10. Central Committee, Chinese Communist Party,
"Kuan-yü t'u-ti wen-t'i te chih-shih" _/_ Directive on
the Land Problem_/_, in *Chien-fei hsien-k'uang hui-
pien* _/_ Collected Documents on Current Conditions of
the Traitor Bandits_/_ (Taipei, 1950), Vol. VI,
p. 40.

11. Jack Belden, *China Shakes the World* (New York:
Harper & Brothers, Publishers, 1949), p. 169; and
Crook, *Revolution*, p. 125.

12. "Kuan-yü t'u-ti wen-t'i te chih-shih," pp.
40-45.

13. Shantung Provincial Government, "Resolutions
on Land Reform in Shantung Province," October 25,
1946; Shensi-Kansu-Ninghsia Liberated Area, "Regulations for the Draft Purchase of Landlords' Land,"
December 1946; Central China Bureau, "On the
Resolution on Measures to Solve the Land Problem
During Rent and Interest Reduction and Settling Ac-

counts," June 9, 1946. In addition, the governments of Shansi-Chahar-Hopei, Shansi-Hopei-Shantung-Honan, Shansi-Suiyüan, and Kiangsu-Anhwei liberated areas passed similar agrarian legislations. See Li (ed.), *Chung-kung te t'u-ti*, p. 214.

14. Nosei Chosakai (ed.), *Sengo Chūgoku ni okeru tochi kaikaku* / Land Reform in Postwar China / (Tokyo, 1952), pp. 13-14.

15. Mao Tse-tung, "A Three Months' Summary," *Selected Works* (New York: International Publishers, 1962), Vol. V, p. 116. There is no precise figure on the size of landholdings in the liberated areas. The Chinese Communist Party Central Committee had stated in the "May 4 Directive" that 8 percent of the population in the liberated areas were landlords and rich peasants, with poor, hired, and middle peasants constituting 92 percent. One 1945 study estimated that 62 percent of the population in North China consisted of poor peasants with 27 percent of the land; 25 percent were middle peasants with 33 percent of the land; 8 percent were rich peasants with 28 percent of the land; and 5 percent were landlords with 12 percent of the land. In South China, 71 percent of the population were poor peasants with less than 16 percent of the land; 20 percent were middle peasants with 20 percent of the land; 6 percent were rich peasants with 17 percent of the land; and 3 percent were landlords with 47 percent of the land. See Ch'en Han-seng, *The Chinese Peasant* (Oxford Panphlets on Indian Affairs, No. 33, 1945), especially the introduction. One recent study questions the degree to which class differences and rural instability permeated the Chinese countryside. The author, however, recognizes that war, inflation, and famine could debilitate large segments of the peasantry. Thus, although assessments of tenancy patterns may differ, it is probable that there emerged a sizable number of peasants in North China during and after the anti-Japanese war for whom agrarian reform had an enormous appeal. See Ramon H. Myers, *The Chinese Peasant Economy: Agricultural Development in Hopei and Shantung, 1890-1949* (Cambridge, Mass.: Harvard University Press, 1970), pp. 285-86. For another evaluation of tenancy in China in relation to the development of Chinese Communist movement, see James Pinckney Harrison, *The Long March to Power: A History of Chinese Communist Party, 1921-72* (New York: Praeger Publishers, 1972), pp. 406-407.

16. For various estimates of troop strength, see Jerome Ch'en, *Mao and the Chinese Revolution* (Lon-

don: Oxford University Press, 1965), Appendix E, p. 375. About 400,000 of the Chinese Communist forces were not regulars. See United States Department of State, *United States Relations with China with Special Reference to the Period 1944-1949* (Stanford: Stanford University Press, 1967), Vol. I, p. 313.

17. *United States Relations*, Vol. II, p. 1042; and Lionel Max Chassin, *The Communist Conquest of China*, trans. by Timothy Osato and Louis Gelas (Cambridge, Mass.: Harvard University Press, 1965), p. 59.

18. William Hinton, *Fanshen: A Documentary of Revolution in a Chinese Village* (New York: Monthly Review Press, 1966), p. 200; and Belden, *China*, p. 123.

19. Belden, *China*, pp. 342-43.

20. Report of a UNRRA worker in south Hopei as recorded in *China Weekly Review*, January 24, 1948, p. 236.

21. Graham, "Communist China's Land Reform," p. 321.

22. Shen, "Red Land Reform," p. 259.

23. This point is emphasized in Belden, *China*, pp. 233-36, 353, 374. See also Harrison, *Long March*, p. 393; and *United States Relations*, Vol. I, p. 314.

24. Jacques Guillermaz, *A History of the Chinese Communist Party, 1921-1949*, trans. by Anne Destenay (New York: Random House, 1972), pp. 397-400. See also Liao Kai-lung, *From Yenan to Peking* (Peking: Foreign Languages Press, 1954), pp. 61-64; and Mao Tse-tung, "Strategy for the Second Year of the War of Liberation," in *Selected Works*, Vol. V, p. 142.

25. Ozaki, *Sengo Chūgoku*, p. 17.

26. The Chinese Communist strategy for the second year of the civil war required that the troops operating in enemy territory should seek replenishment from these areas. Initially, 80-90 percent of the captured Kuomintang forces and a small number of junior officers were expected to be recruited. This figure was later shifted down to 60 percent. See Mao, "Strategy for the Second Year," p. 145; and "On the September Meeting -- Circular of the Central Committee of the Communist Party of China," *Selected Works*, Vol. V, p. 272. There were also major recruiting drives in the liberated areas to prepare for the counteroffensive in the second year of the civil war. See John Gittings, *The Role of the Chinese Army* (London: Oxford University Press, 1967), p. 63.

27. Ozaki, *Sengo Chūgoku*, pp. 15-16.

28. Graham, "Communist China's Land Reform," p. 321.

29. Crook, *Revolution*, p. 156.

30. Until the autumn of 1947, the Chinese Communists only considered large landlords the class enemies of the masses. They argued that small landlords, who suffered "feudal" oppression from larger landlords and Kuomintang officials, might be better off as independent farmers under an honest and efficient government. The Nationalists, however, began to restore all landlords' former rights in the areas recovered from the Communists. Since the landlords and rich peasants had not proved as cooperative as anticipated, the line of division in the class struggle assumed the form of poor and middle peasants versus landlords and rich peasants. See Michael Lindsay, *Notes on Educational Problems in Communist China, 1941-1947* (New York: Institute of Pacific Relations, 1950), p. 31.

31. John Wilson Lewis, *Leadership in Communist China* (Ithaca: Cornell University Press, 1966), p. 110.

32. Chao Han, *T'an-t'an Chung-kuo kung-ch'an-tang te cheng-feng yun-tung* / Talks on the Rectification Movement of the Chinese Communist Party / (Peking, 1957), p. 23.

33. Shansi-Suiyüan jih-pao (ed.), "Wei ch'un-chieh tang te tsu-chih erh tou-cheng" / Struggle to Purify Party Organization / in *Wei ch'un-chieh tang te tsu-chih erh tou-cheng* / Struggle to Purify Party Organization / (Hong Kong, 1948), pp. 33-38.

34. Belden, *China*, pp. 166-68; and Hinton, *Fanshen*, p. 259.

35. P'eng Chen, "P'ing-fen t'u-ti yü cheng-tun tui-wu" / Equally Divide the Land and Reorganize Our Ranks /, in *Wei ch'un-chieh tang te tsu-chih*, p. 16.

36. Crook, *Revolution*, p. 136.

37. Mao Tse-tung, "The Present Situation and Our Task," in *Selected Works*, Vol. V, pp. 165-66.

38. *Ibid.*, p. 174. When the Central Committee fled Yenan on March 19, 1947, it split into two main groups. Most of the leaders in the Central Committee Secretariat, including Mao, Chou En-lai, and Jen Pi-shih, wandered throughout the Shensi-Kansu-Ninghsia liberated area. The other group, called the Working Committee of the Central Committee, was headed by Liu Shao-ch'i and settled at Hsipaip'o Village, the site of the National Land Conference. See *ibid.*, p. 132. The main Central Committee group was at Chiahsien during the conference and from

that site promulgated the Outline of the Land Law.
See Ch'en, *Mao*, p. 284.

39. Central Committee, Chinese Communist Party,
Chung-kuo t'u-ti fa ta-kang / Outline of Chinese
Land Law / (North China, 1948). An English translation of the Outline of the Land Law is reproduced
in Hinton, *Fanshen*, Appendix A, pp. 615-18.

40. As the People's Liberation Army switched to
the offensive, its rate of recruitment increased.
In the second year of the civil war, it launched a
recruitment drive as preparation for its counteroffensive. See Gittings, *Role*, p. 63. The step-up
in military conscription paralleled the intensifi-
cation of agrarian reform. According to Mao Tse-tung,
from July 1946 to September 1948, the People's
Liberation Army grew from 1.2 million to 2.8 million men. These gains resulted from 800,000 captured
Nationalist soldiers and 1.6 million peasants who
obtained land and were mobilized to join the
army. See Mao, "On the September Meeting," pp. 269-
71.

41. *Chung-kuo t'u-ti fa ta-kang.*

42. Yi Lin-p'ing, "Overhaul Party Organizations
Constantly in Battle," *Nan-fang jih-pao*, December 22,
1960, as translated in *Survey of China Mainland
Press* (United States Consulate-General in Hong Kong),
No. 2431 (February 3, 1961), p. 7. Hinton des-
cribes the conference of 1,700 activists from the
Shansi-Hopei-Shantung-Honan liberated area that met
at Yehtao in October 1947 in his *Fanshen*, p. 263.

43. Lindsay, *Notes*, p. 150.

44. The "supplementary measures" for the Northeast can be found in Tung-pei jen-min cheng-fu nung-
min pu (ed.), *T'u-ti cheng-ts'e fa-ling hui-pien*
/ A Collection of Land Laws and Policies / (Mukden,
1950), pp. 6-9. For an English Translation of
the "supplementary measures" for Shansi-Hopei-Shantung-
Honan, see Hinton, *Fanshen*, Appendix B, pp. 619-22.

45. Ozaki, *Sengo Chūgoku*, p. 20.

46. Mao and his group "zigzagged north to Wang-
chiaping, east to Tsaolink'ou, then west-northwest to
Wangchiawan in April and Hsiaoho in July, turning
east-northeast to Suiteh, and north to Chukuanchai in
September and Shenchuanpo in October, before turning
south again to Yangchiak'ou, where they remained
from December 1947 to March 1948." They then moved
eastward through northwest Shansi into western Hopei
to join the other Central Committee members. According to James P. Harrison, "a striking feature of
party history during these momentous years was the
paucity of high-level meetings." No "full-fledged Cen-

tral Committee meeting" took place between mid-1945 and early 1949. The first major party conference after the Seventh Congress was held at Yangchiak'ou on December 25-28, 1947 with only Mao's group and some delegates from the Shensi-Kansu-Ninghsia and Shansi-Suiyüan liberated areas in attendance. The next important party meeting was that of the Political Bureau in September 1948 after the Central Committee had reunited. See Harrison, *Long March*, pp. 399-400.

47. He headed a Land Reform Bureau in the Central Committee. See *Jih-pen t'ou-hsiang hou te Chung-kuo kung-ch'an-tang* ∠ The Chinese Communist Party After the Japanese Surrender ∕ (n.p., 1947), pp. 17ff.

48. "Down with Liu Shao-ch'i: Life of Counter-revolutionary Liu Shao-ch'i," reprinted by Chingkang-shan Fighting Corps of the Fourth Hospital, Peking Municipality, in *Current Background* (United States Consulate-General in Hong Kong), No. 831 (August 17, 1967), p. 10.

49. Liu Shao-ch'i, "Self-Criticism," *Collected Works of Liu Shao-ch'i, 1958-1967* (Hong Kong: Union Research Institute, 1968), p. 30.

50. See T'ien-ching ta-hsüeh, P'ing-shan t'u-kai lien-ho tiao-ch'a-tsu, "Liu Shao-ch'i tsai P'ing-shan t'u-kai chung te tzu-pen chieh-chi fan-tung lu-hsien pi-hsü ch'e-ti p'i-p'an" ∠ We Must Thoroughly Criticize Liu Shao-ch'i's Capitalist Reactionary Line in the P'inghshan Land Reform ∕, April 7, 1967. This Cultural Revolution document also criticizes P'eng Chen for advancing a "kowtow policy" in land reform and party purification work that led to excessive attacks on cadres.

51. An early version of this speech is printed in Chieh-fang she (ed.), *Mu-ch'ien hsing-shih ho wo-men te jen-wu* ∠ The Present Situation and Our Tasks ∕ (n.p., 1949). See Mao Tse-tung, "Tsai Shan-Sui kan-pu hui-i sheng te chiang-hua" ∕ Speech at a Conference of Shansi-Suiyüan Cadres ∕, April 1, 1948, esp. pp. 77-78. For an English translation, see Mao, *Selected Works*, Vol. V, pp. 231-32.

52. Old liberated areas had been under Chinese Communist influence before 1945. Semiold areas experienced liberation between the end of the anti-Japanese war and August 1947. New liberated areas were those occupied by the Communists since the beginning of their counteroffensive.

53. See the articles on land reform in newly liberated areas in *Ch'ün-chung* ∠ The Masses ∕, February 12, 1948; and in *Chin-Ch'a-Chi jih-pao* ∠ Shansi-

Chahar-Hopei Daily_/, February 7, 1948.

54. *Chin-Ch'a-Chi jih-pao*, February 8, 1948.

55. Li (ed.), *Chung-kung te t'u-ti*, pp. 226-27.
See also Mao Tse-tung, "Speech at a Conference
of Cadres," in *Selected Works*, Vol. V, pp. 227-39.
Perhaps the most moving (and detailed) accounts of the
land revolution are Hinton, *Fanshen*, and Crook,
Revolution. Both villages described in these two
works had undergone the "antitraitor" and "settling
accounts" movements. By the time of the "May 4
Directive," large landholdings had already been redistributed. There was little land left for those
still in need, and middle peasants came under attack. Thus, severe "left" deviations occurred months
before the Outline of the Land Law was promulgated.
In these villages, the Outline of the Land Law
was not implemented until early 1948. Although misclassification of peasants continued, implementation consisted mainly of work in party purification
and ironing out past mistakes in land redistribution.

56. T'an Cheng-wen, "Shan-hsi Kuo-hsien shih
tse-yang chin-hsing t'u-ti kai-ke te" _/ How Kuo
County in Shansi Carried Out Land Reform_/, in Liu
Shao-ch'i *et al.*, *T'u-kai cheng-tang tien-hsing ching-
yen* _/ Experiences in Land Reform and Party Purifi-
cation_/ (Hong Kong, 1948), pp. 6-20.

57. Jen Pi-shih, "T'u-ti kai-ke chung te chi-ko
wen-t'i" _/ Several Problems Concerning Agrarian
Reform_/, in *T'u-ti cheng-ts'e fa-ling hui-pien*, pp.
12-13.

58. See, for example, Chin-Chi-Lu-Yü pien-ch'ü
nung-hui ch'ou-pei wei-yüan-hui, "Kao nung-min
shu" _/ Report to the Peasants_/, January 20, 1948,
in Hua-pei hsin-hu shu-tien (ed.), *P'ing-fen t'u-ti
shou-ts'e* _/ Handbook for Equally Dividing the
Land_/ (n.p., 1948), pp. 27-34.

59. Mao, *Selected Works*, Vol. V, pp. 157-76. Mao
later criticized Chinese Communist news agencies,
newspapers, and radio stations for reports with "left"
deviations and noted the failure of many propaganda
bureaus of party committees to report such errors
to higher levels. See "Correct the 'Left' Errors in
Land Reform Propaganda," *ibid.*, Vol. V, pp. 197-99.

60. An explicit statement of the objectives
of Chinese Communist agrarian policy in the spring of
1948 can be found in a piece entitled "Questions
and Answers on Agrarian Socialism," issued on July
27, 1948. This article reinforced the moderate
position, challenging "absolute equalitarianism" in
land redistribution. It viewed the land revolution as "neither Communist nor socialist," but as

a means to promote economic development "of a capitalist nature" under "New Democracy." The article defined the objectives of land reform as the elevation of productive power through the elimination of restrictive "feudal" productive relations; boosting incentives to produce and maximizing conditions favorable to agricultural and industrial development. Besides warning against encroachments on industrial property or the holdings of middle or "new rich" peasants, the article went on to state that class divisions would continue in Chinese society after the completion of agrarian reform. It envisioned as an "unavoidable" stage in China's development the continuation of private property and economic competition, but in a "New Democratic" framework that would prepare for the transition to socialism. See "Kuan-yü nung-yeh she-hui-chu-i te wen-ta," July 27, 1948, in *Mu-ch'ien hsing-shih ho wo-men te jen-wu*, pp. 138-45.

61. Jen, "T'u-ti kai-ke chung," pp. 15-19.

62. By "exploitation," the Chinese Communists meant the profit an individual derived from the labor of another (as in renting out land) or from loaning money at a high rate of interest. The extent to which middle peasants could engage in "exploitation" had been raised from 15 percent during the Kiangsi Soviet period to 25 percent during the civil war. See Central Committee, Chinese Communist Party, "Kuan-yü 1933 liang-ko wen-chien te chüeh-ting," in *T'u-ti cheng-ts'e fa-ling hui-pien*, pp. 40-60. The reissued documents on rural classes made it clear that exploitation was the only basis for classification.

63. "New" middle peasants were former poor peasants who had received enough land through agrarian reform to achieve middle peasant status.

64. "Chung-kung kuan-yü tsai lao-ch'ü pan-lao-ch'ü chin-hsing t'u-ti kai-ke kung-tso yü cheng-tang kung-tso chih-shih" /Directive of the Central Committee, Chinese Communist Party, on Land Reform and Party Rectification Work in the Old and Semiold Liberated Areas_/, in Liu *et at.*, *T'u-kai cheng-tang tien-hsing ching-yen*, pp. 26-31.

65. Mao Tse-tung, "Essential Points in Land Reform in the New Liberated Areas," *Selected Works*, Vol. V, p. 202.

66. See the edition of Central Committee, Chinese Communist Party, "Chung-kuo t'u-ti fa ta-kang," in *Mu-ch'ien hsing-shih ho wo-men te jen-wu*, p. 13. The above is my translation of the "note" following Article Six.

67.   Lindsay, *Notes*, p. 171; and Hinton, *Fanshen*, pp. 321-22.

68.   Work teams were used by the party when a new policy was implemented.   Although the teams only dealt with a small percentage of villages, their experiences enabled party leaders to develop policies that could be implemented on a mass scale by local cadres.   The latter received their instructions from county leaders or attended county conferences.

69.   Lindsay, *Notes*, pp. 149-50; Hinton, *Fanshen*, p. 12.

70.   Yi, "Overhaul Party Organizations," p. 7.

71.   Liu Shao-ch'i, "P'ing-shan t'u-kai cheng-tang fan-li," in Liu *et al.*, *T'u-kai cheng-tang tien-hsing ching-yen*, pp. 24-25.

72.   Yi, "Overhaul Party Organizations," p. 7.

73.   Hinton describes the situation in Long Bow Village in Lucheng County after the advent of a work team in March 1948.   The team overlooked real gains in agrarian reform and hastily concluded that land reform and party purification work were unsuccessful. It then dissolved all mass organizations, suspended all cadres and assembled a League of Poor Peasants, which sat in judgment of local Communist leaders.   In terms of class background, the majority of the cadres were former poor or hired peasants, and their abuses of their office did not outweigh their merits.   Nevertheless, they were subjected to two separate public investigations and charged with failure in matters beyond their power to remedy. There were not enough resources in the village to make everyone a thriving middle peasant.   Instead of gaining confidence from the fact that they were still accepted by the people, the cadres became progressively demoralized by each wave of criticism. Measured against unrealistic standards, the Long Bow party branch was for a time on the verge of disintegration.   See Hinton, *Fanshen*, pp. 243-416; and his analysis of the party purification movement in "Hinton Reexamines *Fanshen*," in *Progressive Labor*, Vol. VI, No. 6 (February 1969).

74.   Mao, *Selected Works*, Vol. V, pp. 227-39.

75.   By June 1948, the liberated areas acquired a population of 19 million and 80 cities more than in 1946.   Such well-fortified cities as Shihchiachuang, Yuncheng, Szepingchieh, Loyang, Ichuan, Paochi, Weihsien, and Linfeng had fallen to the Chinese Communists.   Every day brought closer to the reality that the Chinese Communists would stretch throughout the entire mainland.   See Liao, *From Yenan to Peking*, p. 65 and p. 89.

76. Mao Tse-tung, "The Work of Land Reform and of Party Consolidation in 1948," *Selected Works*, Vol. V, pp. 253-59. The call for closer relations between various levels of the party was preceded by a directive on January 7, 1948, for the institution of a regularized system of reports. See *ibid.*, pp. 177-79.

77. The Central Northeast Bureau of the party had issued a "Directive Concerning Land Reform in the New Areas" on November 12, 1948. See *T'u-ti cheng-ts'e fa-ling hui-pien*, pp. 93-94. Other directives included "Outline for the Reduction of Rent and Interest" (Political Bureau, Kwangtung-Kiangsi-Hunan Border Region Forces, June 1949); "Outline for Reduction of Rent and Interest" (Central China Bureau, October 8, 1949); and "Provisional Regulations for Rent Reduction in the New Areas in East China" (East China Bureau, September 1949). See Chao, *Agrarian Policy*, pp. 80-81.

78. Mao Tse-tung, "Tactical Problems of Rural Work in the New Liberated Areas," *Selected Works*, Vol. V, pp. 251-52.

Selected Bibliography

Belden, Jack. *China Shakes the World*. New York: Monthly Review Press, 1970.

Bodde, Derk. *Peking Diary, 1948-1949: A Year of Revolution*. Greenwich, Conn.: Fawcett, 1967.

Chang, Carsun. *The Third Force in China*. New York: Bookman Associates, 1952.

Chang Kia-ngau. *The Inflationary Spiral: The Experience in China, 1939-1950*. Cambridge, Mass.: Massachusetts Institute of Technology Press, 1958.

Chassin, Lionel M. *The Communist Conquest of China: A History of the Civil War, 1945-1949*. Cambridge, Mass.: Harvard University Press, 1965.

Ch'en, Jerome. *Mao and the Chinese Revolution*. New York: Oxford University Press, 1965.

Chiang Kai-shek. *Soviet Russia in China: A Summing-Up at Seventy*. New York: Farrar, Straus and Cudahy, Inc., 1957.

Ch'ien Tuan-sheng. *The Government and Politics of China*. Cambridge, Mass.: Harvard University Press, 1961.

Clubb, O. Edmund. *Twentieth Century China*. 3rd edition. New York: Columbia University Press, 1978.

Crozier, Brian (with the collaboration of Eric Chou). *The Man Who Lost China: The First Full Biography of Chiang Kai-shek*. New York: Charles Scribner's Sons, 1976.

Eastman, Lloyd E. *The Abortive Revolution: China under Nationalist Rule, 1927-1937*. Cambridge, Mass.: Harvard University Press, 1974.

Esherick, Joseph W. (ed.). *Lost Chance in China: The World War II Despatches of John Service*. New York: Random House, 1974.

Gillin, Donald G. *Warlord: Yen Hsi-shan in Shansi*

Province, 1911-1949. Princeton: Princeton University Press, 1967.

Guillermaz, Jacques. *A History of the Chinese Communist Party, 1921-1949*. New York: Random House, 1972.

Harrison, James Pinckney. *The Long March to Power: A History of the Chinese Communist Party, 1921-72*. New York: Praeger Publishers, 1972.

Hinton, William. *Fanshen: A Documentary of Revolution in a Chinese Village*. New York: Vintage Books, 1968.

Hsia Tsi-an. *The Gate of Darkness: Studies on the Leftist Literary Movement in China*. Seattle: University of Washington Press, 1968.

Hsiao Tso-liang. *The Land Revolution in China, 1930-1934*. Seattle: University of Washington Press, 1969.

---. *Power Relations within the Chinese Communist Movement, 1930-1934: A Study of Documents*. 2 vols. Seattle: University of Washington Press, 1961 and 1967.

Israel, John. *Student Nationalism in China, 1927-1937*. Stanford: Stanford University Press, 1966.

--- and Donald W. Klein. *Rebels and Bureaucrats: China's December 9ers*. Berkeley: University of California Press, 1976.

Johnson, Chalmers A. *Peasant Nationalism and Communist Power: The Emergence of Revolutionary China, 1937-1945*. Stanford: Stanford University Press, 1962.

Kapp, Robert A. *Szechwan and the Chinese Republic: Provincial Militarism and Central Power, 1911-1938*. New Haven: Yale University Press, 1974.

Kataoka, Tetsuya. *Resistance and Revolution in China: The Communists and the Second United Front*. Berkeley: University of California Press, 1974.

Kim, Ilpyong J. *The Politics of Chinese Communism: Kiangsi under the Soviets*. Berkeley: University of California Press, 1973.

Kubek, Anthony. *How the Far East Was Lost: American Policy and the Creation of Communist China, 1941-1949*. Chicago: Henry Regnery Co., 1963.

Lary, Diana. *Region and Nation: The Kwangsi Clique in Chinese Politics, 1925-1937*. London: Cambridge University Press, 1974.

Linebarger, Paul M. A. *The China of Chiang Kai-shek*. Boston: World Peace Foundation, 1941.

Liu, F. F. *A Military History of Modern China, 1924-1949*. Princeton: Princeton University Press, 1956.

Loh, Pichon P. Y. (ed.). *The Kuomintang Debacle of*

1949: Conquest or Collapse? Lexington, Mass.:
D. C. Heath & Co., 1965.

McLane, Charles B. *Soviet Policy and the Chinese Communists, 1931-1946*. New York: Columbia University Press, 1958.

Melby, John F. *The Mandate of Heaven: Record of a Civil War, China 1945-49*. Toronto: University of Toronto Press, 1968.

North, Robert C. *Moscow and Chinese Communists*. 2nd edition. Stanford: Stanford University Press, 1963.

Pepper, Suzanne. *Civil War in China: The Political Struggle, 1945-1949*. Berkeley: University of California Press, 1978.

Price, Jane L. *Cadres, Commanders, and Commissars: The Training of the Chinese Communist Leadership, 1920-45*. Boulder: Westview Press, 1976.

Pye, Lucien W. *Mao Tse-tung: The Man in the Leader*. New York: Basic Books, 1976.

Rue, John E. *Mao Tse-tung in Opposition, 1927-1935*. Stanford: Stanford University Press, 1966.

Schram, Stuart. *Mao Tse-tung*. Harmondsworth: Penguin Books, 1966.

---. *The Political Thought of Mao Tse-tung*. Enlarged and revised edition. Harmondsworth: Penguin Books, 1969.

Selden, Mark. *The Yenan Way in Revolutionary China*. Cambridge, Mass.: Harvard University Press, 1971.

Sheridan, James E. *China in Disintegration: The Republican Era in Chinese History, 1912-1949*. New York: Free Press, 1975.

---. *Chinese Warlord: The Career of Feng Yu-hsiang*. Stanford: Stanford University Press, 1966.

Sih, Paul K. T. (ed.). *Nationalist China During the Sino-Japanese War, 1937-1945*. Hicksville, N.Y.: Exposition Press, 1977.

--- (ed.). *The Strenuous Decade: China's Nation-Building Efforts, 1927-1937*. Jamaica, N. Y.: St. John's University Press, 1970.

Smedley, Agnes. *Battle Hymn of China*. New York: Alfred A. Knopf, 1943.

Snow, Edgar. *Red Star Over China*. Revised and enlarged edition. New York: Grove Press, 1968.

Thompson, James C., Jr. *While China Faced West: American Reformers in Nationalist China, 1928-1937*. Cambridge, Mass.: Harvard University Press, 1969.

Thornton, Richard C. *China: The Struggle for Power, 1917-1972*. Bloomington: Indiana University Press, 1973.

---. *The Comintern and the Chinese Communists, 1928-1931*. Seattle: University of Washington Press, 1969.

Tien Hung-mao. *Government and Politics in Kuomintang China, 1927-1937*. Stanford: Stanford University Press, 1972.

Tong, Hollington K. *Chiang Kai-shek: Soldier and Statesman*. 2 vols. Shanghai: China Publishing Co., 1937.

Tong Te-kong and Li Tsung-jen. *The Memoirs of Li Tsung-jen*. Boulder: Westview Press, 1979.

Tsou Tang. *America's Failure in China, 1941-50*. Chicago: University of Chicago Press, 1963.

Van Slyke, Lyman P. *Enemies and Friends: The United Front in Chinese Communist History*. Stanford: Stanford University Press, 1967.

White, Theodore H. and Annalee Jacoby. *Thunder out of China*. New York: William Sloane Associates, 1946.

Wilson, Dick. *The Long March: The Epic of Chinese Communism's Survival, 1935*. New York: Viking Press, 1971.

Young, Arthur N. *China and the Helping Hand, 1937-1945*. Cambridge, Mass.: Harvard University Press, 1963.

---. *China's Nation-Building Effort, 1927-1937: The Financial and Economic Record*. Stanford: Stanford University Press, 1971.

---. *China's Wartime Finance and Inflation, 1937-1945*. Cambridge, Mass.: Harvard University Press, 1965.

Contributors

F. Gilbert Chan (Ph.D., Columbia): Associate Professor
of History, Miami University; Regional Coordi-
nator for China and Japan, *Canadian Review
of Studies in Nationalism*; coeditor, *China in the
1920s: Nationalism and Revolution* (New York: New
Viewpoints, 1976); editor, *Nationalism in East
Asia: An Annotated Bibliography of Selected
Works* (New York: Garland Publishing, Inc., 1980).

Samuel C. Chu (Ph.D., Columbia): Professor of History,
Ohio State University; President, Midwest Con-
ference on Asian Affairs, 1979-1980; author,
Reformer in Modern China: Chang Chien, 1853-1926
(New York: Columbia University Press, 1965);
coauthor, *Passage to the Golden Gate: A History of
the Chinese in America to 1910* (New York:
Doubleday & Co., Inc., 1967).

Donald A. Jordan (Ph.D., Wisconsin): Associate
Professor of History and Director of Southeast
Asia Studies Program, Ohio University; author, *The
Northern Expedition: China's National Revolution
of 1926-1928* (Honolulu: University Press of
Hawaii, 1976).

Robert A. Kapp (Ph.D., Yale): Assistant Professor of
History and East Asian Studies, University of
Washington; Editor, *Journal of Asian Studies*; au-
thor, *Szechwan and the Chinese Republic: Pro-
vincial Militarism and Central Power, 1911-1938*
(New Haven: Yale University Press, 1974).

Ilpyong J. Kim (Ph.D., Columbia): Professor of Politi-
cal Science and Chairman of East Asian Studies
Committee, University of Connecticut; author of
*The Politics of Chinese Communism: Kiangsi under
the Soviets* (Berkeley: University of California
Press, 1973) and *Communist Politics in North Korea*
(New York: Praeger Publishers, 1975).

Noel R. Miner (Ph.D., Stanford): Assistant Professor
of History, University of Colorado at Boulder.

Jane L. Price (Ph.D., Columbia): Lecturer of
East Asian Languages and Cultures and Research
Associate of East Asian Institute, Columbia
University; author, *Cadres, Commanders, and Commissars: The Training of the Chinese Communist
Leadership, 1920-45* (Boulder: Westview Press,
1976).

Hung-mao Tien (Ph.D., Wisconsin): Chairman and Professor of Political Science, University of Wisconsin at Waukesha; author, *Government and Politics
in Kuomintang China, 1927-1937* (Stanford:
Stanford University Press, 1972).

Index

Abo Kiyokazu, 109
Apresoff, Garegin, 136, 137, 147*n*
Ataturk, Kemal, 63
August 7 Emergency Conference, *see* Chinese Communist
    Party
Autumn Harvest Uprising, 10, 198

Blue Shirts Society, 14*n*, 27, 28, 30, 35*n*; *see also*
    Whampoa Clique
Boycott of 1931-1932, 6, 91-124 *passim*
Britain, 93, 99, 100, 111, 112-13, 114, 118, 127, 133,
    136, 138; *see also* England
Bukharin, 206, 207
Bukulin, 140

C. C. Clique, 27, 33*n*
Chang Chia-ao (Chang Kia-ngau), 15*n*, 31
Chang Chih-chung, 30
Chang Ch'ün, 29, 30, 159, 160
Chang Chung-sun, 224
Chang Hsin, 131, 138
Chang Hsüeh-liang, 41, 96, 97, 104, 117
Chang Jen-chieh, 29, 80, 81, 83, 84
Chang Kia-ngau, *see* Chang Chia-ao
Chang Kuo-t'ao, 201, 208, 212*n*, 214*n*
Chang P'ei-yüan, 130, 132, 134, 135, 136
Chang Tso-lin, 128-29, 136
Ch'en Ch'eng, 30
Ch'en Ch'i-mei, 29, 30
Ch'en Chi-t'ang, 21, 24
Ch'en Ch'ün, 31
Ch'en Chung, 131, 134
Ch'en Eugene, 96
Ch'en Hsiu-ying, 148*n*
Ch'en Keng, 224

261